T0209625

MEMOIRS' OF A N●BODY

SELF-PROCLAIMED

BEST SELLING AUTHOR

A.C.TAYLOR

authorHOUSE®

AuthorHouse™
1663 Liberty Drive
Bloomington, IN 47403
www.authorhouse.com
Phone: 1 (800) 839-8640

Published by AuthorHouse 02/12/2020

ISBN: 978-1-7283-3453-0 (sc)
ISBN: 978-1-7283-3452-3 (e)

Although inspired by true events, some parts are fictionalized for dramatization purposes.

DEDICATION

Dedicated, to my Lord and Savior Jesus Christ of Nazareth. You have been my refuge even at times when I didn't deserve it. You've held my hand through the hardest times of my life without you there is no me. Thank you for loving me when I didn't know how to love, thank you for using me hopefully as an instrumental to let that little girl or boy in foster care know to steadfast on the word of the Lord and he will strengthen thine heart.

I love you and I'm sorry for all times I've let you down and lost my way. Please forgive me if anything in this book is not of your will; my only desire is to make you proud of me. Thank you for still loving me through it all. I give the praise to The father, The son, and The Holy Spirit.

Honorable Mention:

Claybelle "Claire" Durant my loving grandmother. Thank you for taking me. I would trade all of my tomorrows for one more yesterday.

"Push, PUSSH! It's a girl!" The doctor exclaimed in glee. "How come she so tiny, I mean I know she is premature but is she okay." My mother asked. My name is Taylor. My birthday is the day I decided to take the world by storm. If I had known what I know now I probably would have decided to take my time. Hey I guess that's me; always in a rush to do what I think is right but somehow always ending up wrong. I had been alive for a few short years by this point. I have gotten to know my mother and daddy pretty well. They are definitely my favorite people in this world. I hate it when they fight. I'm always so scared. Ramon was arguing with Kymela again. I could just imagine how this was going to turn out. I laid in bed looking at the ceiling....

"Kymela didn't I ask you to bring more beers out the kitchen?" Ramon asked. "I figured we should slow down on the beer a little bit." Kymela responded. Ramon turned around with a look that Kymela was far too familiar with. Ramon took off his glasses. They were thick. I heard people refer to them as coke bottle glasses whatever that meant. He only took off his glasses when he meant business. His curly hair helped his appearance although he had a very distinguish face. His look was something to be desired to say the least. He wasn't the most attractive man, but he was Kymela's man nevertheless. Ramon turned back to Kymela with words of hatred pouring from his mouth. "Did you think since we have company that, that gives you the right to defy me, get loud, and talk back!" With a swift effortless stroke of his right hand he slapped

Kymela down. Kymela looked up to his friend who was standing next to him in the kitchen for help, but he turned around and headed back to the living room. Kymela's eyes quickly surveilled the room for a weapon. There wasn't anything close enough for her to grab. At that moment she knew it was on. Kymela began to cry while mumbling. "I'm sorry, I'm so-so sorry." Although she knew in her mind it was too late Ramon was mad. He grabbed Kymela off the kitchen floor by her hair. As soon as she was on her feet, he slapped her down again. He began kicking her all over as if she was some common street thug that had broken into his house and he wanted to teach him a man to man lesson. He raised his foot with his standard issue marine boot attached and came down on Kymela's face. Kymela began saying her prayers as she fell in and out of consciousness. I had already come out of the bedroom. I tip-toed to the end of the hallway. I had to know what was going on. When I had gotten to the end of the hallway I'd seen three men sitting on the couch. They were drinking that bitter yellow stuff in some bottle that father always drink. Ewe. Just then I heard my mother's pleading again with Ramon. I looked at the couch at these so-called men. They didn't do anything to help my mommy. I didn't know what to do or how to erase what I had seen from my memory. I turned around and headed back to the room. I walked inside my room and sat on the bottom bunk. The whole time I was thinking to myself how I hoped he didn't hurt her too bad. Sometimes you can't tell when they fight but other times she didn't look to good. I started to cry because my mommy was being hurt and I didn't know what to do. I tried to wake my sister Karin but she just turned over. So I sat on the bed with nothing to do but cry. KOOM-BOOM, SLAAM, SLAAM! "Stop Ramon, please stop!" That was all I could hear. Between the cabinet doors slamming with the pots and pans hitting the floor I was becoming increasingly scared for her. This thing was getting serious. I began to pray harder for my mother. By now my sibling was getting up one by one. There are four of us in total. "I think he is going to kill her this time." Karin said "Don't say anything that stupid." I said. "Well there are three men in the living room. They are just sitting on the couch drinking that nasty stuff Daddy's always drinking." I continued. "That would be beer and I like it." Karin said "I'm telling momma on you." I replied. "If you do, I'll punch you in the face." Said Karin. My sister Karin is skinny with light colored skin. She also hits me a lot. I don't hit her back because she is my sister and I love her. I don't think she likes me too much though. Every time my mommy or daddy turns their back she hits me. I never say anything. I don't want her to get in any trouble; but every chance she gets she is pinching, slapping, or punching me. She even be pulling what little bit of hair I got. I do my best to show her I love her but she can't stand me. I don't understand why she would want to hurt me. She is always putting on that shy smile then saying she is sorry. I fall for it every time. Then she turns right around and do something else mean to me again. "Run Y'all. RRRR UUUU NNN!" my mother yelled. With that I stood up off the bed then turned to my sisters. "Come on y'all, let's go!" I said We all took off running out of our tiny bedroom door down the hallway through the living room out the front door. We had successfully made it to the front porch. We all trotted down the three steps that connected the front porch to the concrete. I grabbed India's hand she was a year younger than me, which meant she couldn't run that fast. I mean how could she I'm only three years old. I started running down the block. It was raining really hard. Karin is laughing but I don't find anything funny. I can barely see my mother through the rain. My thin ponytails were now heavy from the rain. They kept hitting me in the face. I managed to make out my mother through the rain. She had our brand new baby sister in her arms with no shoes on. I kept running. I began squinting harder so that I could see better. I lost my grip of India's hand. India fell, I looked back daddy was gaining on us fast. I had to keep running. I swung around to see my mother at the end of the block. How could she move so fast? I thought. In my mind I had to catch up with her. I had almost gotten to the end of the block. My mother turned around and began to speak. "Come on, come on baby." I turned back around to see where my daddy was. Daddy was way back there, we were dusting his butt. Then at that very moment my life changed. I swung back around and my mom had disappeared. Just that fast she was gone. I stopped running while the confusion overcame me. I couldn't believe she left me. I was soo close and she left me. I swung around in slow motion. I called my mommy but she didn't answer me. My daddy along with his marine buddies had my sisters. They were crying, kicking, and screaming as they picked them up and headed back toward the house. The rain seems to be coming down even harder. The mixture of salt water, tears, along with snot streaming in my mouth were beginning to make me nausea. Daddy finally caught up to me. He extended his left hand. I looked up to see the smile plastered on his face. I took my daddy's hand. We turned around then walk back towards the house. My entire body went limp. I fell to the ground. My dad picked me up. He carried me into the house. I suddenly began kicking while screaming. I deliberately attempted to scratch his face off. He had hurt my mommy and now she was gone. I glanced around the house. I didn't see my sisters or hear them. I was too busy trying to take Ramon A.K.A. Daddy the fuck out. I bit Ramon's arm. He screamed. "Bitch!" Ramon dropped me on the floor. I jumped up then ran for the door. Ramon grabbed me and yelled. "Taylor, sit down now!" I stomped on his toes. He began laughing until I hit him in his privates. Ramon grabbed me by both of my arms squeezing really tight. He picked me up then sat me down real hard on the couch. "Enough!" he said. At that moment I looked into the eyes of what I believe to be the devil. He stared back into my eyes. I started screaming for his marine buddies to help me. "HEEELP, HELLLP, HHHEEELLPPP! PLEASE HELP ME!" Both of them appeared outta nowhere. They stood over me looking down while I sat on the couch with fear in their eyes. Finally one of them said something. "Ramon man she's scared talk to her." My dad responded. "This bitch is not scared. She is dramatic just like her mother. She can sit there crying while making herself sick all night for all I care." he said. I watched as all three men made excuses to leave one by one. My head was spinning along with my stomach hurting. I stretched out on the couch and fell into a peaceful sleep. I opened my eyes in a white room with drawings on the wall. It had all different colored children playing holding hands in a circle. There was a dog in the picture with some butterflies, a ball, along with birds on what seemed to be a beautiful summer day. This is not good, I thought. The door swung open abruptly. My mommy appeared through the open door. I could see her in another room sitting at a rectangular shaped wooden table along with my sisters. I ran to the table to be with my family. God had answered my prayers. Ramon was gone plus I was able to be with my mommy again. The family was back together. Kymela was smiling even though tears were streaming from her eyes profusely. I knew something had to be wrong. My siblings were oblivious though. They were sitting there laughing, playing, and coloring. I could just sense something was not right. I just stared at Kymela. Mommy was so pretty even though she didn't know it. She had thick long hair with deep dimples along with perfect white teeth. Her honey brown complexion matched her oldest daughter. Kymela had big breast, her hips are wide, a flat stomach; but her shoe size is a twelve. Plus she stands at about five feet seven inches. Kymela was pretty in her own right with a singing voice to die for. She was shy, very-very shy. She only felt comfortable enough to sing in front of her children. She would sing us lullabies, church songs, R & B records and would actually sound like the people on the radio. She would sing to us constantly, and now here she sit trying to tell the people she loved as well as trusted the most in this world that she have to leave. How do you tell your children you won't be seeing them for a while? Ramon and Kymela dabbled in drugs. LSD, cocaine, marijuana, hash well if you name it they did it at least once. She and Ramon had gotten too high when the last fight broke out. She knew she had to get out of there. Ramon took that as the ultimate betrayal. She left him. She tried to call Ramon on the pay phone to apologize and then go back home. It's not like she had anywhere else to go. Ramon picked up the phone with glee. He knew exactly who it was and what she wanted. He laughed as he told her he called child protective to take away her precious children. Kymela wasn't thinking when she hung up on him. She called the police and requested for them to take her to her children. Her mind was on getting her babies. Had she been thinking she would not have arrived high with no shoes on. Plus she admitted she had nowhere for her and her children to go, never mind the fact that she was only twenty-one years old with four children under the age of five. The police took her to the place where everyone was being held. The social worker took one look at Kymela and knew her kids deserved better. There was no way Kymela would ever get them back under her watch. Those innocent children were never going back to the likes of her. Now Kymela had stop reliving in her mind everything her children had not seen. Kymela came to the realization that her little princesses was leaving her. How could she explain this to them. Plus this bitch of a social worker made it very clear she wasn't going to be getting her kids back anytime soon. Kymela began to speak. "I need to talk to you guys for a minute. Karin stop coloring for a minute please. Mommy has something to tell you. Come on, all y'all gather around get in close. I have to go away for a while." Her smile was still strong but the tears were streaming steadily. "Why mommy?" asked India. "Well mommy needs some help, I am a little sick right now." Kymela replied. "Are you going to die?" Karin asked. I swear for her to be the oldest she can be so dumb sometimes. "No, No nothing like that. I just have to find a place for us to live. I also have to take care of some other stuff." was her response. "I don't mind mommy." I said. I figured she needed that. "As long as we never go back with Ramon." I added. I thought I was helping the situation but I was making things look worse for mommy. Kymela got up from the table to leave. Then all of these white people came piling in the room. They had smiles on their faces but my gut told me this was real bad. My mom told us to go with them and be polite. Instantly everyone started crying. We did as we were told following these strangers to some unknown place. The fear was paralyzing and we hadn't made it out of the room yet. I overheard my mom say she didn't want us separated. The white lady said she'll do what she could but it was going to be hard. Kymela walked away with tears pouring from her eyes. There was no sound coming from her mouth, the look of despair was heartbreaking for anyone to witness. I swear it looked as if that was the lowest point in her young life. Her mind was racing, if only she could rewind the hands of time. She would go back to yesterday morning when her gut told her to leave Ramon. She would've followed her first instinct packed her bags; taken us and left. If only's kept tracing through her mind. I walked outside to this huge blue car with drawings along with some writing on it. I didn't know what it said but I would learn those words all too well. All three of us piled into the car one by one. A white man came around the corner to put the baby in the car seat. The white lady from the room was standing watching everything. She sat down inside the car. As she fasten her seatbelt she turned around with the same annoying smile on her face. It was nothing to be smiling about. "Aww don't cry I'm going to take you guys to a better place." she said. Then she turned back around and proceeded to drive. My mind was going a mile a minute with all kinds of thoughts until we arrived to the first house. Karin was up first. It was a big pretty house. The lady got out the car walked around to the passenger door then opened it. "Karin, come on sweetie don't be scared." she said with a smile. Karin got out the car, she never even looked back. There were a whole lotta steps that they had to climb. Once at the top the lady rang the doorbell. Karin began to cry as soon as the door opened. Some black woman was in the doorway smiling but Karin started screaming "I want my mommy!" India and I started crying as well. The lady at the door just smiled as she took Karin inside along with the white lady. I started hugging India while I was crying. What in the world is going on? The white lady came back to the car with the same silly grin on her face. "Everything is going to be alright." she said. Where was Karin? I was too afraid to ask but that was all I was thinking. She followed her same seatbelt routine, and then we pulled off. It didn't seem like we were driving that long when we made another stop. This time she took my baby sister out of the car. She was still asleep; she had been since Kymela had feed her in the white room with the drawing and things on the wall. She walked around the house then disappeared into a side door of the house. She came back to the car alone again. I didn't cry because India had told me her head was hurting. Plus she felt like she was going to throw-up. The last house was big. Not as big as the first one though. She unfasten her seatbelt turned around and said this is it. India had fallen asleep with her head resting in my lap. I was really starting to get scared. I woke India up. The social worker lady, well that's what everybody kept calling her, ask us to get out of the car and follow her. We did as we were told. We went to the front door. There was a dark skin man along with a brown skin woman standing there. Their smile was different then everybody else's it felt real. They told us to come in. I felt like they were weird they had plastic mats on the floor in front of the door. They asked us to take off our shoes. We did as we were told. It was prickly things sticking us in the feet. I glanced around the entire living room was white. It had a lot of ceramic or porcelain looking things everywhere. They even had plastic on the couches! They walked us down this long hallway that lead to the kitchen. They offered us some food I said no thank you. India clung tightly to my leg. I looked down and asked her if she wanted something to eat. She looked up with her big brown eyes as if she was silently pleading me for the right answer. I asked her again was she hungry. She shook her head no. I knew she was lying. I couldn't remember how long it's been since we ate. So I asked her again, this time I told her there is nothing to be afraid of. If you're hungry then you should eat. India shook her head yes this time. They made something that looked and smelled good. I still wasn't touching the stuff; even though I was starving. The white lady left after dinner. Trust me there was no love lost there. The brown-skin lady began to speak as soon as the white lady left. She told us we would be staying with her for a while. The man was standing there with the same goofy grin on his face. "My name is Mrs. Adkins and this is my husband, but you can call me whatever makes you comfortable." she added. "Well let's get ready to take our bath. We walked upstairs. The walls were painted blue in the bathroom. As India and I piled in the bathroom; she put the top of the toilet seat down. She sat down on the toilet and motion for me to come over to her. She stripped me of my clothes and my dignity. Her "husband" was standing in the doorway, with the same goofy smile. He was really starting to sicken me. I tried to cover myself with my hands. Ramon had taught me nobody was supposed to look at my business. "My butt my business." he would say all the time. For some reason the lady began to laugh at me. I guess I looked funny to her. She picked me up then placed me into a hot bath. Just what I needed; I thought. I laid my head back in the tub looked up at the ceiling then just released a sigh. "Mmm-ahh". Mr. Goofy as well as Mrs. Adkins began to laugh again. How annoying, here I am three years old and even I know today would not be the day for all the smiles followed up by laughter. I've always been very mature for my age. Little did I know that as I got older I would be very naive when it came to the wrong things. While they were still engaged in their snickering; our foster mother picked up India then placed her in the tub as well. After we soaked for a few minutes she began to wash us up. "Come on, guys." she said. She picked India up out the tub. She then instructed me on how to be safe on getting out. I was kind of jealous of India getting all the attention. Mrs. Adkins began to speak. "Look Thomas. Look at this ring around this tub. These children are downright filthy." she said. I rolled my eyes at Mrs. Smart-Mouth. What she didn't know is that Kymela let us go outside to play all day long. Although she ran our bath water Ramon instructed her to let us eat before we took our bath. We had finished eating at different times. One by one we went into the living room; climb on the couch then fell fast asleep. I started to say something but after the day I just had, I really didn't have time to deal with Mrs. Smart-Mouth or her goofy "husband". She led me out of the bathroom down the hall into this very traditional looking room. There were flowers all over the walls; it had matching bedspreads and curtains. I guess this isn't too bad, I thought. I laid down too exhausted to fight the world anymore today. I fell into a helpless sleep. The days ahead with Mrs. Smart-Mouth and her "husband" was going to be trying to say the least. The more she tried the more I fought her on EVERYTHING. As time crept along we settle into a routine. The white (social-worker) lady would come to pick us up every Saturday. We went to see Kymela in the white room with the painting of children playing on the wall. All of us would arrive with our different social worker people. We sat there laughing, playing, coloring, and bickering. Just basically having family fun. The social worker people would began piling in around the same time. With their usual phony plastered smiles along with them. Telling us it was time for them to take us home. Seriously home, they have got to be kidding me. It was always an emotional scene when it was time to go. Mrs. Smart-Mouth would do something nice for us when we got there. This particular Saturday when they said we were going home I wasn't so terribly offended. It was starting to feel like home. When we got there we were allowed to go straight outside. India was happy. In the backyard we had a sliding broad, with this big peach tree, we also had an apple tree with little green apples. We weren't allowed to eat those though. Mrs. Smart-Mouth said it would make us sick. I absolutely hated the peach tree. There was always some kind of bugs falling out into my shirt. At night the lightning bugs would come out. India and I played a game to see who could catch the most. I loved catching them closing my hand so they would light up. Then when I'd get bored and I'd squash it and catch another one. India use to let hers go. So I tried to make it the rule of the game but India wouldn't play with me. So I changed it, we had to put it in a jar at the end of the night if they made it we would let them go. The seasons changed as time flew bye. As Karin got older she gave Kymela a hard time at every visit. Kymela would sit there and cry at every visit the entire time. My baby sister Gerren was soon extracted from the visits. Her foster mother said it was too emotional for her being that she was so young. She couldn't understand why this lady would pick her up and tell her how much she loved. Plus kept mentioning the fact that she was her mother. She would complain about how long it would take to calm her down once she got home. The one thing I did notice was that Ramon never came to the visits. It was early Saturday morning the first one of spring. The birds were chirping, the sun was shining followed by a warm breeze. "Can we go outside pleeaase?" I asked. "Of course you can, just don't get dirty." said Mrs. Smart-Mouth. I knew we were supposed to go see Kymela today. She always told us how pretty we looked when we walked in so I didn't want to get dirty. Mrs. Smart-Mouth followed her normal routine of watching us through the window. I swear she acted as if we couldn't see her through the curtains. I waved at her. She looked surprised at first then she waved back. She turned out not to be that bad after all. She was actually really rather nice. I jumped off our newly installed swings and headed over to the sliding broad. India slid down the sliding broad. She saw me running in her direction. she tried to run around to go back to the sliding broad before I got there. I made it at the steps the same time she did. "It's my turned" I said. "That's why you're not my sister." she replied. "Don't say nothing stupid like that I am your sister!" I yelled. "No you not! They took your real sister and switch her with me." India said in a cold voice. I instantly began to cry. "I'm sorry don't cry said India, I am your sister. Remember the day I cut myself on the sliding broad. I got a scar on my stomach. See look right here; she said while pulling up her shirt. If you're ever wondering if I'm your sister just look for my scar okay." she finished. I shook my head yes. I was so happy they didn't take her away. Mrs. Smart-Mouth called us out the window. The white social worker lady was here to take us on a visit. We arrived in the white room again. This time I was paying more attention to the painting on the wall. Everyone seemed so happy. The smiles on their faces while they were holding hands made me feel like everyone in the world should play together it looked like fun. Kymela arrived while I was in mid thought. She looked different. Her hair was comb but not in its usual manner. It seemed kinda of messy. Plus she was getting fat. I thought she had more food to herself since us along with Ramon was gone. I figured she finally had some time to relax. Karin glanced at her then paused. Karin quickly figured out Kymela was pregnant. She went off. Karin glance turned into a stare. She began squinting her eyes as if the devil had just taken control of her soul. "Mom are you pregnant?!" she asked. India stopped what she was doing. We all were now staring in the direction of our mother. "No." she answered. "Yes you are, you left us here while you go out and party. Now look at you! You're starting a new family, without us! God only knows with whom!" Karin spat out. Kymela began to cry and panic all at once. She didn't want the rest of us to feel that way. Kymela knew in heart she loved all her daughters and would never leave them. She omitted the fact that Ramon called begging her to go back to New York City with him. How he told her that they could start a new family. Then in a moment of weakness she gave into her love, hate, mixed with passion for Ramon. They had an intimate encounter for just that one night. Now here it is four months later, and again she was with child. Ramon assured her it was an accident but she knew better. After declining Ramon's last attempt out of desperation, he went back to New York City without her. Kymela was looking for the right words. Trying to muster up the nerve to talk to Karin without spilling the ugly truth about Ramon. "That is not true, Karin. I could never even think of doing such a thing!" she managed to say. Karin looked over at us. "Yes she would ya'll." she said with venom seeping from her voice. India had a look of panic on her face. The white social worker lady bust through the door. "I happened to overhear, just checking to see what is going on." she said. Before Kymela could answer, she began degrading her. "I thought I told you to tell them. This wouldn't have happened had you listened to me. Now would it?" she asked in a condescending voice. The white social worker lady turned to us with her same plastered smile. she began to speak. "Girls, why don't we go and get some snacks out of the machine. Karin and mommy needs to talk for a bit okay." she said. We all started towards the door. The white social worker lady made it her business to tell Karin that if she needed anything to yell, with a fake smile across her face. Then she rolled her eyes at Kymela while walking out the door. What she didn't know was that although Kymela put on a smile while talking to her daughter, that day changed their relationship forever. She now viewed Karin as evil and downright disrespectful. The white social worker lady decided to cut the visit short. We were escorted out of the building to separate white cars. All of them had the same writing and drawing the outside of them. On the way back to Mrs. Smart-Mouth house I gazed out the window daydreaming about yesterday. How happy we were. Now I could slowly see that the family I once knew was fading away. Gerren still didn't come to visit. She was a chocolate little baby, the last I saw her. Now I was sitting there wondering what she looks like. Now we were arguing amongst each other. Quite frankly I'm was happy to be going back to Mrs. Smart-Mouth's house. After the argument between Karin and Kymela. Karin never came back to the meetings. Two years slowly drifted by with the same routine. Only difference was now we had a little sister named Rose who would accompany Kymela on each visit. She was by far the prettiest of all us. It appeared she had managed to inherit every positive quality Ramon and Kymela possessed. She had big brown eyes that could put the moon to shame. Her sandy brown hair matched her caramel skin tone. Rose's deep dimples enhanced her smile that flashed off her perfect white teeth; she also had thick long hair. One night we were all sitting around watching Entertainment Tonight. My mind was wandering. I hated watching this show. The ringing phone scared me out of my thoughts. Apparently Ramon had been in a terrible car accident. They weren't sure if he was going to live or not. My foster mother was unsure if they should tell us being that we were so young. I being a child was there but unseen. They were talking about him as if I didn't know what was going on. It seemed after Kymela left, Ramon became a workaholic. He managed to land himself two government jobs after being discharged from the marines. One for the post office sorting mail.

The other was New York City Transit. He traveled from one full time job to the next. It left him with very little time to sleep in between. I guess this was how he coped with losing his family. Meanwhile Kymela spent her days and nights in church. Praying to the Lord to bring back the only love she ever knew and her kids too. "They said he fell asleep behind the wheel." Mrs. Smart-Mouth said to her "husband". "Then he had a head on collision with a city bus." she finished. Mrs. Smart-Mouth never mentioned the incident again. I cried a lot when I was alone. I figured Ramon was dead; she was just too nice to tell us. Allot of time went by along with a lot of unanswered questions. Unbeknownst to me, Ramon had undergone multiple surgeries that resulted with a plate being placed in his leg. Perhaps Ramon couldn't take the loss of his family anymore then decided to end it all. No one really knows what happened that night. Ramon pleaded with Kymela to come see him. She declined. Her mind was focusing on the parenting classes she had to attend. Along with the many court dates she had scheduled. Her heart wanted her to run to him but she couldn't be there not the way he wanted. She couldn't be his twenty-four hour babysitter. Plus one of the conditions on possibly getting custody of her children back was attending a domestic violence therapy group, and not to have us around Ramon until he attended an anger management program. After numerous phone calls to Kymela, Ramon started to realize that maybe he had taken things too far this time. He just knew with everything that was going on Kymela would've been by his side. Ramon laid in the hospital bed many nights alone. Days turned into weeks. Weeks turned into months. He couldn't believe how alone he really was. Every once in a while one of his brothers or sisters came up. If his mother could get the time off of work she would be there too, but nothing from his family. Although he was healing physically, emotionally he was in turmoil. He couldn't believe that after all that had gone on he still had not seen his children or his wife. Slowly he forgave Kymela for what he deemed as her betrayal. He wanted his family back. He laid in the hospital for months on end waiting for the day that he could see his daughters again. He wanted to make it up to them. Everything! When Ramon first arrived at the hospital; immediately after his surgery his mother brought in a lawyer. They discussed things that he really didn't remember. Every so often in the beginning of his recovery the lawyer would call to verify more information. The conversations were short. Ramon was barely able to speak. Even his phone calls to Kymela was dialed by someone else and lasted for only a few minutes at a time. In the process of getting better along with his soul searching he had forgotten all about the lawyer. He was quite surprised on discharge day when the lawyer showed up. In his hands was a check for one million dollars. It seemed his mother had been making all the decisions on his behalf when he was enduring his recovery. Now with his new found wealth Ramon was going against the system. He had every intention on seeing his daughters by any means necessary. It wouldn't take long to find out Ramon got exactly what he wanted. Once Ramon's cast was removed he set off to Virginia. Ramon arrived early in the morning. He wanted it to be a surprise. That it was. I was outside playing with India. We had rushed through our homework along with our snack. It was time to go outside. We were playing school; I'd looked over the train tracks that was some distance away but close enough to see when the train was crossing. I couldn't tell but it looked like a tall skinny man was crossing the tracks. He walked with a horrible limp. As the figure came closer I could make out Ramón's face. It was Ramon! I took off running towards the train tracks. Mrs. Smart-Mouth dashed out the house behind me. Of course she was standing in the window peeking thru the curtains as usual. unbeknownst to me I had begun to scream. "Daddy, daddy, daddieee!" I shouted. India didn't know what was going on but she took off running behind me. He swiftly grabbed me while picking up both of us up all in one motion. "Hey, Hey, Hey!" he said. I hadn't realized to that very moment how much I missed Ramon. I couldn't control my emotions. As the tears rolled down my cheeks, I realized why he was my daddy. We had a bond that could never be broken that was connected through our hearts. No matter what we were a part of each other for life. He told us we were going to spend the day with him. I held on to his neck so tightly I never wanted that moment to end. Ramon had a whole day of adventures planned for us. We went shopping then out for pizza. We had a blast. While in the pizzeria the white social worker lady showed up. Uh-oh went thru my mind. She talked about some agreement Ramon had made with her. Involving him being able to see us unsupervised. Ramon went in his pocket and took out what appeared to be a lot of money then handed it to the white social worker lady. The smile on her face spoke words that needed not be mention. "Thank you." said Ramon. "Anytime" she responded. She looked at us with the same sicken smile as usual. "You guys enjoy the rest of your day." she said as she headed towards the door. We finished our meal then he took us back to our foster mother's house. Saying goodbye wasn't that hard for me. Ramon had promised he was going to come back and I believed him. Two days later Ramon came back. He had all my sisters in the car along with Kymela. I ran to the car. "Daddy where did you get this car from." I asked. "Well I figured if I have to keep going from house to house I needed it. Plus with us traveling back and forth to the mall, in addition to going out to restaurants and stuff; it would be better to rent a car. Is that alright with you?" he answered. "Yea, I guess so. I betcha' my big wheel can beat your car!" I said. "No, I don't think so." said Ramon. "Yes it can!" I replied smiling so hard that my cheeks hurt. "I'll prove it. Let's race!" I continued. "You're going to lose." Ramon insisted. "I bet I won't". I responded still smiling. Ramon put India in the car. I jumped on my big wheel. Ramon put up three fingers in the window to indicate the count down. Three fingers, two fingers, one finger, no fingers. Go, I thought. I pedaled as fast as I could. Ramon was at the end of the block by the time I had got out of the driveway. Ramon was at the stop sign. Ramon began turning the corner. I started screaming daddy wait you win. I jumped off my big wheel. I started to run after the car screaming, but the way he turned the corner as if he didn't see me I knew it was no use. Yet again, I found myself standing in the middle of the street looking for one of my parents. Mrs. Smart-Mouth came out the house. She asked me what had happened. I explained to her everything in detail. How I was going to race Ramon. That I had lost and Ramon left me. She did her best to make me feel better. But the truth of the matter was her and I never really got along. She just kept me around because India was so attached to me. In her mind India was her daughter. She allowed her to sleep in the bed with them since day one. India got all the attention while I was ignored. The only person who knew I was there was India. I would find myself begging

India to sleep in the room with me just so I would not feel alone. I fell asleep replaying the events of the day while crying. I was to the point that my stomach along with my head was starting to hurt. I was awaken when India bust in the house talking about the great time she had with mommy, daddy, and all the rest of our sisters. I looked up at my father with my eyes watering. Ramon looked down and began to speak. "Now the next time daddy tells you a car is faster than a big-wheel you'll listen to him right." he asked. "Yes sir." I responded with a smile. I was secretly thinking you fool. You made me miss the only outing we had as a family in years just to prove a fact. Something you know a child at the age of five would dispute but is clearly wrong in everyone else's eyes. Your point was proven when you reach the end of the block. You didn't have to leave me! I didn't say anything because I didn't want him to leave me again. I wanted him to stay a little while, so that I could spend time with my sisters. Little did I know at that very moment I started a pattern of not speaking up for myself. Also the feeling of abandonment and loneliness were starting to become a permanent fixture in my life. I still couldn't quite figure out what lesson Ramon was trying to instill. Maybe it was; don't ever question your daddy. I know what I learnt was don't speak up for yourself. Also that I was completely alone in this world. My mom let him leave me and my sisters were in the car too. The foster parents were home; no one stopped him. I was definitely alone.

CHAPTER 2

Home Sweet Home

Kymela finally did it! All the parenting classes, court dates, visits were over. Today was the day we've all been waiting for. It had finally arrived. We were going home! The white social worker lady arrived to pick us up. I quickly jumped in the car and put on my seat belt. The excitement was invigorating. The white social worker lady kept talking. She said everybody was coming home today just at different times. She kept talking until we pulled up in front of a two-story house. There was a tan station wagon in front of the house. "Is that my mom car?" I asked. "No." she replied. "I think it's hers, I mean it is parked in front of her house." I continued. "No, that's not your mother's car." she said again. I unlocked my seat belt and got out of the car. India and I were the first to arrive. I walked up to the front door. Rose bust out the screen door and jumped directly into my arms. I walked up to my mother. She was standing beside a heavy-set, light-skinned lady. She was smiling just as hard as my mother. My mother explained to us that the lady standing beside her was the pastor. She had rented us the upstairs of the house. The downstairs was the church. I had never met a lady pastor before. Her husband was the minister of the church. As far as members they were only her children and one elderly lady that she took care of in her home. The house was beautiful. There was sliding double doors that lead from the living room to the den. There was a new set of double doors that lead from the den to the dining room. I walked from the dining room straight into the kitchen. I ran to open the door to the back yard. It wasn't as big as Mrs.

Smart-Mouth house, but I was grateful. As far as furniture we didn't have that much. It was a couple of chairs around the wooden kitchen table, a love seat in the living room and beds upstairs in our bedroom. Kymela was determined not to ask Ramon for anything she did the best she could and we appreciated it. Karin was the next one to arrive. she went thru the house like we did. She sat down on the couch and glared at Kymela as if she wasn't impressed, with her or this whole reunion thing. India and I just began talking to her. After a while she started to loosen up a little bit. We sat there and waited a long time for Gerren. The pastor lady left. She told us she would see us in church on Sunday. When she left we were still waiting for Gerren. A social worker arrived and asked Kymela to talk to her in private. Kymela told her it was okay to talk in front of us. The social worker began to explain what she thought would be the best thing for Gerren. She began to explain to Kymela how it wouldn't be fair to Gerren to take away the only mother she has known so suddenly. Kymela began to cry. She explained how they had snatched her baby as an infant, how she had to jump through hoops and now the judge says she can have her back and that's what she wanted. Gerren still didn't return until a couple of weeks later. Things were going great at first. We went to church every Sunday. The pastor lady had a lot of kids. Some older some our age that we'd play with. The pastor lady started to tell Kymela how unruly we were. How she needed to spare the rod or spoil the child. Which Kymela took very seriously? We started getting pinched if we embarrassed her. Most of the time it didn't seem like we did anything to be punished for. Like for example they would have dinner after a church service we would go get plates sit down and eat our food then ask for more. Kymela would pinch us and tell us we were trying to let everybody at church know there was no food in our house. She knew we hadn't eaten all day and there really was no food in the house. Then one Sunday they were having dinner after church we rushed to get our food as usual this was going to be our only meal all day. Someone made a comment let them go first, you know they be starving. Kymela couldn't wait for us to get upstairs. She started punching us to the ground one by one saying we were going to stop embarrassing her. Then she told us the next time they had food after church we were not to go and get any. So every service after that we would sit next to Kymela and wait for second service without any food. If someone would come up to us to ask if we wanted anything we were instructed to say no thank you with a smile. We all did as we were told we didn't want to get punched any more. Some time had passed Ramon was coming for a visit? Kymela went to Woolworth to buy a new outfit. We smiled as Kymela showed off her new dress. It was a pretty print with white buttons down the front. It was kind of low cut in the front to show off some cleavage. We were happy for Kymela she had us back and now she was going to get Ramon back. Life was finally starting to look up for Kymela and us as well. With Ramon coming back Kymela would stop being so mean to us. Things were bound to go back to the way they use to be. Back to when were a happy family. When we had fun. Heck maybe Ramón can get Gerren to stop sitting in corners staring at us like we crazy or something. I mean at first I understood she didn't know us. But now it's been months and she still doesn't talk unless spoken to first. She's kinda weird. Bang, Bang, Bang. "Momma, momma, there is someone knocking on the door!" We all yelled in unisense. I ran to the room with a bright smile on my face. We all knew who it was. Ramon! The look in Kymela eyes made me stop smiling instantly. At that moment I wish I hadn't come into the room. I just stood there I knew I had to speak. "Momma, there is someone at the door." I said in a low voice. "What did you say to me?" She asked in a flat tone. "Momma there is someone at the door." I repeated in a voice barely audible. Kymela raised her hands and slapped me with all of her mite. The slap was so powerful it knocked me halfway off my feet. I grabbed the edge of the bed to keep from falling all the way to the floor. I stood there looking dumb founded. I didn't know what I had done wrong. I tried to replay what I had said to Kymela when her voice interrupted my train of thoughts. "From now on when you address me you say excuse me ma' first. Whatever I'm doing is more important than anything you will ever have to say to me. Do you understand me? "Kymela said in a calm voice as if nothing just happened. "Yes ma'am." I said while fighting back the tears. "Now say it again." Kymela instructed. "Excuse me ma', there is someone knocking on the door." I repeated. "I already know that" said Kymela with a smile. As she started towards her room

19

door she turned around and told me to fix my face. As she left the room I followed her in silence. When she got to the front door and her nervousness was starting to prevail. Kymela turned around with a bright smile on her face showing off her dimples and perfect teeth. "How do I look ya'll?" she asked. "You look great!" said India. As soon as the door opened we jumped into Ramon arms, smiling, laughing while grabbing our gifts. We wrestled Ramon down to the ground. He was laughing so hard, he could barely speak. Ramon is back was all I could think with a smile. I knew one thing for sure he was going to fix little Miss Kymela's ass if he catches her hitting us like that. Ramon stayed for a while. Life was great. When we came home from school Kymela was smiling, cooking or cleaning up. None of those things which she did when Ramon was not there. Ramon stayed laid up in the bed smoking cigarettes. He was even talking about finding a job in Norfolk. He was going to try and see if he could get a job for Virginia Public Transportation. Then one day our whole routine was interrupted by a knock at the door. It was the pastor lady. She came inside the house. She told Kymela how she had missed her in church the last couple of Sundays. Then she asked her when was she planning on coming back to church. Kymela did her usual shy smile and simply said she didn't know. The pastor lady told her don't turn her back on God after all he had brought her through for some man. Kymela told her she wasn't turning her back on God by spending time with her husband. By now Ramon had heard enough. He walked down the hall to where they were standing to really see what was going on. Ramon engaged the pastor lady in some pointless conversation who's God? Does he exist? Yah-dah, Yah-dah. The pastor lady got real mad started calling Ramon the devil. Then he said he never heard of a woman pastor and that she was a false prophet. The pastor lady turned to Kymela and told her if she would like to continue to rent her house Ramon had to go! Ramon was infuriated. He yelled what kinda christian would tell a woman to leave her husband a fake one that's who. The pastor lady husband heard the commotion. He got out the car and came inside the house to defuse the situation. It was too late. Ramon had enough of bickering back and forth he turned to Kymela and posed one question was he going or the pastor lady. Kymela put her head down, with that

Ramon walked out the door. I figured he would be back being that he didn't take any of his stuff. Little did I know it would be a while before we would see Ramon again. When Ramon left Kymela turned into a drill sergeant. We'd come home from school and have to clean the entire house. Her motto became cleanliness was next to Godliness. We had to wash the dishes, clean the stove, wipe off the table, clean the bathroom, our rooms, the living room, dining room, den, along with washing out some clothes by hand, hanging them on the clothesline to dry, bring the clothes in from the clothes line, iron them, sweep and mop the floors. Then if we didn't make her mad we could eat dinner. Trust me it wasn't hard to make her mad. So two to three nights out of the week one or more of us went to bed without dinner. The more chores we were given the more physical Kymela became. The physical abuse went from pinching, slapping, punching, to knock outs. When that didn't fulfill Kymela's temper tantrums the real beatings began. Kymela moved off of the pastor lady's property. She then tried to call Ramon to come back. Ramon wasn't having it. Kymela went into a deep depression. To cope with her depression she revolved her entire world around making the finest little girls Virginia had ever seen; who knew the meaning of hard work. By the time I was seven years old I'd taken on the role of mom. In order to survive we needed food. India started off stashing food in her bedroom closet. It was not much just apples and oranges from school that she didn't eat at lunch. We quickly became her co-defendants. We started adding all non-perishable items to the closet. We weren't allowed to touch the food until a night when we were told to go to bed without dinner. That would ensure there would be food or something left for the next unfortunate soul. At school things weren't much better. I had no friends plus everybody picked on me. I grew from pudgy to full blown fat. My hair never did grow in. It was still a thin stringy see through mess that it had always been. In the looks department, I was hurting. My skin was darker, I have a gap in my front teeth and I walked like a duck. Kymela went to every church service available. Morning, noon, and night. All we owned were hand me down church clothes. Kymela didn't have any sense of style nor could she afford the latest fashions. We were the object of ridicule in church. When we first started going to church my enjoyment came from knowing God loved me unconditionally. Then it became a place of solitude. A place to get away from Kymela. The ridicule was initiated by the pastor lady usually. Her children were pretty nice to us if she wasn't around. The pastor lady mocked us. She made fun of our clothing, when Kymela was not around. After a while she began to act this way in Kymela's face. She was cunning. She would find a roundabout way to humiliate Kymela. If we were all standing there she would say something to the effect of Sista Wilson, now you know those girls hair could've been done a little better. Or sista Wilson those girls' clothes are filthy. I'm just telling you these things because I care. It took me awhile to figure out what was going on. I thought she was helping her. She would say it so nicely. I thought she was only being helpful, when visitors came to the church guest pastors' and their congregation. I realized she just had a nasty streak. It became apparent why she wanted it to seem like she was so concern. As soon as one of the guest pastor or congregation came close enough to the pastor lady she would start talking about Kymela. She would make it a point to let them know that we were always dirty. She would point out spots on our clothes. Ring around our collars, no stockings or that our hair was a mess. I could constantly overhear her saying how Kymela was just nasty and there was no excuse for her. If we would tell Kymela she was teasing us or calling us names behind her back, she would convince Kymela that we were kids and we were misconstruing things. She would sometimes tell her I told you sista Wilson. They must've overheard one of the other pastor's bring it up. It was never the guest pastor it was always her making cruel unnecessary comments. All of the guest pastors' were not innocent some of them would join in; but for the most part it was her. The rest of the guest who didn't like that behavior would often tell Kymela she should consider switching churches. She thought they just wanted to recoup her for their church she never paid them any attention. Thus I started to learn quickly that this so-called pastor lady was a sneaky, lying, manipulative, conniving witch. I knew we were going to clash on more than one occasion. Perhaps she was embarrassed by the way we looked as a representation of her church. Maybe she didn't know how to handle it, maybe.

Life for me started to go from bad to worst. There was hardly ever any food in the house. Kymela's budgeting skills was non-existent. One day out of nowhere we received a phone call. One of Ramon brothers had died. Ramon wanted his children to be there. He explained to Kymela how it would be faster to fly everyone out there. He really didn't want his children to be all cramped up on the bus. Kymela was scared to fly but she understood. My mom hung up and told us the bad and exciting news. Ramon brother had died. He had hung himself. The most important thing we heard was that we were going on an airplane. Furthermore our destination was New York City. I couldn't wait to tell everyone at school. I figured if they knew I was going to New York City they wouldn't pick on me as much. We had only been there once or twice since we lived in Virginia. If we went before that I couldn't remember. I got to school and made sure I rubbed everybody face in it. Kymela picked us up before school was over. She had only sent us to school to do some running around. Then she packed our clothes, picked us up from school in a cab and headed over to the airport. Getting on the plane was so exciting. Karin, India, and I got to sit by ourselves. Well Kymela was in the next row, but still we had a little bit of freedom. I stared out of the window the entire time. It was so breathtakingly beautiful up there. Kymela was still scared. The stewardess kept coming over asking was she okay. She would shake her head yes, but she didn't look okay. The plane landed at JFK airport. It was more people there then I had seen in my entire life. Kymela told everybody to hold someone hand and stay very close. I was starting to think, I wasn't going to like New York City. Kymela told us we had to take the train because Ramon couldn't get off of work to meet us. She told us how the doors opened then closed very quickly and that we would either get stuck in the doors or left if we didn't move quick enough. She also informed us to jump over the crack in between the train and platform because sometimes people foot got stuck and the train tears it off. I did exactly as I was told. I was so scared the doors was going to close on me. I jumped on the train and started yelling. "Momma', Momma I did it!" I yelled at the top of my lungs. Everybody on the train laughed but Kymela thought I was deliberately trying to embarrass her again. She had her hand under my coat pinching me with a big ole smile on her face. I looked up at her with tears in my eyes. "That's nice honey." she replied in her calm but don't mess with me voice. I sat down beside India. I didn't cry; I knew better than to cause any more of a scene. We arrived at this big brick building. There were lights everywhere. We all crammed inside this little elevator. As soon as the doors opened, we could smell food coming from somebody's house. I sure was hungry. We walked down the hallway to the last door on the left. A cute boy answered the door. He kept telling us he was our uncle. 'What's your name?" I asked. "Uncle Calvin." he answered. "Well it's very nice to meet you, Uncle Calvin, I'm Taylor" I said in my most proper voice. I knew Kymela would forgive me for the earlier incident after this. "I know who you are chile. Kymela what are you teaching these kids, they don't even know their own family." he responded in a playful voice. Kymela laughed but as soon as no one was looking she gave me a look I was all too familiar with. I knew when we were alone I was going to get a beating. A guy named uncle Jeremiah walked in. He looked pudgy in all of his pictures but now he was skinny. Kymela said that he was her brother too. I sat there quietly for the rest of the night. I didn't want to say or do anything else to make Kymela mad. They made mention of another brother that was in jail. I fortunately got away from her that night. Our grandmother made all of the children sleep on the pull out couch. Kymela and her went in the room to talk. I could hear them laughing and giggling all night it seem. I finally drifted off to sleep. For a while I knew we were free. Free from chores along with beatings. Kymela was happy thus we were happy. The next day as soon as Ramon got off of work he came straight to Kymela's mother house. He took us and all of our things to his mothers house. After he loaded the car with all of our things it really wasn't any room for all of us. Ramon said he would drop the things off then come back and pick us up. Kymela told him that we would walk over and meet him over there. The whole way over there I took in every sight. I was so excited to be in the big city. It was only three blocks. I remember thinking; they lived so close that, that's must be how they met. After we arrived to my other grandmothers' house all eyes were on us. Ramon kids were in town. We had a lot of aunt's along with uncles over there. It was too many to remember all of their names. They were sad because their brother had committed suicide but that didn't stop them for spoiling us. Every chance they got we were getting something. They would leave all day and tell us they had business to take care of. When they would come back they would have bags and bags of gifts for us. Our other grandmother was getting mad that we hadn't come back. So they decide to start splitting the trip. One night we would stay at Kymela's mother house then the next night at Ramon's mother house. The funeral had come and gone yet we still hadn't left to go back home. I didn't think too much of it. I was secretly hoping we never went back. I loved Ramon's house. Half asleep I got up to go to the bathroom. I had to walk pass Ramon's room to get to the bathroom. The smell seeping from every portion of the house was outrageous. They had about three cats and two dogs. No one ever cleaned up. The smell of feces was overpowering as I walked up the steps. I stepped into something wet on the way. In my mind I cringed I know it had to be dog pee. As I kept walking I could hear Ramon along with Kymela's voices coming from inside Ramon's room. By the time I got to the bathroom there was all type of gritty stuff in under my feet. I sat on the toilet. I then started rubbing my feet together vigorously to get the grit off the bottom of my feet. After everything was off of my feet I sat there listening to what seem to be an argument coming from the wall leading to Ramon's room. "I think it's time for you and the kids to be heading home." Ramon said. I couldn't hear what Kymela response was. All of a sudden I heard a familiar increase in Ramon voice. "Look, Kymela the funeral is over. You knew what the deal was when you came up here." Ramón continued. I didn't hear any response from Kymela. I walked back down stairs back to my room then fell asleep. The next morning I was still surprise when Kymela told us we were leaving. She said we were going to our other grandmother house. No one wanted to go over there. She was nice and everything but we got more stuff at daddy house. Kymela told my sisters that Ramon had to go back to work. Mm-hum was all I thought. We took a dollar cab back to the other grandmother house with all of our things. Even though they said we were splitting the trip the truth of the matter was we hadn't been over to her house in about a week. When we got there she wasn't very nice to Kymela. After about two weeks she was downright mean to her. Kymela mother had a discussion with her about our schooling and how she should be getting us back. I thought to myself how could my grandmother not see Kymela was trying to get our family back together. Needless to say we were on our way back to Virginia. When we got home Kymela became worst. Apparently she had spent all her money in New York. So we had no food or rent money. She took it out on us every minute she got. We struggled a little while; until the first came. Life was back to normal. Kymela dictated orders. We cooked and cleaned as we were told with no complaint or hesitation. That didn't stop Kymela from beating us every chance she got. We took some more trips to New York for birthdays or Christmas. The last time we went to New York we stayed even longer than the first time. We arrived for Thanksgiving but the next thing I knew Christmas was rolling around then New Year's eve followed by Karin birthday. We were there for so long that Kymela's mother started being mean to Kymela again. Then she said we had to be in somebody's school. Again Kymela went over to Ramon's but I guess that didn't work out because we left again, right after Karin birthday party. Kymela was so hurt by what had transpired while in the city. She tried not to let it show; but again we were out of money, and again all the bills were due. This time she was more than three months behind in rent. On top of that the house had been burglaries. Upon further investigation it appeared someone had tried to set the outside of the house on fire. Luckily it only brunt a little bit of the outside of the house. All of our Christmas gifts were stolen. We didn't have much furniture but they seemed to have found anything of value. Kymela didn't call the police because she felt it was one of the neighborhood children who didn't like the church lady or the dirty girls. Kymela assumed they didn't know what they were doing. Kymela seemed not to be able to let go of whatever had enraged her in New York. Therefore the simple life as we came to know it was over. Kymela learned how to perfect the art of torture. The next night we had all finished our chores. We sat down to play candy land. We had to do something to occupy our time; since they had stolen our television. I looked up to see the kerosene heater was on fire. Kymela had brought the heater to cut back on the electric bill. I shot a look of fear at Kymela. She looked in the direction of the kerosene heater. She grabbed Rose then ran out of the front door. India and Gerren was sleep on the couch. Karin was in the downstairs bathroom. I couldn't believe she left us. I didn't see the fire start. I don't even remember where I was coming from. I stood there staring blankly between the front door and the fire. The kerosene heater was engulfed in flames. Kymela had it place almost directly in-between the living room and the den, so this way it could heat up the entire downstairs. I thought maybe we could squeeze by. I said a silent prayer while I woke India and Gerren up. I called Karin from the bathroom. I don't know why but it never crossed my mind to use the back door. Maybe I subconscienely didn't want to make Kymela mad. She never let us use the back door, without permission. I just knew we had to get out of there. I told everyone to hold hands. Upon my instruction we held hands formed a line and very carefully we was going to walk around the fire. I gently pushed each sibling past the fire. I did Karin first. That girl was crazy; who knows what kinda of stunt she would've pulled. I did the same for Gerren and India. Each one as they made it stood on the other side of the fire. They stood there praying that the next sister made it across safely. Once we were all over the threshold I told them to head to the door. As we were walking outside I could hear some loud mouth lady yelling. "Her kids are in there!" she said to the firefighter. "How many?" he responded. I could see Kymela by the fire truck crying. I think she could feel my eyes burning into her very soul. She looked up at me. The loud mouth lady followed Kymela's eyes. As soon as she made us she began yelling. "There are the kids! How did you guys get out?" she asked. India pointed at me. I just shrugged my shoulders. As if to say I didn't know. Had I'd known what I know now I would've said through Gods' grace and mercy. Kymela tears had begun to dry up in the midst of the commotion. We went running towards Kymela screaming "Momma, Momma! "The loud mouth lady congratulated me then told me to always look after my sisters. I assured her I would. The firefighters asked Kymela if we needed to go to the hospital. She declined. As we walked through the front door, some of the firefighters had kicked in the backdoor. Kymela sat down on the couch. She just kept staring at the back door. The firefighters tried their best to fix the door for the night. The landlord heard through the grapevine of the fire. The first thing the next morning he came over to inspect. He'd seen all the damages from both fires, Kymela was always late with her rent. He couldn't take it anymore, we got evicted. Kymela tried to call Ramon to tell him what was going on but he thought it was some sort of trick by Kymela so she can move back. Kymela had no choice; we had to move into a shelter. They were nice there. Kymela didn't hit us that much there. I think it was because she had friends and people to talk to. Plus they could report her to social services. My birthday was approaching rapidly. I was all kinds of excited. I just had a feeling it was going to be great. It was my birthday. The ladies had put their food stamps together. They were going to throw me a party with their combined funds. They had been asking me questions all week like what's my favorite kind of cake, what kinda icing I liked. I pretended I didn't know what was going on. I overheard Kymela tell them they didn't have to do anything for me. They told her "we are all in a bind we have to help each other out. Plus that is our little helper she takes all of our babies feed them, change them, play with them. Gurl you know how much you be needing a break sometimes. We all know to go find her she'll be good with the baby for at least an hour or two." she said thru her giggles. At first I was mad at Kymela for trying to stop them. I'd quickly gotten over it. I had gotten up extra early. I continued walking down the hallway. I got to the bathroom. I had to stand outside and wait. One of the ladies was using it. She opened the door to see me standing there waiting patiently. "Well if it isn't the birthday girl! Happy Birthday!" she said. "Thank you." I responded with the biggest smile. I walked inside the bathroom reliving the last few moments. It was my birthday! I had so many things running through my mind. I was thinking about what I was going to wear. I had an outfit in mind. I had to look nice. If Kymela picked out my outfit, I knew I would've looked a mess. My mind darted toward what measures I had taken not to get into trouble. I thought about how I didn't pee in the bed the night before, so I couldn't get a beating for that. I washed extra hard so that the smell of soap remained on my body, so I couldn't get a beating for "pretending to wash." Even though I knew I always washed, that was Kymela saying. I left the bathroom extra clean because I didn't want to get a beating for that. Plus she would've beaten me real bad for embarrassing her. I walked back down the hallway to see another lady coming towards me. "There she is; the birthday girl! Hurry downstairs for your breakfast!" she said with a sneaky smile on her face. I had an extra pep in my step accompanied by a smile so bright I could've single handedly lighten up the night. They had asked me last week what my favorite breakfast was. They tried to do it in passing at breakfast one morning but I knew exactly what was going on. I didn't let them know I knew what they were doing. I just told them cheese eggs, toast, with sausage. Now I was excited about breakfast. Ooo-weee this was going to be a good day. I thought. I entered the room they had placed us in with excitement plastered on my face. Kymela was standing there. I froze as soon as I seen her. "Did you wash?" she asked. "Yes, Ma'am." I replied. "Get over here. Let me smell you." Kymela continued. I raised my arms with a smile. All I could think was this was my ninth birthday and nothing was going to spoil it. She dismissed me, then walked out the room to the bathroom. I sat there hoping the lady didn't leave a mess because Kymela would've thought it was me. I started getting Rose dress, before she even asked me. I even did Gerren's hair really pretty. I didn't say anything at breakfast or for the rest of the morning. I knew Kymela was looking for something to punish me for. The time had finally arrived. It was time for my party. They made spaghetti for dinner. That was my favorite. One of the ladies went in the back to get my birthday cake. It was beautiful. The cake was long, not like the round cakes I was used to. Strawberry cake with strawberry frosting; along with strawberry ice cream on the side. Oh my absolute favorite. It was time to light my birthday candles. Oh the excitement. Kymela sent me upstairs for a lighter. I ran upstairs barely containing my glee. I glanced around for the lighter. Kymela told me it was in the closet with all of our stuff. I didn't see it. I made myself calm down to really look for the lighter. I still didn't see it. My heart started pumping with fear. I knew better then to go downstairs without the lighter. I had no other choice. When I got down stairs Kymela immediately accused me of half looking then sent me back upstairs. When I got to the closet I moved some things around then placed them back. I started to cry but fought back the tears. I went back downstairs only to get the look from

Kymela, then sent back upstairs to really look. This time I took everything out of the closet one thing at a time. Even though our entire life was packed in this one closet I knew this could turn ugly. I stacked everything in the corner very neatly and precisely how it was in the closet. I didn't want to put anything back wrong. At this point anything could set her off. Still no lighter. My heart became heavy as I stacked everything back in the exact coordinates they were removed from. I walked slowly backed down stairs my smile had now dissolved into the look of despair. "Excuse me ma', I looked in the closet and I didn't see the lighter." I interjected into her already existing conversation. One of the women told Kymela that our entire life was packed into the closet and maybe it will be better if she looked. Kymela told me to come with her. My stomach began to turn in knots. I did as I was told and followed her. As soon as we got around the corner, and out of sight Kymela began to pinch me. She began to speak in low but deadly tone. "If I find that lighter I'mma tear your butt up. I began to pray. Oh, Lord please don't let her find the lighter. When we got upstairs she looked high and low. I was beginning to get happy that she did not find the lighter. Then the unexpected happened. Kymela turned around and told me I had hidden the lighter from her. I began to speak. "Excuse me ma'." As those words left my mouth a powerful slapped went across my face. "Now look in the closet over there!" said Kymela with intensity in her voice. My first thought was that she had found the lighter. The palpitations in my heart were visible to the naked eye. I stuck my head in the closet in the direction Kymela was pointing. I never saw her pick up the metal lamp in the corner. I felt a sharp pain in the back of my head. I stumbled into the closet. I held onto one of the boxes in the closet. I turned around swiftly. I'd seen the lamp in Kymela's hand. Tears were streaming down my face. White spots of light were everywhere. "Shut-up." demanded Kymela in a cold calm yet firm voice. I began sniffling while wiping my face. I tried to stop crying but it hurted so bad. I kept touching the back of my head with my hands. Then I would inspect my hand. "What are you looking for blood?" Kymela asked. I shook my head no. Kymela smacked me to the floor. Blood was leaking from the side of my mouth. Kymela instructed me to get up and shut-up. I did as I was told. In the midst of the hitting I didn't recognize the fact that Kymela had pulled out everything we owned and threw it all over the room. I was too busy trying to block the next blow. She told me I could come downstairs after I put everything back then cleaned my face. I started putting everything back in the same order if possible. Kymela was enraged; and I didn't want a repeat of that. My head was pounding so hard. The tears would not stop coming. I felt alone and abandon in that room. It was my birthday. I guess this was my gift from God as well as Kymela. Why didn't God help me? I couldn't handle the knowledge of knowing God didn't answer me. Kymela seemed to hate me. I laid across the bed when I was done putting everything back. I cried myself to sleep questioning God's where abouts in my time of need. I awaken the next morning feeling more like myself. Yesterday was yesterday. I'd seen one of the ladies in the shelter. She informed of the mess Kymela said she had found when she got upstairs last night. She also told me how numerous women from the shelter tried to wake me but I wouldn't budge. One lady came up to me with a suspicious look in her eyes asking me what happened last night. I simply told her that I cleaned the room then fell asleep. She smiled and told me how she left me a big piece of cake. I didn't want it that was a birthday I would like to forget. As I walked away I knew I had done the right thing Kymela had us trained that if we told anybody what was going on in the house they would take us away again. After that day time just seemed to creep right on by. The next thing I knew we got into something called housing. I didn't quite understand what it was but according to the ladies it was a marvelous thing.

CHAPTER 3

Introduction to the Hood

We left the shelter. Kymela was happy. Kymela had a few friends now; so every now and then she would have some company. They would come by to talk with Kymela all day. Kymela had gotten so comfortable with one family that she even let them move in. Kymela had gotten a job at a fast food restaurant. Life was good. One day when I came home from school they were gone. I didn't know why they had left but my soul cried. I couldn't openly express my disappointment. Kymela was just looking for a reason to get anyone. I knew with their absence it was life as usual. It didn't take Kymela long to go back to her old habits. Now she was more enraged than before. She had become downright diabolical. We were not allowed to eat anything in the house without permission from Rose first. We would have to beg a five year old for breakfast, lunch, and dinner. Rose being a child thought this was cute. We would stand humiliated asking Rose. "Rose may I eat?" "No!" she would often say with a smile. Then she would run to Kymela to collect her reward. Kymela would often give her the food we were asking for. She would congratulate her with kisses leading to laughter followed by hugs. We stood there hungry while longing for the attention Rose received. It was obvious she hated Karin, Gerren as well as myself. Rose along with India was the ones she loved. We were loved in that exact order and we all knew it. That was my home life. It was normal so I thought. We were adjusting to a new neighborhood. I was afraid of our new environment. It was called the projects. Bowling Park was nothing that I had ever been used to.

Guys would stand outside on the corner all day long. They would play horseshoes until all times of night. Kymela made us stay inside the house for the rest of the summer. There was a park right outside our back window but we weren't allowed back there.

It was the first day of school. I was scared yet excited. It was a new start. No one knew my name or our history. I was looking forward to school. We had to walk across a big field to get to the school. I walked into the classroom. The children in my class immediately began to giggle at my appearance. I slide into my desk. I sat there unprepared as usual. No paper or pencils. At my old school my teacher knew that I never had anything and would give me the materials needed for the day. The teacher asked me why I wasn't prepared. Then made a smart comment. The kids in my class continued to laugh. I didn't care it was part of my life, I've grown accustomed to. Finally it was time to go home. I arrived to the big field that we had to cross in order to get home. Kymela told me that I had to wait for India after school. I stood there waiting for her. We began walking thru the field. Instantly we were surrounded by at least ten to fifteen children. The children started asking us what school we were from. Where did we use to live? I was eagerly answering the questions. We finally were going to have friends of our own. I knew this would work out. New school, new friends. We would have people to walk home with every day. Life was about to turn around for us. India seemed to be acting distant towards our new found friends. By the time we had reached the middle of the field one of the girls turned to India and began to speak. "I thought your sister was supposed to beat my sister up after school." she said. I looked at India. It was too late for a response; the girl hit me right across my face. It didn't hurt. This little girl could never hit me as hard as Kymela. I just stood there looking at India with my eyes screaming how you could. I had never been in a fight before. India ran and left me in the field getting beat up. Once the rest of the children seen India had ran away scared; they jumped me. Everybody was hitting me. The children who looked scared that was standing there watching started yelling free licks. I was getting hit from every angle. I didn't know what free licks meant but I sure could feel them. I fell to the ground. I balled into the fetal position to protect myself as much as possible. They kicked and punched me until they were exhausted, which was after about fifteen minutes. Once they got tired they just walked away and went home. I laid in the grass for a few minutes I wanted to make sure everybody was gone. I got up off the grass and walked the rest of the way home alone. I got to the end of the court. From there you could see our front door. Kymela was standing there looking out the screen door. I started to smile when I'd seen her. She cared about me. I could see the concern on her face. When I got inside the house and told the story about how I'd gotten beat up; she tried to act nonchalant but I knew better. I'd seen the relief in her eyes when I was coming around the corner. After I was done with my recap Kymela let it be known she didn't want us outside fighting anyone. Kymela also added if we were outside fighting and she caught wind of it she would beat us. Being that we weren't allowed to go outside Kymela had an idea to turn us into the next Jackson five; by forcing us to sing. We sounded okay everyone except for Karin. She was tone death. We would stand there singing for hours sounding like shit. Even though it was Karin's fault she couldn't help it, the girl just didn't have a voice. Kymela would stand there slapping, hitting her for hours demanding that she sang right. Kymela did that until she got bored. Then it was back to business as usual. After we did our chores I would go upstairs and lay down. Sometimes we would be called to sing and that made life worst. It seemed like school was no better. Every day I would walk through the field with my heart racing. I'd wait for the first unexpected, yet expected blow. Beating me up every day after school was now a tradition. I mean who wouldn't hit the girl that never hit anybody back. They didn't know how afraid of Kymela I was. Every afternoon India would take off running through the field. I would come in hair a mess and my clothes dirtier. My life was not the best but it was still my life. I never complained and I thanked God every Sunday for it. With Kymela's non-existing budgeting skills life seemed to be getting worse. She would get her food stamps at the beginning of the month. She would buy silly items. We would have a cabinet full of snacks and all the Pepsi you could drink. She would purchase some lunch meat, a couple packs of hotdogs, pork and beans with a big bag of rice. By the second week of the month we would be out of food. On top of that we rarely got any of those things, unless

Rose gave us permission. I was so tired of the beatings inside as well as outside of the house. I needed to find a way to make money and leave the house. I was tired of starving. India found out the rental office loaned out lawn mowers to the tenants in case they wanted to cut the little patch of grass in front of their house. It was a nonelectric lawn mower that you had to push to cut the grass. I decided to sign the lawn mower out walk around to the private houses and charged them five dollars to cut their grass, if they wanted it. I would then bring the money to Kymela to buy us food. I would make anywhere from twenty to thirty dollars a day. I would sneak out to cut the grass come home and give the money to Kymela to buy us dinner. After all my sisters learned of my new found activities; we decided we could make more money if we cut grass together. So we paired off in two's. Now we had double our profit. Kymela still spent the money foolishly. We would have hotdogs one night, and then with the rest of the money she would buy Pepsi, B.C. powder, and a whole bunch of little Debbie cakes. I got tired of working for nothing. I thought she would be ashamed that her children ten and under had to work to put food in the house. She knew it was mainly me. A nine year old! I awaken really early. By eight o'clock I was in the rental office signing out the lawn mower. I did two lawns by myself. I saw India with Karin walking in my direction. They had their own lawn mower. I told them of a really big yard where we could try to get twenty dollars for. We knocked on his door he gave us permission to cut his grass. I was excited with the fifteen dollars I already had we were going to have thirty-five dollars and the day was young. By the time we had finished for the day we could have at least sixty dollars! We spent all morning on his yard. First he wanted us to rake the leaves and pine cones, place them all in this bag, then mow, and rake the lawn. We gave up after about two hours. The man was so mad when we took off running with our lawn mowers. He started yelling after us. "Don't knock on my door no more! You kids came here bothering me!" We had did his entire back yard. By the time we had gotten to the front we were exhausted. The twenty dollars we had asked him for was all we could think about. We had no concept of the bigger the yard the more money we should ask for. We thought we were getting over asking for twenty dollars. His lawn exceeded twenty dollars and he very well knew it. We did a couple more yards. We headed back to the rental office to return the lawn mowers. All together we had earned thirty dollars for the day's work. On the way back across the street I could see Kymela looking at us thru the window. I couldn't let her rob us again. I stopped my sisters and explained to them that if we went across the street and gave Kymela the money she was only going to send us to the corner store. We would get b.c. powder, cakes, a pack of hotdogs, and some Pepsi. I informed them that we wouldn't have food for the next day, and then we would be back at square one. I suggested we walked to the nearest supermarket and pick out things Kymela would have to cook. The nearest supermarket was three miles away. We walked all the way there laughing and playing along the way. I didn't want it to get dark before we got back so I quickly ran around the store grabbing things I either seen Kymela cook or knew she could make. I grabbed cabbage, cream style corn, whole corn, pork beans, two cans of each and rice. That should cover four days of sides. All of which I thought would go over rice nicely. Then it was off to the meat section. I picked up two packs of family size chicken, a pack of hotdogs, along with one pack of chicken gizzards. I then sent India to get Kymela a two liter of Pepsi, with a box of little Debbie cakes. I did this so Kymela could have her snack and she wouldn't be that mad. I wanted to buy us something to eat or drink on the way home but we didn't have enough money for all that. When we finally got inside the house Kymela was smiling asking for all the money we had made. I spoke up first. Since it was my idea. "We brought groceries; we also brought your Pepsi and cakes." I added to soften the blow. Kymela face went from a smile to a frown. I mean what was she going to do beat us for not giving her the money we had worked for. What had we did wrong; buy food. Check mate, I thought. Needless to say Kymela had years of experience at being a bitch. She politely walked over to the bags pulled out the soda and box of cakes. Kymela began walking up the steps; midway she stopped lend over the banister and replied "Since y'all are so smart, cook it yourself." Kymela continued to her room. I wanted her to see the food that I had brought. I wanted to teach her how to shop. This just wasn't fair to my sisters they had worked so hard for a decent dinner now they wouldn't have one. I had to make it up to them. I began cutting the cabbage. I put on a big pot of water. Then I put on a big pan of grease. I tried to season the chicken with a lot of pepper. The grease was popping and smoking. I hurried up and threw flour on the chicken then threw it in the pan. I didn't want to get popped by the grease. So grease splattered everywhere I placed the cabbage in the water. I put on another big pot of water for the rice. I dumped half the bag in the pot. I was determined to make us dinner. The chicken came out brunt on the outside while raw and bloody on the inside, the rice was hard, and the cabbage was mushy. We ate as much of it as we could. My entire day was a bust. I felt like I let my sister's down. I sent them upstairs. I washed the dishes, wiped off the stove, kitchen table, along with the counter tops, swept and mopped the floor. I could not wait to get into the bed. The next day we got up early for church. We got to church and endured the usual ridicule. As church was letting out all I kept thinking was how I was not in the mood for Monday's madness either. On the way out of church I heard Kymela tell the pastor lady that we would be helping them sell donuts next Saturday morning. I looked at Kymela; there goes our extra cash for food. Every time I think I've come up with a plan I tend to lose. When we got home I just went upstairs to my room. I figured Kymela would cook them dinner if I was out of her sight. I awaken the next morning late. I had peed the bed the night before, but if I didn't go to school Kymela would make me scrub my bed and do a lot of other miscellaneous chores around the house. I quickly walked over to the barrel with all of our clothes in it. I just grabbed anything out of the barrel. I didn't have time for a smell check of the clothes. I knew the barrel was filled with clean clothes and dirty clothes. We couldn't afford dressers so that would've had to do. I threw on my clothes then ran out the house without taking a shower. I'd already had horrible body chemistry. My natural scent could've been sponsored by Frito Lays because it definitely was corn chips. Ever since I could remember a corn chip odor use to follow me. I knew all of this yet I still left the house without a shower. When I arrived in class the scent that followed me was shameful. That's the day stinking girl was born. While I sat in class everyone walked past holding their nose. The teacher opened all of the windows in the classroom. It was in the middle of winter. The room was freezing the teacher allowed them to put their coats on while she aired out the room. Everyone knew it was me. The embarrassment I felt was indescribable. I honestly didn't know that I was going to smell that bad. With my natural smell mixed with piss and dirty clothes it's a wonder everybody didn't pass out. I never came to school smelling that bad again. I must admit I did have a few bad days after that. When your natural scent is corn chips it's hard not obtain an odor. As soon as you work up a sweat here comes the corn chip smell. My teacher finally got tired of my stench so she sent me to the nurses office. I had to explain how I washed, how often I washed; things of that nature. I just wanted to fall directly through the floor. During our conversation she explained how my body chemistry is changing. I don't even think she believed I was washing at all or the fact that my natural odor was corn chips. As I walked home I made a conscious decision that I would never let this happen again. I walked in the house and told Kymela all that had happened at school that day. I thought that would motivate her to wash my clothes, even though I was the one who pissed in the bed. Kymela covered her nose and told me to go take a shower. I went in the shower and began washing up. The fishy smell hit my nose like a ton of bricks. I reached for the window in the bathroom. I opened the window to air out the bathroom. I began to scrub I had to get to the bottom of this odor. Kymela busted in the bathroom with an extension cord in her hands. She began beating me relentlessly, in the shower. Every thrash felt like fire hitting my body for a split second; then leaving behind a burning sensation. The gut hurtling screams coming from my little body thru the bathroom window had everybody in the projects on pause. They wanted to know what was going on in the church lady house. They began to wonder and whisper about the little girls that never ever came outside. After the beating I was sent to bed without dinner. I cried myself to sleep. I got up extra early and tried to run out of the house. Kymela was up and waiting. Kymela told me to come here. I did as I was told. She took one look at the blisters on my skin. Some of them had welted up so big they had fluid in them. "Go back to bed, you're not going to school today." she said as she turned and went into her room. In my mind that was so wrong on many different levels. I knew she didn't want me to go to school because of the marks all over my body. However, all I could think of was; now I wouldn't get breakfast or lunch. On top of that I would have to do numerous chores. I probably have to clean the entire house by myself. I knew better than to complain, so I climbed back into bed. I stayed in the room all day long. I didn't watch television all day. I didn't want Kymela to know I was awake. I just read books all day and slept. Kymela left me alone; I was so grateful. The next day I got up at my normal time. I looked at my body to see if the blisters were gone. They were. Kymela walked up to me. I showed her my arms so she could see the visible bruises was gone. Kymela told me I wasn't going to school today. I truly didn't understand why. I walked back in my room contemplating what Kymela could've been up to. I tried to re-enact yesterday by staying in the room; Kymela had other plans. Kymela came to my bedroom door and told me today I was going to learn how to wash. She demanded that I got into the shower. I did as I was told. I got in the shower fearful of what Kymela was going to do. While I was in the shower Kymela sat down on the back of the toilet seat. If Kymela would move I would jump or flinch. "Stop jumping; like you scared or something. I know better than that." Kymela said. I lathered the wash cloth really good. I wet my entire body. I stayed in the back of the shower to work up a really good lather. I just wanted Kymela to see that I knew how to wash. Also to ensure she wouldn't have any complaints. "Get to the front of the shower! That's why you stinking now!" Kymela said. Kymela left the bathroom while I was rinsing off and let me know on the way out that there should be no more excuses for my smell. Kymela got me up early on Sunday to re-enact the shower scene from Wednesday. I did everything the way she had instructed. Kymela took out my clothes and laid them across the bed. She told me to sit in the pew next to her in church. Kymela had told me she didn't want me to work up a sweat. So I had been sitting somewhere she can watch me all day. After about three hours of church I started smelling the slight efflorescence of corn chips. I was waiting for the slap me but Kymela kinda looked sorry for me. When one of the pastors children walked, they shout me a look of discuss. Kymela told her to hold her nose when she walked back pass me. I looked down to the ground. Kymela knew that I didn't do anything to deserve this. I couldn't understand why she would just trade on me like that. I mean, there I was sitting there not doing a blasted thing then corn chip effloresces hit her nose. We left church with me feeling so low. I know Kymela probably was embarrassed but I am her child. How could she? I mean, how could she? Instead of Kymela taking me to the doctor or anything it became acceptable that I carried a slight odor. Time drifted by and summer was here.

It was hot plus school was out. We still weren't allowed to go outside to the park. We spent our day washing clothes by hand, which never came clean. Our routine consist of us mopping, cleaning, scrubbing daily in addition to our Jackson five rehearsals, church and selling donuts every Saturday morning for the church. We had a routine that we dared not stray from or we would've felt the raft of Kymela. She was so easily enraged with little or no provocation at all. I got up early Kymela told me that India and I we're to go to the store. We were to get her a zero candy bar, oatmeal pie cake, and a Pepsi. This big girl walked over to us. She told us she was going to smack the crap out of us. I didn't know what we had done wrong. She was sixteen or seventeen years old I was terrified. Another girl walked up, then spoke up for me. "You are not going to do anything to her." she said. The older girl slapped the mess out of my new friend. I just stood there as my new friend cried. She waited for the girl to walk away with her friends. "Why the fuck didn't you help me?!" she asked. "I'm sorry; I didn't know I was supposed to." I replied. "Are you serious?" she asked. "Yes." I replied. I think she must've heard the innocence in my voice because her facial muscles began to relax. "Where the fuck is you from?" she inquired. "Well I'm originally from New York City but we live here in Norfolk the majority of our life." I responded. She started laughing. "No, what projects did you come from?" she asked. "Projects what's that?" I asked "Oh boy, where did y'all live before y'all moved here." she said in a very slow tone. "OOOH! We lived in a house on Church St." I finally answered. "Where all the prostitutes and pimps be." she interjected. "I never seen such a thing." I protested. "Then you've lived a very sheltered life 'cause there are hoes on Church St." she jokingly replied. "Well we don't go outside. What is a prostitute/ hoe anyway?" I asked. "Are you serious?" she asked. "Well I think a hoe is a woman that sleeps with a lot of men, but I don't know what a prostitute is." I answered truthfully. "Well a prostitute does special favors for money and a hoe does special favors for free." she replied. "You are special; there are not many people like you that are so innocent. Where y'all going?" she continued "We have to go to Sparta Market for my mom." I replied. "Imma walk with y'all; 'cause y'all need protection." she said. We both started laughing. "My name is Venita." she said "And mine is Taylor." I added. Needless to say Venita and I became best friends. We laughed, talk, in addition to joking all the way to the store and back. When we got to the front of the courtyard I could see Kymela glaring at me from one of the top room windows. I quickly got rid of Venita and walked briskly to the house. I walked inside the house, Kymela didn't say anything.

CHAPTER 4

Hood Up or Lay Down

Venita was the only person in the world that wasn't afraid of Kymela. Plus Kymela was surprisingly nice to Venita. No matter how many times Kymela said no Venita would come to the door and asked can I come outside. Every once in awhile Kymela would say yes. Venita didn't care that everybody else called me stinking girl or that nobody talked to me. It wasn't like she was weird or anything. She had a lot of friends. She would walk away from anyone of them in a heartbeat to come over to me. I would often hear her say things in my defense; as she was walking away. We were best friends and that's all that mattered to her. I could only really see Venita when it was time to go to the store. I would make it my business to go get her. If I could I would sneak through the field after I ran out the back door. Venita was my escape from pain and misery besides church. As soon as I got up one morning Kymela let me know I had to go to the store. She also informed me there would be capital punishment if I took my time getting ready. I could hear the attitude in her voice as she told me her list of things to buy from the store. As I headed for the back door Kymela stopped me in my tracks. "Go out the front door. I don't have time for you and Venita to play around all day!" she said "Yes, ma'am." I replied. I knew to do exactly what I was told. I walked out the front door, through the courtyard. I turned the corner just in time to see this boy name Kirk. I tried to walk past him. Kirk grabbed my arm abruptly. I swiftly turned around with my heart thumping almost right outside of my chest. Kirk pushed me into the bushes then threw me against the cold brick wall. The shirt that I had on was cut into a V in the front and back. As the chill from the wall sent shivers down my back, he began to speak. "Do you know my name?" he asked "No." I answered very calmly. "Yes, you do." he kept repeating with malice in his voice. "No, I don't know who you are." I kept reassuring him. Although the tension was still building in my chest something inside of me told me that if I didn't do exactly what he wanted the situation would get considerably worst. "Your name is Mark right." I said adding my dumb little girl voice. He had to buy this. He had a bulge coming from inside of his pants. I didn't know what that was or what it was for but I became increasingly scared. My heart was racing so fast you would've thought I'd just ran a marathon. He came in closer to me and did nasty things to me. I knew if Kymela caught me she would kill me. Kymela would never believe I didn't engage in such an activity unwillingly. He began to pick up the pace. He grabbed a hold of both of my arms tightly while biting down on my neck then he let out this loud grunt as if something was hurting him. He let my arms go. My heart was still beating rapidly. What was to become of me now? He looked deep into my eyes as if searching my very soul and asked me again. "What's my name?" his voice was stone cold. As soon as the words left his mouth I knew my answer would determine his next action. So without hesitation I replied as innocently as I could "Your name is Mark right." I answered. He turned around and walked quickly away. I sighed a deep breath of relief. I continued to walk to the store. I wanted to go home right away but I was too afraid to go home without Kymela stuff. As soon as I hit the door Kymela asked me what took me so long. *I stood there telling Kymela the entire story from the beginning to the end. She declared there would be no exceptions, no one is to go to the store by themselves. No anger, no compassion, no emotional response whatsoever. Is she human? Does she care about me at all? Now I hafta watch this Kirk fellow around my little sisters.* I went to my room it was nothing left to do but cry. I felt so violated in addition to dirty. Dirty because deep down inside I knew I enjoyed everything that he did to me. A part of me knew it was wrong I just didn't understand why it was wrong. The next morning I got up extra early. I snuck to Venita house. I had to tell her what Kirk had done. I didn't know if she would believe me or not but I had to tell her. Kirk was a couple years older than us. He was a nickel and dime drug dealer. Kirk was chocolate with deep dimples. He was no dog, and I wanted her to know that someone thought I was cute. He always had on the latest fashions and he kept a little bit of money in his pockets. I was kinda flattered that he chose me. Plus I have one up on Venita. I had to rub this in the Venita's face. I cut through the back of the projects I'd seen India in the window; I stopped and blew her a kiss. I got to the front door I asked Venita's mother if she could come to the door for a few minutes. Her mom said she had to clean up. I begged for a couple minutes outside of the door. Venita came outside and sat on her front steps. I told her every little detail plus added a few I wanted her to be jealous. I couldn't contain myself I had a big smile on my face. Venita hung her head down then she started to cry. Venita told me how sorry she was that had happened to me. I didn't understand why she was so upset. She began to explain to me how Kirk had taken advantage of me. I knew I was upset earlier but that was mainly because I felt bad for enjoying it. She continued to tell me that if he would've put "it" in that I would've been rape. I didn't know what "it" was and before I could ask her she had to go back in the house. I walked back to the house hoping I made it back before Kymela got up. I was successful. I went inside my room. I began to cry again. I thought about the way Venita cried. If what he had done effected Venita in such a way then he took a whole lot from me. I just didn't know exactly what it was, but I knew one thing for sure, I was going to miss it. I spent the rest of the day gazing out the window. Venita was so sad I wished I hadn't told her. Monday morning, I walked across the street to school. That morning, one of the popular girls came walking towards me. "Taylor, I'm tired of people always picking on you." She said "Do you want to learn how to fight?" she continued in her most concern voice. "Yes!" I responded without hesitation. The excitement in my voice left a trail of glee in the air. "Come around the corner with me and I'll teach you." She offered. As I walked around the corner I was impressed by her character. Here she was a bus rider and she made it her business to stop by to help me today. My silly ass should've known better than that. She instructed me to stretch my arms out wide. I thought this was a warm up exercise. She pulled her fist back as far as she could and punched me in my stomach. The first period bell rung as I doubled over in pain. I couldn't believe that she would be so devious. What a way to start the day. I tried to pull myself together as much as I could. I spent the rest of the school year away from those animals. Except for my daily ass whupping, along with the name calling they didn't bother me too much. School was coming to an end. I was thrill to say the least. Summer was coming in. My mind had envisioned so much fun intended for me. I had waited impatiently for the first day of summer. It had finally arrived. I had to go to the store. Which I had learned was a new found blessing with Venita always waiting around the corner for me. Plus it was my freedom away from Kymela and her bullcrap. On the way to the store the local boys were outside playing horseshoes. It was a game designed to throw a metal piece of iron shaped like a horseshoe on a metal pole if the horseshoe stuck then you got a point. I thought it was one of the dumbest games I had ever seen. I walked around the young boys that were playing the game. It was always one pretty light complexioned girl, with deep dimples, juicy lips, and perfect teeth. Plus to make matters worse she had one of the baddiest bodies you could ever imagine. Her standing there with the boys wasan everyday ritual. I personally think she was the prettiest girl in Bowling Park Projects. I hurried by her as she was sitting there telling jokes. I don't know what she said about me but everybody just looked in my direction and laughed. I was scared. Venita wasn't out there and everybody knew her so nobody would've messed with me. I always felt safe when she was around. All the girls were envious of her. They knew better than to ever express their jealous because at any given time she could get one of the boys who were fighting for her attention to slap whomever she chose in the face. I'd seen that happen on more than one occasion. The girl would often vow that she would return with her brother or some other boy. She would continue on her rampage about some great fate that would bestow unto them but they never resurface. I would often wonder what it would be like to spend a day in her shoes. I picked up the pace. I couldn't let my daydreaming give her an opportunity to try and hit me. One of the drug dealer boys called her name. She began walking in the boy's direction. Another boy went to take his turn throwing the horseshoe. For some reason she tried to run across as the boy threw the horseshoe at the same time. I heard a loud scream. I stood there motionless watching as everyone ran over to her. The horseshoe hit her directly in the middle of her forehead. That was the first time I'd seen high velocity blood splatter. She only let out a scream for a quick second. Sashe was knocked out cold. My heart palpitations were off the richter scale. I started praying for her in my mind. "Lord, please don't let her be dead, Lord please don't let her be dead. I repeated in my head over and over again. Throughout all my praying I thought she was dead by the way the boy kept shaking her and calling her name. The majority of the boys had tears in their eyes and the one who threw the horse shoe looked as if death would enter him any minute. The more he shook her the more blood gushed from her forehead. I covered India's eyes. She didn't need to see that shit. I turned around to go the other way. I'd seen a pay phone at the end of the block. I dialed 911. I explained the situation and expressed the need for an ambulance. I gave my name then discontinued the phone call. It was obvious those fools wasn't going to do it. I guess they figured they would shake her back to life. On the way back from the store I had seen an ambulance speeding down the street. I wonder if it was the one I had called for the pretty girl. I said a silent pray for her as I continued to walk. I couldn't get too wrapped up in I wonders. I snuck and brought India candy from the store. She was taking all day to eat it. I didn't want to be mean but I was going to have to throw it away if she didn't hurry up. So my main concern was her. Later that night I heard a commotion I knew the pretty girl was home from the emergency room. Everybody was outside, the girls was just sitting out there hoping she wasn't as pretty. The boys were out there for the same reason but they wanted her to still be pretty. I ran to the window I wanted to see too. I was hoping she was still pretty. I couldn't really get a good look at her face from the window. It was dark and the lightning was bad. It must've been awful from the questions everybody asked her. "How many stitches did you get? Will that scar go away?" I gave up on getting a good look. I was just about to get out the window when the pretty girl spotted me. "Hey little girl what's your name?" she asked. "My name." I said in a voice that revealed my surprise. "Yes, your name. What's your name little girl?" she asked again. "Taylor." I responded. "They told me a little girl with that name called the ambulance. Was that you?" she continued. "Yes." I answered in a faint voice. "Oh, I thought that was you. You're the only one round here with that white girl name. Thank you though. If you ever need anything just let me know word up yo'." She finished. "Alright." I replied with glee in my voice. I laid across the bed with a smile on my face. I knew I had just made a new friend. I spoke every time I'd seen her after that sometimes she spoke sometimes she didn't, but I always spoke. Her face never did heal completely. Well her scar never fully went away I should say.

The house was achingly hot. The projects brick walls in addition to the concrete floors, oh the humanity. It felt like the world was coming to an end. Especially if I have to spend another day in the house. Kymela came out of nowhere and told us we had to get our hair done. Rose asked her why. I overheard Kymela tell her that we were going to vocational bible school in Robert's Park Projects. Yes was all that ran thru my head. Everything was working out great. I was even more excited that vocational bible school was a part of the free lunch program. That meant we got breakfast, lunch, plus a snack. No more starving until dinner, if we were allowed to eat. I gave God the praise life was good. We were going to church to learn more about God whom I hold very dearly. I knew he was going to help me out the situation I was in. Two weeks into bible school Karin promise one of the boys she was going to do something with him or for him. I don't know what it was but when she didn't he got really mad. He informed her that after vocational bible class he was going to smack her. I wanted to go straight in and tell Kymela but the look of fear in Karin eyes I knew it would be better if I didn't. We walked thru Robert's Park Projects. We reached the curb. India seen the boys surrounding us. It had to be five or six of them. We all knew what was going on but India decided to speak up. "Excuse me Ma'. That boy told

Karin he was going to smack her when we got out of vocational bible class." She said while pointing at the boy. "He is not going to do nothing with your mother standing right here. Let's go." Kymela said. I guess nobody told him because he hauled off and smacked the shit outta Karin. Kymela turned around with fire seeping from her eyes. Kymela hit the boy so hard in his face he stumbled back in disbelief. India took off running through the projects to one of my mothers' friend's house. The rest of the boys swarmed Kymela throwing punches from all direction and angles. I guess they jumped in to help their friend that was still standing there looking dumb founded. I stood there motionless. Poor Kymela was getting jumped by fifteen and sixteen year olds. There was a broken tree branch on the ground from a previous storm that nobody ever cleaned up. Kymela picked up the branch. She was swinging at them for dear life. She was getting a couple of good licks in but she was out numbered. One of the boys started charging towards me. I took off running through the projects. I was nowhere near as fast as India; but I kept going. I tried to lay down in the grass. I don't know what was going on in my head. I figured it was dark outside, plus I had on all black, they wouldn't be able to see me. The boy was walking really slow up to me. I guess he probably thought my fat ass passed out or something. I'd seen my mother's friend from church husband running in my direction. He knew the boy was going to reach me before he did so he yelled out to him. "Hey!" he shouted. The boy took off running in the other direction. "Go to my house!" he added as he ran in the direction of Kymela. I don't know what happened after that. We had to stay the night at the church lady house. Kymela woke us up early, then took us home. As soon as we got in the house Kymela wanted to know why I didn't help her. I knew I was in trouble so I couldn't think of anything to say that would make this go away. So I stood there looking simple minded as she would say. The truth of the matter was I didn't help her because I was scared. I wasn't going to run off and leave her like the rest of my siblings had done. I just was too afraid of getting beat up by the big boys. Kymela didn't like the fact that I kept standing there with no verbal response. She kept posing questions that I knew there was no right answer to. Kymela told me she was going to teach me how to fight. Kymela instructed me to ball up my fist. I did so. She then told me to place my hands in front of my face this would help me to block the hits from my face. I began to smile. I started thinking how I was going to finally learn how to fight. I couldn't wait to use everything I'd learn on the kids at school. I also was smiling because she was taking an interest in me. Kymela swung the first blow. It connected to the side of my face. The shock was apparent on my face but I was still smiling. Kymela barely spoke to me unless she was hitting me or ordering me around. I was ecstatic she was putting in this time with me. Kymela started landing random blows to my face along with various other parts of my body. My simple self was still smiling at first because of the attention but then it dawned on me that even though she was smiling this was not a game. I was getting beat up. This was obviously payback from last night. The blows were fast and furious. I tried to block every area she was gunning for. I was unsuccessful each time. I started to cry after a while. Kymela laughed wholeheartedly. She encouraged my sisters to join in her relentless taunting. Kymela said things like; go in the room cry baby, or oh' you're crying because it hurt. Look y'all she's crying. I walked in the room tears streaming from my eyes. At least I stayed I thought. I didn't blame India and them for joining in. I knew that if one of them would've said anything in my defense they would've been the next object of her insanity. I laid across my bed and prayed that God would help me. That was beginning to become my nightly ritual. I awaken bright and early. It was Saturday morning so I knew we had to sell Krispy Kreme doughnuts for the church. This Saturday I was mad about it. I walked around complaining in my mind about how it's the same thing every Saturday. We walked from door to door selling doughnuts. It wasn't that I mind working but we never got paid plus the pastor lady children didn't have to be out there every single Saturday. Sometimes if we would ask where they were she would say she'd dropped them off in different neighborhoods but I didn't quite believe that. I felt like they got to enjoy their Saturday morning cartoons. The pastor lady wouldn't even offer us a box of doughnuts for our trouble neither. No matter how many doughnuts was left if we didn't sell them she would put them in her van and pull off. Sometimes she looked mad as if we weren't selling them on purpose. Plus I was aggravated because of the heat. I usually tried to get Venita to come with us. At least that would make my Saturday morning go a little faster. Venita only went one Saturday once she realized we didn't get anything for our troubles she vowed to never do it again. Kymela made sure we were completely dress before the pastor lady showed up. If we were late the pastor lady or one of her children would talk about us. We all piled into the church van as the pastor lady drove us around the corner to the residential neighborhood. We got out and planned what area we would be targeting. Last but not least what time we would be meeting back at the van. I was usually the last one back. I spent the majority of my time daydreaming while talking to God. It was time to get back to the van. I strolled up just in time to see the pastor lady counting the boxes of doughnuts that was left versus the money she had received. She got to Karin then her facial expression changed. So I started to speed up. Karin was always good for some type of entertainment. As soon as I got within ear shot I heard the pastor lady explaining the mathematics to Karin. "Everybody was sent out with eight boxes of doughnuts. They are two dollars a box. You only gave me fourteen dollars. Karin that means there is a box of doughnuts missing." Said the pastor lady in an inquisitive tone. Karin began to cry instantly. "I-I-I was robbed." She stuttered through her tears. The pastor lady seemed very concerned as well as Kymela. I was upset as well. "Now Karin calm down and tell me what happened. Do you know who robbed you?" She replied with concern still lingering in her voice. "A blind man took my doughnuts." She responded. My eyes widen by what that fool just said. Kymela face instantly betrayed her. The embarrassment that she was feeling was seeping through her pores must be; because it was written all over her face. Despite myself glee was written all over my face. I turned in the direction of the pastor lady to find her look of concern had been replaced with disgust. The pastor lady looked directly at me in disappointment due to the smile on my face. I couldn't help it, was this girl crazy. The pastor lady turned back in the direction of Karin for some more probing. "Karin how did the blind man know you had doughnuts?"

She asked. "He smelled them." She muttered. "Well which way did he go? We'll jump in the van right now and catch him." The pastor lady said continuing to bait her. "He jumped on his motorcycle and drove away." Karin finished while still crying. I let out the loudest laugh ever. Unfortunately for me I was standing directly next to Kymela she pinched the shit outta me. I didn't stop laughing even though tears escaped my eyes. The shit was funny. The pastor lady began to laugh then Kymela joined in. They asked Karin what she really did with the box of doughnuts. She finally confessed to eating them. I walked away with my side hurting from laughing so much. After that incident Kymela did her best to save up two dollars even if it was in change to purchase us a box of doughnuts every Saturday.

The next couple of days were boring. Venita only came over when she was extremely bored. That wasn't that often because she had a multitude of siblings like me. One of her visits she convinced Kymela to let us join the clean-up crew. The clean-up crew was an organization that was supposed to teach us how to take pride in our neighborhood. The program was designed whereas we would sweep the street and pick up trash for free. Our only reward was a snack at the end of the day. That worked for us because we knew we were going to get something to eat. That would have to cover breakfast and lunch. Most of the time it was Combos with a Capri Sun. Plus it was a way to get out of the house. It would have to substitute for vocational bible school. It was the fourth week of the clean-up crew; everybody was tired of hard work for no pay. We weren't complaining, that was the only time we ate some days. It was a normal morning except for the complaining, which was starting to become a habit. I guess it was as normal as it could be for the hood. We worked what seemed like all day. It was only three hours of work and they always let us go after two and a half hours. They decided to make us stay the entire time on this day. I guess that was their way of getting them back for all that smack they were talking earlier. It was time for snack. I was always the last one to get a snack I think it was because I was pudgy. I figured the adults thought I already ate too much. I turned around India had gone outside. I got so mad. She knows she's supposed to wait for me. I'd seen a group of kids bum-rushing the door. Although I really wanted my snack; I knew Kymela would kill me if India walked in the house alone. I finally got to the front of the door. I pushed it wide open. I was scanning for India, if I caught her before she got in the house I could still get my snack. I had my evil eye going. When I caught up with her I was going to shake her real good for leaving me. There was a man yelling something I couldn't make out. In my mind it was the projects somebody was always yelling about something. There she goes right there I thought. KAA-BOOM! I heard the loudest pop. It felt like my ears was going to bleed. The birds began to fly in the opposite direction. The birds were chirping awfully loud. I take it the blast hurt their ears too. Even though everything was happening so fast it felt like the world was moving in slow motion. I'd seen the sawed-off shotgun in an older man's hand. Then I'd seen a young black man running away from the older man. He was holding the spot where his elbow once was. Blood was squirted through his fingers profusely. "I warned you about messing with my daughter" a man yelled, while slowly walking behind the running man. My heart dropped India was just standing right there. One of the rental office workers grabbed me by my arm. I didn't realize it before the lady touched me, but they were snatching up all the children that were outside the door and taking them back inside. I had to break away from this lady. I started yelling to the top of my lungs. "My sista, my sista!" The rental office lady tried to grab my arm tighter to take me back inside of the office. Also I think she wanted to show me who was in control of the situation. I pinched her as hard as I could; then stomp on her foot. As she bellowed out in pain I took off out the door. I turned back towards her with a look of sorrow in my eyes. I didn't want to hurt or disrespect the lady but I had to help India. The look that she returned let me know my apology was acknowledge and accepted. My attention was redirected to the task at hand. India was standing right there in the midst of it all. The look of confusion along with fear had my heart at a standstill. I had to help her; some-how. My mind was racing. How could I let something like this happen? I was still going in the direct line of fire. Ka'Pow! The bullet tore through its intended target. I watched the blood along with bone fragments splatter from his knee. He was severely wounded. The image was being burned into my long term memory. With his partially amputated arm he attempted to hold his injured knee. He was using his good hand to nurse his arm. The shit looked sick. My stomach was turning in knots. I began to pray Lord, Jesus please help me find my sista'! The poor man was beginning to sub come to his injuries. He started doing a slow hobble dragging his leg behind him. His white t-shirt was now burgundy. I remember my goal; finding India. I snapped out of whatever trance I was in. It was like watching a horror flick unfold before your very eyes. I wanted to turn away but you just had to see the end. India was nowhere to be seen. Oh, please God help me find my sister. The feeling was returning to my legs. I was back on my mission. I continued to walk right to the middle of the shootout. I could hear the candy lady yelling get that child. I guess she was talking about me. Little did she know I was determined to find my sister. I would not have advised anyone to touch me or they were going to receive an butt whooping with help from the lord. I kept walking pretending like I couldn't hear the gasps from the onlookers as I got closer to the gunman. I knew I was protected by the Holy Spirit. In my mind I just had to see if India was over there hurt. I was so close now I could see the smoke traveling from the gun barrel. I'd begun to smile because the old western GunSmoke title suddenly made sense. Clever title, I thought as I continued to walk. Shuk-shuk, Boom. The sound was deafening. It felt as though the sky would rip apart. The sound echoed so tremendously. I'd felt as though God himself shed a tear as the bullet penetrated every vital organ on the man left side. The visual graphics were horrifying. It looked as if someone took a bite out of the side of his body. The man let out a cry filled with agony and pain. My ears were ringing so bad it felt like they may very well began to bleed. The young man fell to the pavement on the bullets contact. For the moment my attention was not on India. I looked down to watch as the man struggled to get away from the gunman. He looked like an injured soldier doing a one arm one leg army crawl. My heart saddened as I watch the man gasped for air. His eyes closed slowly. It was over. He was dead. The candy lady voice became clear through all of the chaos again. "Get her! She's in shock." She yelled. I stood there staring blankly. To everyone else it appeared that I was staring into nothingness. Little did they know I was actually concentrating on where all that blood was going. I thought to myself it was no way they could clean all that up. Perhaps the rain would take care of it. Then I'd seen the blood formulate a straight line stream. My eyes followed as it flowed effortlessly. The blood went down the sewage drain. I'd felt my arm being yanked kinda of hard. I think they were trying to snatch me out of my "shock". I turned around slightly. "Have you seen my sister?" I asked. Just then India appeared out of nowhere. I should've thank God; but I'd seemed to have forgotten all about him in the midst of my happiness. The candy lady walked India and me down the court to our house. Kymela was standing in the screen door, her usual; looking on-ward. The candy lady informed Kymela of my "shock". Kymela smiled and nodded her head as the candy lady told the story. When the lady was finish with her version of the events Kymela told us to come in the house. When the door closed Kymela wanted more information about what had happened. She began to ask us all types of questions. I filled her in while smiling from ear to ear. Again I was just happy she was showing some kind of interest in me. I continued to smile as I repeated the story over and over again of the man dying in front of me. Anything for her acceptance. After the fourth or fifth time of the same story Kymela excused us for bed. I asked India where she had disappeared to. She informed me how she had ducked behind a car shortly after the shooting began. With a lot of encouragement from the rental office and Venita we were allowed to finish the final week of the clean-up crew program. It was the last day of the clean-up crew and we were going to find out about our special prize. The rental office staff told us they had a gift to show us that loving our community always paid off. I was excited all day. The grand finale was here. We would be going to Busch Gardens for our hard work and dedication. They provided us with bagged lunches. We were to ask our parents for additional monies for souvenirs or anything else we wanted to purchase. The trip would be on the following Saturday morning. Kymela didn't have any money to give us. I was just glad we could go at all. Busch Gardens was great. I waited all week with the excitement festering in my soul. The big day had finally come. I couldn't sleep a wink the night before. We meet at the departure destination. They told us we had to meet them back at the gate at four o'clock. Venita and I wondered off in the theme park. We rode the Big Bad Wolfe repeatedly. Karin was mad because the rental office ladies had brought their children on the trip and had previously denied our little sisters a spot on the bus stating it wouldn't be fair the other children that worked. Eventually Karin got over her anger and began to enjoy the theme park. By the time we arrived back home everyone was asleep, except for Venita and me. We spent the entire bus ride talking about nothingness. Only thing I remember was that we promised to always be best friends. That was the end of a very unforgettable summer.

CHAPTER 5

Living in Hell

I was walking home from school with my hair a mess from my daily ass-whooping as usual. I began walking down the court to our house. I'd seen the laundry hanging on the clothes line, which meant Kymela fat ass had to do some work; and wouldn't be in a good mood at all today. So I'ma get my ass whupped again. I started walking up the ramp to our house thinking to myself...this some bullshit. The door swung open before my hand could actually touch the knob. Kymela was standing smiling. "Come in, come in." Kymela said in a pleasant voice. I walked past her with my heart racing. What in the world is she up to? I braced myself for the hit that I was about to receive. I turned around to see the blow coming, but she was really smiling. I turned back around and walked further into the house slowly. Her smiling...what the hell is going on? I thought to myself. As I round the corner to the living room I saw him sitting in the wicker chair. It was Ramon. I ran into his arms. This nigga brought out the best in everyone, so I thought. He also brought his youngest sister with him to assist us with shopping. Her name is Deeann. She was about nineteen years old and very pretty. I wondered if I was going to grow up to be pretty like her. Deeann also brought her friend Gretchen. Gretchen was even prettier than Deeann. She was light-skinned with big brown eyes along with dimples and perfect teeth. If you ask me she was a prettier version of Kymela. I could tell this was going to be a problem. Ramon seemed oblivious to Kymela's random glances in Gretchen directions. Ramon just sat there and waited for each person to arrive, I guess to surprise them the same way he surprised me. Once we were all present in the house he made an announcement. He was taking us all shopping for school clothes. I was extremely happy when Ramon added we were getting money according to our size not our age. Being that I was the biggest, I'd always get the most money. I use to think that was something to be proud of. We went to all the low budget stores, along with some expensive ones. Kymela tried to pick out majority church clothes; but when Ramon seen we had more dresses and skirts than jeans he quickly put them back. It was the year of the binki pants, all the girls were wearing them. Ramon let Karin and I get a pair despite Kymela protest. We all went out to eat afterwards. It was a big day. Ramon played with us until Deeann mentioned that she wanted to go out. Deeann told Ramon that she was not going to be downsouth and not check out the clubs down here. Ramon asked Kymela if she knew of any good clubs out there. Kymela told of one she had heard of. They all got dressed and went out. They must've had a blast because I could hear them walking up the courtyard giggling and carrying on. I knew if I was up when Ramon was there it wouldn't be a big problem. Kymela didn't say much when he was around. When they walked in I swarmed them, asking questions and seeking attention. Auntie Deeann told me about a new dance called the Electric Slide. She was trying to get the steps down pack, so when she went back to the city she would have a new dance to show them. I explained how I couldn't dance that well but maybe India or Karin could show her in the morning. It was time for everybody to go to bed. They rushed me upstairs to get the sleeping arrangements out of the way. None of them wanted to sleep in any of our rooms because we all peed the bed. I reached the top of the steps and sat down. I knew they would still be talking; hopefully I would hear something they didn't want children to hear. Something good and juicy. Kymela began to speak she told Auntie Deeann's friend that she would not be sleeping with her "husband" tonight and that she would have to make other arrangements. Auntie Deeann's friend must've gotten offended because she told Kymela that she wasn't sleeping with her husband that night nor would she any other night. Auntie Deeann and her friend began laughing uncontrollably. Kymela simply gave them all blankets to make a pilot on the floor. Now usually when Ramon came; our parents would send us to bed and Ramon would spend the night in the room with Kymela. This time things were different Ramon was downstairs on the floor with his sisters and her friend. I'd awaken early to try and convince Kymela to let us stay home from school. No such luck. I wasn't all that disappointed though; I had a brand new outfit. The night before we all picked out what we were going to wear. I had on my bikini pants with a dark blue stripe down the sides along with my light blue pull over sweater with my electric blue Etonic's. I just knew I was matching with all my blues on. Karin had on the same outfit except hers was all different shades of pink. I was just so excited I was going to school clean for once. Brand new clothes no hand-me-downs. Karin and I stood at the bus stop freezing. The wind was whipping around the corner a mile a minute. The bus pulled up and my heart was pounding. Karin shayshed on the bus twisting her hips with every turn. Her walk was proud as if she knew every boy on the bus wanted her at that moment. When she finally sat down the whole bus busted out laughing. Oh no, I thought. Now I had to walk down the bus to find a seat, if they laughed at her surely they were going to laugh at me. I placed my books directly in front of my belly to try and hide some of the fat. I walked as fast as could down the tiny isle, every boy just stared at me as I walked passed. I sat down in my seat then turned my head toward the window. With every heartbeat I awaited the sudden outburst of laughter. To my surprise it never came. A boy yelled to the back of the bus in my direction; it must be jello 'cause jam sure don't shake like that! The rest of the boys started grunting, shaking their heads in agreement. I let out a sigh of relief never taking my attention away from the window. The whole day was filled with compliments. I was so flattered. That afternoon I couldn't wait to get home. Ramon had to hear all about my great reviews. I turned the door knob with so much excitement and anticipation. The air in the house had changed. I couldn't figure out what was going on but something was amiss. I looked in the living room where Ramon things were and they were gone. Everything was gone. I put my head down to fight back the tears. Kymela came up behind me. I turned around startled. "He had to go back to work." She said. I smiled at Kymela then turned to walk up the stairs before she could make me do something. I'd miss ole Ramon; again.

Kymela spent the next couple of weeks in her room. She didn't care what we did as long as we were quiet. We ate plenty and made sure the house was clean for the day that she would emerge. Finally the door swung open. I knew she was back. I could see that she wanted payback from the furry in her eyes. There was no telling the aftermath of Ramon trip this time. Kymela had a smile on her face. I didn't know what was going on but I was happy that she was smiling. Kymela made an announcement. She was going to the hair salon then out to the club. Kymela came back from the hair salon. She had cut off all of her beautiful hair. She got this new hair-stlye called the salt-n-pepa. One of the friends Kymela had made in church was going out with her. We had to get dressed to go to her friends' house. Kymela friend had children of her own. The plan was for us to watch each other. This went on for about three weeks. Every Friday night Kymela would have us get dressed to go over to her friend's house. We would spend the whole weekend over there. I was happy about Kymela new lifestyle choice we had friends of our own now and so did she. One Friday night after our parents had left one of the little girls put on a movie called Eating Chocolate. I was ready. I thought the movie would have all different kinds of chocolate with different ways of eating them. The movie had a women being hurt in her private area. She was screaming. Our new friends along with some of my sisters were laughing at me. I started asking all kinds of questions like; why was he hurting her like that? Why would they want to watch something like this? The list goes on and on. When our parents came home I couldn't wait to tell them what was going on while they were away. My mother's new found best friend children started lying on us. They told their mother we found the tape and put it in. I couldn't believe children in the church would tell such lies, especially in front of us. We all got a beaten being that our parents couldn't decide who was lying. Kymela never went back over to that friends house again. She told us she didn't want us to be tainted. I didn't quite understand what that meant but I knew it had something to do with being harmed in some way. Kymela started going back to church. I was happy the first Sunday we showed up. The pastor lady gave us a special shout out from the pull-pit. Everyone seemed as if they generally missed us. I told Kymela I was glad we were back in the church. The next day it went back to business as usual we arrived home from school with too many chores to even consider doing any homework. Kymela was back alright cleanliness is next to Godliness and spare the rod or spoiled the child was her phrases every minute of everyday. The house sparkled at night before we went to bed. Everyday I went to school to get beat and every night I came home to clean and get beat. I was in a lose-lose situation. We went to every church sermon in order for Kymela to repent for her sins. I laid down and asked God to please help me out of the situation I was in. It seemed as if he didn't hear me or the answer was no. Either way I was trapped in hell. Kymela had started a nightly ritual with each one of us that none of us were aware of. Kymela would signal out one person by telling them they didn't do their chores properly. In all actuality Kymela would fondle that particular daughter that night and perform some kind of explicit act with that person. One night she went further with Karin then she had with any of us. We went through minor touching, rubbing, and humping. Karin and her went all the way. The next morning Kymela left the house early. Karin was in our room just staring out the window. I asked her what was wrong. Karin turned to face me with tears in her eyes. She began to tell me in graphic details everything Kymela had done to her the night before. The rest of our sisters slowly started to walk in the room to hear the story. One by one we started with our own individual stories realizing that she had done similar things with each and everyone of us. No one person was alone. We cried and hugged each other that's all we could do at that moment. We generally didn't know what else to do. How could we get out of this? Where can we go? What can we do? Karin told us she was going to put a stop to this now! Karin said she could no longer stay in this house with Kymela. We cried even harder. Had she gone completely mad where would she go? We begged Karin to stay but she said she couldn't let Kymela hurt us anymore. Karin didn't take anything she just walked out the front door. Tears streamed down Karin face as she exited the courtyard. "I'm going to get us help!" she yelled, while trying to fight back the tears but failing miserably. We couldn't stop crying. We stood in the doorway for a long time holding each other and crying. Our oldest sister was gone at the tender age of thirteen and we were scared for her, but most importantly we were scared of what Kymela was going to do to us when she came home to find Karin had left. A few hours had passed and Karin knocked on the front door. I let out a sigh of relief. Karin told us to go to the neighbors house. I absolutely was not leaving the house. Karin had convinced everyone to go to the neighbors house besides me. Kymela was going to kill them when she got back. They could all lose their damn mind with Karin if they wanted to. The neighbor came to the door and instructed me to his house. I did as I was told. When I got inside the house all my sisters were smiling telling their stories like it was Showtime at The fucking Apollo or some shit. I was mortified. I couldn't fix this and I knew it. If they would've given me some time I would've came up with a plan. I stared at them as they shared our families darkest secrets with complete strangers. What the hell can they do to help us. I refused to comply with the madness, when one of the guys in the house asked us a question I act like I was mute and turned my head. In my mind they won't have another story for the project's gossip wheel on my say so. One of the men in the house got upset when I didn't answer his question that he posed with a wide smile on his face revealing the fact that he was taking pleasure in our story; thus our pain. He started to tell everyone in the house I enjoyed everything Kymela had done to me that's why I was refusing to share. Are you insane I thought. Your sitting here with a smile plastered across your face trying to figure out why I don't conform for you, please; I thought. Did he not know we spent the morning crying? Does he care what was taken from us? Does he not know that social services will separate us? Does he know we're all we got? Can he not tell that they are smiling because someone anyone has showed them some attention? Can he not tell they don't understand the magnitude of what they have done? Do he not see the pain in my eyes as he taunted me. Telling me how I enjoyed these indescribable acts? I sat there quietly. After awhile he sent us back to the house. Before I left I tried to reason with him about calling the police, I told him let me try and call my father or somebody first. He told me it was his responsibility to tell the police. What if one of you go back in that house and tried to commit sucide he added. I shook my head as I left the house. I got in the doorway and asked him why would he send us back then. He informed me that Kymela was exposed and she wouldn't hurt us tonight, she'd be too scared he added. Karin refused to go back to the house. When Kymela came in and asked where was Karin India was the first one to speak. India along with the rest of my siblings started explaining to Kymela how I had went the neighbors house and told them everything! Kymela didn't respond to my sisters lies. I thought to myself they were going to get me seriously hurt. Kymela made dinner and sent us to bed. The next morning Kymela told me to get in the shower. I was afraid of what was to come. Kymela came in the bathroom and began to scrub me all over. My skin burned from terry cloth fabric scrapping my body with such force. When she scrub my privates I wanted to cry because they hurt so bad but I didn't want to get hit. Kymela told me there was no way in the world a child could be born with such a smell. Kymela then accused me of letting a boy down there. Kymela picked out all of our clothes. We had breakfast for the first time at home. Kymela told us that Judas was gone and now we could live a normal life. Kymmela had us lined up by the front door. She told us we were walking with her to school today. I was shocked but pleased. It seemed that Kymela had changed and for the better. Kymela was taking a great interest in us. I sat in class feeling like it was a new day. A new beginning, we were going to be alright. Just then my name was announced over the loudspeaker. I had to report to the principals' office at once. They also added for me to bring my things. I got up and went into the principal's office. There was a black lady standing there. She had an inviting smile but I knew better." Hi my name is Ms. Corethia Gates. I'll be your social worker." she said. My heart skipped a beat. I thought that maybe it would all go away. The sinking feeling in my stomach was nothing compared to the racing of my heart. Was this lady serious? She said it as if I knew she was coming; like this was part of our normal routine. "So do you know where I will be place? Will my sisters be accompanying me? "I replied. "well for right now you'll be staying with your pastor. She has agreed to take you guys in until we can find a more suitable placement."

CHAPTER 6

On My Own

My corn chip aroma convinced the pastor lady I was going in the bathroom "pretending to wash." My nastiness was something Kymela had embedded in me." she added. The pastor lady still communicated with another pastor that she'd often fellowship with. She would still talk about us to her. Now she would just do it on the phone all day. The pastor lady told me she had reached her wits end with me. The other pastor lady agreed to let me stay with her. I arrived at the new pastor lady house. My leaving wasn't as devastating as I thought it would be. I knew this pastor. She was genuine. She often dismissed the other pastor lady's gossip. I arrived with all of my bags. Upon arrival I was told that there was only one rule I couldn't wear jeans or pants. She said her husband felt like it was not lady like. Plus her being a Christian she said it was a rule she really didn't mind much. She had one daughter Bethany. Bethany was older than I was. She had too much going on than to worry about me. She was pregnant and planning her wedding. I liked Bethany a lot but she really wasn't that fond of me. She had been an only child for sixteen years and now there was this new little person in the house asking too many questions all of the time. I would ask things that were inappropriate but I didn't know any better. I would sit constantly in her boyfriend face asking questions. One day I just came out the blue with another one of my questions. "Is the only reason why you're marrying her is because she got pregnant?" I asked. Bethany told her mother I was too nosy. Being that we had adjoining rooms she felt that one day I would open up the door to try and see what her and her boyfriend was doing. Plus she had already told me she had wanted the room for her baby. I didn't want to believe it but I knew my days were numbered in that house as well. Two weeks went by Ramon called with some very bad news; another one of his brother's had died. I pretended to cry on the phone. The truth of the matter was I had too much on my plate to let that stress me out. I guess a part of me started to feel jealous that he was at peace while we were left here to do the work. I hung up the phone then excused myself to the room. The pastor lady was so worried about me that she asked Bethany to be a little nicer to me. Bethany obliged her mother. They felt awful that I couldn't go to my favorite uncle's funeral. I milked the attention for all it was worth. I started following Bethany around again still asking questions. First thing in the morning I would knock on the room door for her to unlock it from her end. She always let me come right out. That was the conclusion her and her mother had arrived to; since she was scared I was going open the door and catch her in "the act". The truth of the matter was I wasn't mad about it. Nor did I feel anyway, because I was planning to open the door. I wanted to know real bad what they were doing in there. Bethany walked into the bathroom. I followed her while she began to brush her teeth I began to talk. "How did you get pregnant? Did you get pregnant in your room? Do you think he is marrying you because you're pregnant?" I asked Bethany. She didn't answer me she pushed me out the bathroom then closed the door in my face. My constant blabbering was becoming increasingly agitating to Bethany. Bethany went to have another talk with her mother about my mouth. The new pastor lady came in my room. The room was intiationally her sewing room although she hadn't been in there for months. It was still early in the morning so my natural aroma had the room humming. I had gotten quite comfortable so I didn't do the usual maintenance to keep the room from smelling. I usually woke up and jump in the shower instantly. Then I would grab all my clothes and put them in plastic bags and place them in the suitcase. I'd finished my ritual by zipping the suitcase to conceal any odor. Inside I was ashamed that I could have slipped in such a manner. From the look on her face I knew that I had sealed my own fate. Her nose was scrunched up. Then she looked in the direction of my clothes. All my clothes were thrown around on her new fabrics. she talked to me for a few minutes but I could tell something in her had changed. I would have to go. I so loved living there. As I suspected the next morning I was told to pack my things my worker would be coming to get me. I wanted to cry but I had to be strong. I got all my things together quietly. I knew Bethany would tell all the kids at my church what happened. I gathered my things kicking myself along the way. The doorbell rang. I took a deep breath as I hauled all my things down the stairs neither Bethany nor her mother was anywhere to be seen. I at least wanted to say goodbye to them. I climbed in the social worker car. I knew somewhere they were watching I yelled out the window as the car pulled off. "I'll miss you!" I knew she thought I was being a little smart mouth but I wasn't. I knew I would never see them again. I turned around and stared straight ahead. I had a new adventure to attend to. The car pulled up to my new foster home. It was a townhouse located in an upper middle class neighborhood. I walked inside the foster home. It was nicely decorated. There were three people waiting there for my arrival. My new foster mother; along with her boyfriend, and a girl that looked like she was close to my age. I was extremely interested in meeting the little girl until I'd seen the look on her face change from joy to disappointment. 'Oh, boy.' I thought. I guess I wasn't her ideal playmate. My new foster mother walked me through the house with my social worker at my side. She explained how Angel was her biological daughter. She always wanted more children but after Angel it was impossible. The social worker and my new foster mother left me in the room with Angel to unpack. Angel definitely did justice for her name. She had the most angelic face one could lay eyes on. Her skin tone was a carbon copy of Werther's Original piece of candy but she was not as sweet. Yet her dimples gave the illusion of innocence. I held a minor conversation with her. It was still a new place plus I didn't know her. I heard the front door close. The school teacher stood in my doorway. "Angel, why'd you sit there and let that girl unpack all of her stuff. You know we're getting on the road." She asked. "I told her not to mommy." Angel replied. I turned in shock. She had said no such thing. "Well you have to take whatever is left in those bags. We're already late I should've been on the road hours ago." She stated. The teacher lady was so excited to be getting her first foster child that she had planned a trip for me to meet her mother upon my arrival. We got into the car to drive down south. Her mother lived in St. George, South Carolina. On the way down south we stopped off to pick up Angel's best friend Jennifer. She wasn't as pretty as Angel by far, but she would soon prove to be an all around better person. The ride seemed to take forever. It was day, then night just to turn right back into day. I couldn't wait to go inside her mother's' house. I didn't know her but the only thing I wanted to do was stretch out. I got to the door her mother and father were standing there. They had the biggest smiles plastered to their faces. It was even hotter down there than in Virginia. After I sat there for a little while feeling uncomfortable I went outside to catch lightning bugs. That was my absolute favorite pastime. I would catch them in my hands. Then I would peep inside to see them light up a few times then I would squash 'em. I would run around trying to catch another one to start my ritual of torture all over again. They called me inside. I hadn't even realized how much Angel and I was getting along. The whole time she was outside by my side playing with me. All three of us came running inside. We raced to the bathroom to wash our hands. It was time for dinner. I couldn't wait to eat. I plopped down in between Jennifer and Angel. "What's for dinner?" I asked. "Homemade biscuits, baked macaroni and cheese, stuffing, fried chicken, string beans, topped off with banana pudding for dessert." My new foster grandmother answered. "Oh man!" I yelled. "How much do you want?" She asked "I want a lot!" I responded with a smile that was brighter than any star in the sky. She did just as I asked she packed my plate. The joy had to be glistening my eyes 'cause when I received my plate everyone at the table let out a slight giggle. I bit into the biscuit first. It was disgusting. I picked up some fresh string beans. We had sat outside and snapped; they were still hard. The chicken taste like it was fried in pure fat. Well nobody could mess up macaroni and cheese I thought. It had the same nasty taste to it as the biscuits. The whole meal was a bust. I sat there picking at my plate. I didn't want to be rude or obvious. I shoveled a couple spoonfuls in my mouth every six to ten minutes. My foster mother picked up on the fact that I was not eating. She asked me what was wrong. I told her it tasted funny. She was livid along with embarrassed. For that I was going to pay. "My mother cooked all this food for us, and you're going to sit there and be ungrateful like this. You didn't even have food in your house when they picked you up." My foster mother words were the equivalent to her throwing a steak knife across the table that penetrated my heart; well that's the way it felt anyway. How dare she insult my mother! Kymela did the best she could under the circumstances. Welfare only gave her a limited amount of money. They told her she had to be at the poverty level in order to receive the funding. She wouldn't be allowed to get a job just to earn a little extra money. They didn't give her much but they paid the rent. With Kymela only finishing junior high school she wasn't qualified to do too much of nothing. She would only be able to work for minimum wage which was only four dollars an hour. If she would've been allowed to have both she still would've been barely making it; especially with five kids. It was either get assistance or work there was no room for both according to the government. It was a catch twenty-two even when you win, somewhat you lose. And now to have to sit at a strangers dinner table and watch the smirk on their faces as if they were telling me off, or saying something slick by downgrading a women they didn't even know was far beyond heartbreaking. The teacher lady interrupted my train of thought. "You will eat everything on your plate." My foster mother repeated with just as much furry as before. "Yes ma'am." I replied. I sat there cramming spoonfuls of food in my mouth in order to avoid tasting it. I figured if I barely chewed and then swallowed it wouldn't taste as bad. It tasted like spoiled milk to me. Blood was seeping from the chicken. I kept scuffing down as much as possible. I sat there for hours doing the same thing. After I got done with one bite it would take me twenty minutes to start the process again. To make matters worse they had packed my plate. I was so happy when I first saw the food thinking it was going to be good. They even asked me if I would be able to finish it all. I smiled and yelled "Yes, ma'am!" Now I wished I would've kept my fat mouth shut! "Stop shoving that food in your mouth like that! I know you trying to make yourself throw up." My foster mother interjected into my thoughts. "Yes, ma'am." My response was faint. I finally finished just in enough time to watch the eight o'clock movie on HBO. It was Short Circuit. To my surprise I felt like Johnny five. I was alive but I wasn't allowed to say or do anything. I was a robot in other people eyes. I was never heard or barely seen even though I was too big to miss. The movie ended and my stomach began turning. I told myself it was because I was thinking about that nasty food. They told me where I was sleeping that night. I climbed into the bed and fell into a very peaceful sleep. I was barely awake when vomit started exploding everywhere. The shock was; it was coming from me. As I was vomiting the diarrhea started seeping out. Dog-gone it! I'm doo-dooing on myself. They are going to laugh at me; kept running through my mind. I was trying to navigate myself through my unfamiliar territory trying to make it to the bathroom. I was puking and everything else the whole way. My foster mother came out of her room. Tears started streaming down my face. "I'm sorry, I'm sorry!" I shouted repeatedly. "It's Okay." She responded, trying to reassure me. I didn't know if she was going to hit me or not. I knew Kymela would've for doo-dooing in the bed. Or worst yet, she could've told me I had to leave. She was so mean to me at dinner. I had no clue what she was actually capable of. The more I thought about it the sicker I got. It was starting to be a big commotion in the house. The teacher lady called her mother to help being that I was getting everything everywhere they finally decided to sit me in the tub. I was getting hotter with so many people around. I started feeling light headed. The room began to spin. I heard her mother tell her to call an ambulance. I awaken in the hospital. It had a lot of toys everywhere. I guess I was in the children's ward. My foster mother looked so relieved when I opened my eyes and was actually coherent. She smiled at me. I smiled back at her and began talking up a storm. The doctor came in and told me I had an adverse reaction to the diary products. It seemed the milk, eggs and cheese were too fresh for me. My system rejected it. He told me the reason I was so sick was the apparent over kill of those products. I sat there with a smirk on my face. I told her those biscuits tasted funny and the macaroni and cheese tasted like spoil milk. I soaked up every bit of attention I was receiving. I arrived at my foster grandmother's house to be greeted with love and smiles. Angel was upset she had to spend the last remaining days of summer down south. Apparently I had been in the hospital over a week. As soon as I got inside I was told to gather my things. We jumped into the car and drove back to my new foster mother's house. After some probing I realized that my social worker had no clue I had left the state, furthermore that I had been hospitalized. I was settling into my new room. I loved the decorum. It was more sophisticated than that of a little girl. It was bookshelves from wall to wall. I enjoyed reading. I started to relax until I notice there was no television in the room. I walked back down the spiral stairs to the earth tone living room. I must admit she had style. We could possibly be friends. I loved the fact that she had style. I always wanted a house that looked like a home. She stayed by my bedside the whole time according to the doctor. Maybe she really does care. Unlike some of the other ones that just wanted a check. "Excuse me Ms. Wallace; next month will it be possible for me to get a television in my room." I asked. "No, I don't allow T.V. on the weekdays. Only on Thursday's to watch The Cosby Show and A Different World. They depict what an African American family should embody." She replied. Is she serious! I was devastated. Television was all I had to escape the real world. The endless nights of watching Penny from Good Times get beat or burned with the iron. I knew if she could escape her traumatic life then so could I. Themes songs also pushed me along. Taxi and Hill Street Blues were mysterious yet relaxing. I would often memorize and personalize theme songs from shows such as Kate & Allie, Perfect Strangers, It's a Living, and the Facts Of Life. I would feel inspired as soon as the show would start. What would be my great escape from my gloomy reality? No more Fantasy Island to say the least. I entered the world of reading. I would beg her to let me watch Reading Rainbow. I pointed out that it was educational. She deemed it story time. I just really loved the song; the idea that I could go anywhere was my solitude. Her method proved to be pretty astonishing. I was brighter than I had ever been. I became a straight A student. With a school teacher as your mother there was never any excuse not to improve in any subject matter. I started to feel there was no limit to the things I could achieve. Her reward policy was another thing that kept us inspired. If we got all A's on our next report card we could go to this concert. It featured Heavy D & The Boys. Of course Angel and I were each other's support system for the next couple of months. Angel helped me more than I helped her. Our reports cards expressed our enthusiasm. The next day Ms. Wallace brought our tickets. My first concert. I was at a lost. I really wasn't into worldly music like Angel but I couldn't help but to be excited. I couldn't wait to hear The Boys sing My Lucky Charm. I loved that song. The concert was approaching fast. Angel had her outfit all picked out. Clothes really wasn't that important to me. I just was nervous. I had never been exposed to, too many things of "the world"; as Kymela would put it. I had so many friends in school once I told them I was going to the concert. I was really starting to love living with Ms. Wallace.

It was the big day of the concert. Angel convinced her mother to drop us off early. She didn't want to be seen getting dropped off by her mother. Angel and her best friend Jennifer started to wander around. I stood in the coliseum where I was dropped off at. I must admit I was scared to move. While they were setting up like five guys started jumping up and down on a fold out table. I thought that was weird. Angel interrupted my thoughts by grabbing my arm. "One of the Boyz is in the back, he told us we could come in." She said. I took off running behind her. I wanted a glimpse of the pudgy one. I thought he was so cute. They never came from out back. We were left to sit there to entertain some little boys. They were cute but they weren't famous. I was growing increasingly bored. It must've been apparent from my face because Angel told them we had to go. We headed back to the middle of the coliseum. I thought about how big the place was. I told Angel I had to keep an eye on her. I mean she was my little sister for the time being. The usher took us to our assigned seats. She gave me a little wink of approval for she had overheard my comment to Angel. The lights began to go down. Everybody jumped up out of their seats and ran for the front along with Angel. Angel tried to pull me along with her but people was pushing and shoving so violently we got disconnected. I began looking for Angel. I had every intention of spending the rest of the concert looking for her; but then something magical happened the base-line dropped. The atmosphere began filling with smell good smoke. I got caught up in the excitement. I began letting my head boop to the beat. My fingers started snapping. Then my voice started to reveal my excitement. I was at real concert! "Woo-Who!"

Erupted from my lungs. The hyper the crowd got the louder I screamed. Heavy D jumped on top of the table and started dancing. I was yelling uncontrollably at this point. No wonder why they were jumping up and down on the table. By the time The Boys & Big Daddy Kane came out I barely had a voice. I was standing on a chair jumping up and down screaming and carrying on. The concert ended I was still tingling inside with excitement. After about twenty minutes I began to panic. I couldn't find Angel or her best friend anywhere. I felt a tap on my back. It was my foster mother. I was so happy to see her. The smile on her face made the smile on my face even brighter. All the way home my foster mother tried to scold me for leaving Angel. I thought about telling the truth but why, I had such a good time. Plus I know why she did it. If I was Angel I would've lied to. They couldn't find me. She probably thought she was in some serious trouble. My focus was still completely on the concert. I got in the house and told my foster mother how incredibly dope the concert was. The silence in the house as I spoke was completely non-existing to me. I was too excited to pick up on the signs on how serious she was. The concert was still replaying in my head. I started to fantasize about how life would've been if they would've taken us back stage and we became best friends. My dreams kept growing into what would've happened if I had sung for them and landed a record deal, or what if Big Daddy Kane had fallen hopelessly in love with me. My silliness went on and on until I fell into a dream filled with fairy tales and happy endings. I was settling in well. A couple of months went by. I had stolen this new thing called Slim Fast. It was suppose to help you lose weight faster. I filled the cup up with slim fast. I thought to myself the more I took the more weight I would lose. It was thick and gritty but I forced down every drop. My head began to hurt so badly. My foster mother felt bad for me. She explained exactly how it worked. Then she told me that she would help me with my weight if I wanted her to. Angel and I was becoming close but not as close as her best friend and I were becoming. Unbeknownst to me Angel was becoming increasingly jealous of this fact. Angel began doing little mean things to me. She would tell me I couldn't come in the room when her best friend was over. I tried to tell her mother but her mother told me they've been best friends for so long it's only natural that they would want to do things by themselves. I tried to explain it's not both of them it was just Angel. She dismissed my concerns as childish bickering. I realized it was not worth mentioning it to her mother. After that Angel took it upon herself to get rid of me. She would steal things and tell her mother it wasn't her. Being that I had stolen the slim fast her mother believed her against my ad demit protest. A few weeks went by with the same on and off relationship between Angel and me. This particular day Ms. Wallace seen we were getting along so she left to go to the store. I was sitting on the bed reading one of the novels from my bookshelf. Angel walked into the room with a bright smile highlighting her perfect teeth, deep dimples and beautiful round eyes. By the look on her face I assumed she was up to no good. Angel plopped down on my bed. "Do you wanna see something?" She asked. "Sure". I replied half heartedly interested. I have to admit I was happy she seemed to have time for me. Plus she was being nice to me. Maybe she was starting to come around. Maybe we could go back to being friends. I began to ponder on why she was mad. Maybe I had overstepped my boundaries. This time I wouldn't do that. I had learnt my place. I had decided not to take over their relationship anymore. I would wait for Angel to invite me along and Angel only. Angel pulled out a dirty magazine. It had women in it; looking like they were in pain. This man was sticking his thing in them. I was sickened by the images. I told her I didn't want to see anymore. "It looks like it hurts." I said. "It only hurts at first, and then it feels good." She answered with a giggle. "Why would you do something that hurts at all?" I exclaimed. Angel wasn't making any kinda sense to me. 'Why would you do something that hurt?' I thought. I picked up my book and began reading again. Angel left the room. Angel begged me not to tell her mother then went downstairs. I followed her downstairs to reassure her that I wasn't going to tell her mother anything. Deep down inside I was thinking I had something on her. Angel was quite aware of that fact and was not please with it. My foster mother arrived home with MacDonald's. I ate dinner then went upstairs to take my shower. I often washed two to three times a day to cut down on the corn chip stench. I didn't want to get put out again over "my odor". I put my robe on and proceeded to my room. I sat down on my bed to put on my powder. I extended my hand to grab my deodorant that was on top of my dresser. My door swung open. My foster mother was standing there her face flushed. Her light skin face covered in red was scarier than she could have imagine. I didn't know what I had done but I was sorry for it. I hadn't snuck and turned on the television. There were no dishes. I was completely baffled. She squinted her eyes as her mouth opened. "You showed my daughter a poor-no." She accused. "A wh-what?" I replied, my voice filled with fear. "Don't stand there and play dumb with me! They told me not to get any older children they might corrupt my child, but I didn't listen." She continued. It suddenly hit me she was talking about the magazine. I tried to explain how Angel had showed it to me. My foster mother paused then shot an angry look at Angel. I told her the whole story about me lying on the bed rereading a book. How it was Angel that came into the room with all of that. Her face began to soften Angel realize her mother was starting to believe me. Angel closed her hands into a fist and began banging on the wood door making a tremendous sound of authority. "You are a liar! I never showed you anything!" She yelled. I looked shocked. 'Is she crazy? Do she think she is punking me or something.' I thought. When Ms. Wallace began to smile with pride at her daughter's behavior, I knew I had just lost the battle. I sat on the bed crying. I knew I had to leave. Where would I end up now? I began to blame myself for putting too much faith into this foster home. I figured I would be there for a while. Silly of me. They left my room together. I felt like they should've been giggling and holding hands from the mutual respect in the form of smirks on their faces. Ms. Wallace called the emergency case worker division. She stated that they needed to remove me tonight. Ugh! Was all that kept running thru my mind? Then Ms. Wallace called her boyfriend just in case she needed help with my removal. I silently packed my stuff in disbelief. I'm leaving again with no real destination. Angel and her mother watch me like a hawk. I couldn't blame her though. I brought that on myself by stealing the slim-fast. I began to carry my things downstairs. I sat on the couch with the tears streaming from my face. I opted not to say anything while they sat there at the kitchen table making small talk as if I wasn't there. There was a knock on the door. I assumed it was my social worker, but to no avail it was her boyfriend. My heart beat slowed down to normal pace. I didn't understand why I was so upset it wasn't like I was going to get in trouble. The thoughts in my head were jumbled. I should've, I would've, and I could'ves filled my head endlessly. Where would I go this time of night? How far away from my sisters would I be this time? I was snapped out of my thoughts by the constant taunting from Angel's mouth. 'I just wish she would really shut up already.' I thought. Ms. Wallace decided to join in on the taunting. "I don't know babe, you didn't see Angel in that room. She really stood her ground. I'm impressed. I figured with her size and all but Angel didn't back down." She said grinning like a fat chessy cat. "What did Taylor do?" He asked. "Nothing!" She replied still smirking with pride written all over her face. Now deep down inside I'm really starting to get mad. I have no concept on where my life is going from this point. This mother is a school teacher at that. I couldn't believe she was standing here laughing, and snickering. When she wasn't doing those things she would be standing there with an uncontrollable grin plastered on her face. What was funny that her daughter had disrespected me? Or was it I didn't do anything while I was trying to respect her house. "You weren't scared Angel; I mean she's a big girl." She asked her daughter. Her mother's comment along with that stupid smirk elevated my temper a little more. I wanted nothing more than to wipe that smug grin off her and her daughters face. "I know mom but I'm not scared of nobody; no matter how big they may be!" Angel replied, her smile displaying her gratification with the whole situation. That was it, I had enough! "You need to tell your daughter to watch her mouth. Word-up, Yo!" The betrayal of my voice revealed my nervousness. "Like I said, nobody is going to step to me in my house I don't care how big you is!" Angel responded with rage. My heart began thumping rapidly my face was hot. My breathing quicken. I watch the shenanigans of her mother pulling Angel back. Ms. Wallace was smiling from ear to ear while her daughter spoke this nonsense. This is my life this is not some game. I looked in Ms. Wallace direction. "Look this is the last time I'm going to warn you about your daughters mouth. I don't care how hyper she gets she is not whooping my ass!" I said. My voice was very cold and methodical. Ms. Wallace boyfriend could hear the sincerity in my voice.

"Look that girl is from the mean streets, y'all sure about this" He said. What mean streets. Oh I know, the mean streets of Kymela's house, Sunday school, church. Yea I'm a real misfit. "Ma. Let me get her!" Angel said with anger oozing from her words. To my surprise Ms. Wallace let her go. Angel started racing towards me. Adrenaline shot thru my body like a cannon. Angel stop short in front of me and swung her right fist fast and furious. Surprisingly enough to me I ducked. Angel looked as surprised as I felt. She swung her left fist wildly. I could tell it was done out of desperation. I just remember swinging. I must've been winning because her mother came running. Ms. Wallace yelled "Get your big ass off my baby!" Ms. Wallace grabbed my arms, then my hair. I turned around. Some random lady wasn't about to put her hands on me. She was chunky her damn self. When I turned around in a panic; I began swinging wildly. Ms. Wallace called her boyfriend over to help her. Another fat one I thought. I balled up my fist and hit him as hard as I could. He stumbled back a little bit. I took that moment to survey my surroundings. I could she Ms. Wallace cuddled up in the corner holding Angel while she wept. Angel had blood coming from somewhere on her face. They both had the look of terror in their eyes. I began to feel bad I didn't mean to hurt anyone. I started to relax. Ms. Wallace fat–ass boyfriend tackled me before I could turn back in his direction. As his elbow hit my back I felt all of the wind leave my body. Being thrust forward with such magnitude I lost my balance and hit the floor hard. He plopped his fat butt down firmly on my back. The little bit of air I had in me escaped as I yelped in pain. "You're not so tough now little girl." He said mockingly. I could only yell I can't breathe. My yell became a barely audible whisper. I stop speaking to preserve the little bit of oxygen I had left. A social worker walked in and asked very politely what was going on. Fat ass stood up. I grabbed what I could and walked out the door I was beyond pissed. Angel along with her mother was still standing in the corner looking scared hugging each other. Fat-ass had the same look of fear in his eyes. I said good-bye and thanked her on the way out the door. As I stared out the state issued car window my thoughts were traveling to where I would end up now. I mean what the fuck is up with all this up-downs. My subconscious took over my thoughts. I started thinking about the ins-and-outs of my young life. Would things ever get any better? My social worker inquired about what happened in the house. I continued to stare out the window as if she wasn't even speaking. I mean who did she think she was fooling she didn't care. If she really cares I would be home with my real mother and sisters. It was pointless telling this paid surrogate mother anything. Her job was to pick me up and drop me off at my next holding cell. The car came to a jerk stop. I looked over at her for my instructions. I was beginning to realize that at every house we would have a pep talk. I was told how they were great people and what not to do or say. Plus she added the usual if you need anything; yada, yada, the same old song and dance. I could tell she was just as aggravated from this recycled procedure as I was. I hopped out of the car. I entered the house with the social worker.

CHAPTER 7

Innocence Lost

There were a lot of children standing there. Mostly boys, their faces told a story of agony. I could tell they were all standing there being forced to be polite and "greet the new girl." The lack of excitement or interest in their facial expression made me feel like a fish at the aquarium. The new foster mother was older in age. She invited me in with a warm smile followed by a hug. My new foster father had a very notable gold tooth in his mouth. He smiled and waved at me. "This here is your momma now. I'm your dad, you understand." He said. His voice was nice but stern. I just nodded. I thought they told me I didn't have to call any of these people mom or dad. He kept talking through my disbelief. "These here are your brothers. This is Mitch and Marlon. They are biological brothers. They have been here since they were six and seven years old. Mitch is fifteen and Marlon is fourteen. This here is Elroy he is our special needs son; not biological though. He's been here since he was five; he is sixteen now. He understands well. He just talks with a stutter. He lived here with his brother. His brother just moved out and got his own place. He continued to stay here with us though. These two here are also brothers. The oldest one is David and that one is Davon. They are the same age as you guys; fifteen and sixteen years old. We just got that one over there. His name is Cornell. He is the baby of the family; he is only twelve. And last but not least this is the only girl. That is until you came along. She round bout y'all age too. You will be sharing a room with her. Her name is Wendella." He began to walk through the house. "This right here is the downstairs bathroom, over here is the dining room. We all eat together in this house; dinner is at five-thirty p.m. You come home from school you sit here until your homework is done, and then you can do as you please until dinner. "Over here is the living room. Nobody is allowed in there." He stated, while still being my tour guide. "Over here is the family room this is where we watch television. You also have a T.V. in your room. This is the kitchen Momma doesn't like anyone in there when she is cooking. This refrigerator is always locked. It's the house fridge, it's only things in there for Momma' to cook with. We also have a deep freezer it is also locked we keep the cakes in there. My son works for Hostess. He drives the truck. They give him the cakes that they are unable to sale due to the freshness sticker expiration date. This back here is our spare room that we added to the house. It's an Atri game back here for the children to play on. You can sit back here just to look outside; or read a book or something. We have a couple of german shepherds back here. Only I feed them, pet them. You understand?" He asked, without giving me a chance to respond before continuing to talk. "This here is yawls fridge. It has luncheon meat in there and healthy snacks. It's there for whenever you get hungry. Momma' restocks it every day. We use to keep juice in there, but it would be the first thing to go. Everybody wasn't getting some; it became a problem so we eliminated that. If there is anything y'all can't share or handle it will be discussed. If we can't come to a conclusion it will be eliminated. In this house I do believe in spankings. We don't tolerate unruliness in this house." He said casually; in front of my social worker. I shot her a look. They took me away from Kymela because she beat us now she is going to sit here and let this complete stranger say that he beats us. Isn't that against all of their rules? By the passive way she smiled at me I could tell that's exactly what she had in mind for me. He grinned and winked at her also. Oh Lord, this is going to be fun I thought. He began to speak again. "Wendellla, show her to your room please." "Yes, sir." She replied. While walking thru the house I was able to get a good look at "my brothers". Mitch and Marlon were brown skin. They both had identical dimples that made their perfect white teeth dominating. Both of them had a side box fade with blonde dye at the tip.Tall and slenderly built. Davon and David were equally attractive. Davon along with David had what most black people classified as high yellow skin tone. Davon's hazel eyes where intoxicating he had uneven teeth with a scar on his left cheek that made you feel a sense of danger with a hint of mystery. As fine as he was, his brother appearance was more alluring by far. David hair matched his skin tone; you could see the reddish brown in his low cut deep waved cesar. His deep dimples were unmatched to his enticing green eyes. You could see the cuts in his six packs thru his shirt. His height also gave him leverage over his brother, but the thickness of his whole statue made his brother no competition to him in the looks department. After I did another quick surveillance of the new handsome brothers I noticed they were all evenly buff. I guess that's something they did for fun. While they were in the corner I observe them giggling. I knew they were talking about me by the guilty looks on their faces when we caught eye contact. I followed Wendella upstairs to our room. She sat on the bed and began to talk while I on the other hand began to worry. I didn't want to be the butt of everyone's jokes again. I had no regard in what Wendella was saying therefore I interrupted her in mid sentence. "So do they beat you a lot around here?" I asked. In my mind I needed to know if this was one of those abusive houses that's only in it for the money." Wendella giggled before answering me. "Nah I've been here three years and I never gotten a beating. I think they just say that to scare the new children when they arrive." She stated. "Well how many new children could there possibly be. I mean this house is big but not that big." I inquired. "It's mostly girls, I have three extra beds in here as you can see and they are always trying to get someone to stay in here with me." She said. Once in awhile a boy comes along but the boys run them off pretty quickly." She continued. "Oh." I said hoping my one word response would show her that this conversation was over. "Yea, but the boys aren't that bad. So which one do you think is cute?" She asked ignoring my demeanor and flat tone. Although I thought the boys were cute I would never admit that to her. She had a devilish grin on her face which told me she was more into mischief then getting to know me better. "Well I'm not here for that." I responded as flatly as I had the first time. This time she took the hint and got up to leave the room. "By the way they are very strict on dinner;

we all eat together like a family every night. So if you want to make a good impression I would be on time." She said while exiting the door. I knew the routine. She had to go and tell the other kids what I had. I knew I didn't own much so there wasn't much to talk about except for some holy panties. I politely placed all of my things in the drawer. I couldn't bat away the tears of not knowing what was next. How could they be allowed to beat me kept crossing my mind repeatedly? I fell to my knees as the warmth of my tears streamed down my face. It acted as my only source of comfort in my time of need. I swallowed my cries. I couldn't have the rest of the children thinking I was weak. While on my knees I looked toward the heavens begging God to help me through this time in my life. I kept feeling that the things I was going thru was unfair. I suck the snot back up my nose, wiped my tears, stood to my feet, I was going to make it for God had just told me so. I regained my composure and walked downstairs for dinner. As I was rounding the corner I could hear a boy talking. "She is so ugly." One of them said. I wasn't too sure which one for I had not gotten use to their voices yet. All of the boys turned around to see me standing in the doorway of the dining room. I could tell by the look of uncertainty on their faces they couldn't tell if I had heard them. They also had a look of fear therefore I didn't say anything. I knew if I told on them I would have nothing but trouble in this house for the rest of my stay. I learnt my lesson from the last house. Children will snake you if they feel threatened in any manner. I sat at the table with a smile on my face, but my heart felt as if it was target practice for the entire police force. Inside I was being ripped to shreds; I had God so I knew everything was going to be alright. He told me so. The next day was always the hardest to me. It was the first day of school for me again. Every place had me in school the very next day with new students and new trials. The children didn't bother me as much as they did before. Now I had bigger things to worry about than being called fat. Like how long was I going to be at this place? Will these kids be nice to me when the foster parents weren't around? Would the foster parents be nice to me when the social worker leaves? I spent the majority of my first day in the main office. I started down the hall with my head down. I had gotten bigger in size, which made my head look smaller and the fact that I didn't have any hair made me the new freak walking. I arrived to my class, to my surprise everyone was genuinely nice to me. Little did I know; my new brothers were the studs of the school? The week went by in a flash. Sunday I awoken earlier than usual I knew we had to go to church. I took out my best church outfit. I took my shower then got dress. I found out we belonged to a Baptist church. I didn't know what kind of religion that was but I was hoping they celebrated the same God that I was use to. We pulled up in front of the church to my delight it was next to Rose's church. I couldn't contain my excitement. My smile was radiant. I asked my foster parents if I could go to her church to sit for a while. They allowed me to do so. Rose told me that they had a meeting with my mother but I wasn't there. She inquired why I wasn't there. I told her I was tied up with other things. I knew once I left church I was going to get to the bottom of this. I had a great time. For the first time I thought everything was going to be alright. Life was definitely manageable. I got to see my sister every Sunday; well at least one of them anyway. My mother was now allowed to come to the house for home visits. She had a car which was better for her. My foster sister and brother's were nicer than most. I really didn't have anything to complain about. This foster mother tried to teach me the cleanliness of my period. I showered twice a day because I didn't want to be put out over my odor. I really had no complaints. Within the sixth months the wheels of my life were beginning to turn again. I knew that because once again I was in turmoil. Rose foster mother said she was always upset when I left church on Sundays so I was banned from going next door. So every Sunday I had to stare out the window hoping to catch a glimpse of her when church was beginning or ending. To no avail that never happened. My body was developing rapidly. I thought it was because of the fat that had been added to my stature. The boys however thought it was just big titties. School was out and the boredom had set in. The rest of the children had a friends house that they would go over. I wasn't there long enough for that. I walked around the house all day up under Ma' but I did my best not to get on her nerves.

It was an achingly hot summer day. I was on my second shower. Everyone had left the house. I put on my deodorant along with my lotion.

Then I put on my bra and panties. I was so glad to have a bra and panty outfit that matched. I'd seen the girls in magazines with those on, however I never thought I would have a set. I stood in the mirror sucking in my stomach while pushing in the rest of the fat that was hanging over. My body was hideous. The purple panty set made me look a little better though. I started doing jumping jacks. Jumping up and down in the mirror to watch my breast bounce back and forth. I knew these were the only assets I would ever have in my young life. I turned the radio on they were playing a song that I'd often seen Wendella dance to. I figured I would give it a try. I started trying to bust out dance moves. I looked a mess I kept dancing and laughing at myself. I glanced at the crack in the door that I didn't know I had left. I'd seen the green eyes piercing me. He had a devilish grin on his face. I quickly grab a sheet from my bed and covered myself. How long had he been standing there I thought horrified. My door swung open. I jumped on the bottom bunk in fear. "Don't worry I'm not going to hurt you. I just wanted you to know I like when you dance naked in the mirror like that." David said. My head was still down in shame. He took his index finger and placed it gently under my chin. He ever so slightly raised my face until my eyes were interlocked with his. "You have nothing to be ashamed of; I said I liked what I saw. Can you do it again please?" David asked. I shook my head up and down indicating yes. He walked out the room but left the door slightly ajared like it was. I tried to be as carefree as I was the first time but I was so nervous. I knew he was there, I couldn't deny that, not even to myself no matter how much I wanted to. I kept messing up. David opened the room door and motion for me to come to him with his fingers. I followed him across the hall to the bathroom. I knew what I was doing was wrong but I felt different inside. I began to hesitate. He yanked my arm to pull me inside the rest of the way. It seemed like one effortless motion I was inside and the door was closed behind me all at once. I started to feel like I was trapped for a split second. He erased my fears by staring deep into my eyes. I was memorized. Hell I was paralyzed. My mind said leave but my feet did not move. He told me to lick my lips. I was embarrassed I knew they were chapped and dry I started to put my head down again in shame but this time something very soft and clammy brushed against my lips.

My eyes popped wide open. I was scared. His eyes were closed his face was flushed. My eyes were still wide open I didn't know what to do. I looked like a deer caught in the headlights. He opened his eyes and smiled at me. "What you don't know how to kiss?" He asked. Inside I was jumping up and down; I'm kissing, I'm kissing David! The cutest boy in the house is kissing me. Me, of all people; the one who is considered the ugly duckling. I'm kissing a prince. He took my silence as an admission of innocence. "Don't worry I'll do everything just open your mouth." He stated with superiority and ice cold mint breath. He closed his eyes again and slightly brushed his lips across mine. I still had my eyes wide open. Staring like a crackhead looking for a late night hit. His face was so intense and serious. He opened his eyes this time despite himself he had to let out an inaudible chuckle. "Girl relax, I got you." He said. "I guess I have to start with the basics. Relax, close your eyes and open your mouth." He proclaimed. I closed my eyes and opened my mouth as wide as I could. "Slightly." He added between chuckles. I took a deep breath and followed his instructions. He kissed me on the cheek softly. He nibbled on my bottom lip. A moan escaped my throat from nowhere. I really enjoyed what he was doing. It was making me feel tingly inside. I waited for him to place his lips on top of mine. I wanted him to place his lips on top of mine. He gently grabbed my hair while pulling my head back until the full length of my neck was exposed. I didn't know what he was doing but I liked it. His tongue connected to my neck. As he stroked his tongue up and down along the side of my neck; my legs felt as if they were going to give away underneath me. A hot rushing sensation flutter through my entire body. I couldn't contain myself as another moan escape the pit of my throat. He whispered in my ear. "None of that, you'll get us caught." With that he intertwined my mouth with his. Invading my thoughts with lust, enticing my body with yearning, teasing my mouth with longing. I wanted whatever he had to offer. I needed whatever he was going to give me. My tongue played double dutch with his. His fingers slipped inside my bra. He rubbed my nipples, and then flicked them. He strung along a trail of kisses from my neck to my chest then finding its rightful place upon the tip of my nipples. I gasped in ecstasy. The tingling feeling was back but this time it was in between my legs.

My private parts were throbbing. It wanted something but I didn't know what it was until he slipped a finger inside my pretty new purple panties. He began to stroke my soft spot. I began to slide down door it was too much for me to bare. He was making me feel uncontrollable things. I began to panic. I snatched away from him with all my might. I swung open the bathroom door and headed for my room. He grabbed my arm tightly. "You can't leave me like this?" He said in a question form. "Like what?" I responded trying not to look at him. "I'm going to hurt real bad if you don't help me." He added. I looked up his entire face was red. I didn't know what kind of pain he was in but I didn't mean to do it. I reluctantly walked back into the bathroom. "Well where does it hurt at?" I asked still not making eye contact. "My thing hurt. I need you to put your mouth up there until I tell you to stop." He stated. I put my mouth on his "thing". He began to make vocal sounds. I thought I was hurting him. I stopped then looked up. He pushed my head back onto his "thing". I kept going. Through his moans he told me I had to have done this before because I was a pro. Whatever that meant. I kept the pace according to his instructional thrusting of my head back and forth. He sped up and so did I. Then he yelped I jerked in fear and a milky substance started squirting in my mouth. I thought I had really hurt him this time. His entire body was red. It was pus in my mouth. Oh, lord please let him be alright. He started yelling "Get out, hurry up, And LEAVE!" I ran to my room. Oh, what have I done? I'd hurt him in the bathroom and they were going to find him. I just knew they would send me away for sure. I laid across the bed prepared to cry when the room door opened. David was standing there with a wide smile on his face. "You okay?" He asked. I shook my head yes. My heart was still racing. I didn't understand what had happened. He walked in two more steps. The fear was apparent on my face. "I'm okay." He said, consoling me with his words. "You sure." I asked. "Yea." He said while walking away. He was shaking his head from side to side. Even though his back was to me I could still see his dimples from his side profile. I guess he thought I was funny but I was happy he was okay. I was so grateful to God that I wasn't in trouble. I knew I was never going to do that again. I wasn't quite sure what was wrong with him but I never wanted to do that to anyone else. I kept thinking about his smile. I began to fantasize about pretty green, hazel eyed children running around my house. He was my husband. The wedding was beautiful; yep I had a handsome man. Even though it was mid afternoon I fell asleep. I didn't awaken until Wendella was taking off her clothes for bed. I opened my eyes and ask her what time it was. She told me it was ten o'clock at night and that I had missed dinner. She said Ma' said I was crying in my sleep. She thought I didn't feel well so she didn't wake me. Deep down I wished I could trust Wendella so I could tell her about my day. I just wanted her to know that David was my man! Wendella began talking a mile a minute until she fell asleep. I kept thinking about the bathroom incident. I had slept so long I couldn't go back to sleep. The bathroom scene kept me daydreaming about fairy tales. I knew my mother and sisters would be impressed by my new boyfriend. His looks were undeniable. I knew they would be envious of me. I began exploring my body. I rub the same soft spot that he had rub but it didn't feel the same way it had when he had done it. I clenched my body like I had in the bathroom. I sped up until my entire body began to tremble. I fell asleep. I awaken the next morning with love in my heart and my new man on my mind. I sat at the breakfast table waiting for my oatmeal. David never came. I tried to casually ask about him. One of the other boys smirked and told me he left early. I figured they knew I was his girl. I knew he had told them and I was proud. I floated through the day waiting for him. I put on my other new panty set. I didn't know if he wanted to do that again but I was more than willing; kind of. I arrived home to see David at the dining room table eating his snack. I didn't want to make it to obvious so I didn't sit directly beside him. I sat two seats down and pulled out my snack. I glanced in his direction but he never lifted his head. Maybe he was mad at me about yesterday. I couldn't tell. When the other children arrived at the table I notice he was avoiding me on purpose. I felt used and confused. Why would he not talk to me? I thought perhaps I did something wrong. I didn't say anything to him because I didn't want to get my feelings hurt. I just played along and pretended like nothing happened. Days rolled in as the nights rolled out. He never really spoke to me again. I hadn't really put too much thought into it after awhile. I maintained by being low key. I didn't need that getting back to my foster parents.

One day I came out of the shower. I had my robe on with my matching slippers. I walked to my room to get dress immediately. I would never be used like that again. I heard someone outside my door. I didn't know what to do. I laid across my bunk. My eyes were closed tightly with my back to the door. I wasn't speaking to David and he would never use me again. "I know you're not sleep." A male voice said. I recognized the voice instantly. To my surprise it was Mitch. I didn't turn around. I laid as stiff as I possibly could. Mitch continued to speak. "Can I lay with you?" He asked. I still pretended to be sleep. My heart was pounding. I didn't know what to do. I didn't want to do what I did to David to anyone else. I kept thinking if I pretended to be sleep he would just go away. Again I was astonished by Mitch when he climbed into my bed beside me. My heart was pounding. I guess he could feel my panic. "You don't have to be scared of me." He said softly. I just kept reliving what David had done. I didn't want that. Mitch laid there talking for a long time until I finally answered him. He came right out and asked me could he put his thing inside of me I told him no. He started kissing on me more gently than David had. While he kissed me he wanted me to look into his eyes. I was confused. David wanted my eyes closed. Mitch on the other hand wanted my eyes open. I began to believe it depend on the boy. Mitch kept asking me if he could put "it" in. Through our feverish kisses I would bellow out no every time. "What's the problem you think you're going to get pregnant?" He inquired. "No." I responded, but secretly that was my fear. Kymela would kill me if she knew how I was carrying on. Plus I shuddered to think what Ramon would do to me. "I could wear a condom, if you want. No baby can get through that; it's rubber." He exclaimed. I still shook my head in disapproval. I turned around to pretend like I had fallen asleep again. This time he would definitely get the hint and leave. Mitch got the hint alright he pulled up my robe and began hunching up and down on my fat rolls. He was making noises like David had. I guess he liked it too. He kept asking me what hole he was in. I wanted to tell him neither but I didn't respond at all. His breathing was erratic while he was grunting. He finally wiped something on my back got up and went in the bathroom.

I came downstairs for dinner. I felt somewhat violated. Not totally only because I liked the beginning part so I guess I should've knew about the rest. Maybe I just had sex I wasn't for sure though. He kept asking about this hole I knew he never put it in "the hole". So I guess I didn't. I walked into the kitchen to get my plate Mitch was standing there with a big grin on his face. He waved at me I rolled my eyes and took my food to the dinner table. While at the dinner Mitch kept looking at me but I wouldn't look back at him. I mean that's what David did that's how it's supposed to be done. By the end of the night Mitch eyes had a since of hurt in them. I was too confused to try and figure any of this mess out. I wasn't going to be in my room anymore. I knew that for sure. A whole year trotted by with no further incidents. I got along with everybody. Marlon and I had started a flirtatious relationship. We would joke a lot with each other. I liked him. He was the only one who did not take advantage of me. We began exchanging passionate kisses. They were mutual we both wanted them. For the first time I knew what I was doing and I enjoyed every minute of it. We would sneak to steal a kiss here and there nothing more. I couldn't wait for the house to be empty so I could find my way to his arms to kiss him. Summertime was rolling around. I knew we would have a lot more of those stolen moments and I couldn't wait. Wendella started to act a bit familiar. She was beginning to remind me of Angel. Her actions were devious but she would dish it out with a smile. I sat on the floor to watch Tales from the Crypt. A new HBO series the boys were dying to see. I pretended to want to see it to but I was more afraid of that little corpse than anything else but I wouldn't let them see it. We sat there zoning to the television. Wendella got up tight about something that I didn't think was that important. She told me if I said another word she would put her foot in my mouth. I opened my mouth as wide as I could as if it was an open invitation. Wendella put her foot in my mouth. It was on. I punched her as hard as I could. I pulled her down on the ground. Cornell started screaming for Mom and Dad. We met fist for fist. We rolled back and forth on the floor hair tugging, all while punching. Dad was on his way around the corner Wendella bit me so I let her go. Dad had a rubber racing track in his hand swinging wildly. I was screaming. So was Wendella. Dad was chasing us all thru the house. Hitting us with the rubber race track every step of the way. I turned to explain but Wendella started lying. Mitch jumped in and confirmed that this girl had put her foot in my mouth. We went upstairs into our room no longer enemies but allies. As we stood in the mirror counting our whelps the boys were in the doorway laughing and calling us crazy. Marlon couldn't wait to see me the next day. He told me how everybody was surprise at me. He said I had gotten beat-up but not by too much. I was mad at him until he grabbed my arm and planted a kiss on me. We went back to life as usual sneaking away for our stolen moments in the night. Kissing and rubbing each other every chance we got. Marlon called me outside for our daily rundavoo. We were kissing as usual, and then Mitch walked up. I didn't see him. Marlon had that's why he took his basketball and smacked me in the face with it. Mitch yelled "Oh, my gosh!" He turned and headed in the other direction. Marlon ran after him. I didn't know what to do. I stood there crying. I knew this was bad from the look in Mitch eyes. I went upstairs to my room. The next day I was told to stay home from school my heart was pounding. Ma' came upstairs with a suitcase and helped me get all my things together. She told me I was leaving because I was too nasty for her. I thought she was talking about cleaning up wise. My social worker arrived to take me to my new place. I didn't have the energy to cry this time or to be mad this was my fault. I got into the car. My social worker started her transport therapy. She wanted to know why I had slept with all of those boys. I wanted to tell her how I didn't understand what they were doing to me. How they had taken advantage of me. How I didn't sleep with "all" the boys. Heck I wasn't even sure if I had slept with one boy. I knew no one would listen or believe me. I was just some misguided girl; with boys on my mind according to my worker. She told me there weren't any more homes available I would have to go to a group home until they found me a more suitable place. She also explained that I would be the youngest girl there. They only usually take sixteen year olds. My social worker wanted me to extend my gratitude to them for breaking the rules for me. Being that I was only twelve this was a big deal for them. I didn't know Mitch was jealous and mad. That he went and told mom and dad that I was sleeping around and he was scared that I was going to get pregnant. I guess he liked me more than I was capable of understanding. He felt betrayed. I mean it was his little brother I was making out with. So he was hurt and he got even.

CHAPTER 8

Group Home Life

I walked into the group home. It was a mandatory inspection of my things. I didn't understand why all of my things had to be spooled out on the living room floor. Where the whole house could see. I was told that this was a private procedure. Even though the staff had seen the girls traveling back and forth like I did, they said nothing. Many of the girls lingered about until a staff member would finally speak up. I couldn't make heads or tails of what was going on. They said it was a group home so I had expected iron gates with matching beds to boot. Evidently a group home was just a big house with big rooms with matching twin bunk beds. For all sake purposes I had just left one. As the staff spoke of the house rules along with activities I was more interested in my surroundings. Each girl that passed through I tried to get a glimpse of who she was inside and out with a second at hand. There were so many girls trotting back and forth I finally posed a question in the middle of one staff member statement. "How many girls live here?" I asked. The staff member didn't miss a beat with her response. "Well as of right now we have fifteen girls, but this house is made to accommodate twenty or more at a time. We are really fully stocked but we get new arrivals all the time." She answered. Stocked, I thought. Are we cattle? She continued to talk about the things they felt I needed to know. I was happy for the walk through because that meant this interrogation was finally over. I threw my things back into my bag. I gathered everything and proceeded to follow the staff member to my assigned room. I was told about the kitchen and how we had a personal chef that cooked all our meals. I was informed of meal times and chores that were expected of us. I was showed the sign in sheet; it was for when we left for school and when we were to returned. On the staff office door were all of our scheduled appointments. We had a counselor along with group meetings that were mandatory. They also had other things we could sign up for that was voluntary. I was brought to my room. I had my own space since I was so young and they had many rooms available, they wanted me to be by myself. I figured they didn't want the other girls to influence me. It was almost dinner time. I was mad at myself because I didn't ask about seconds. I was starving I hadn't ate anything since breakfast. To ignore the grumbling of my stomach I began to place my things neatly on the dresser. I had accumulated a lot at my last foster home. I placed my clothes in the draw. I'd walk to the front desk to ask about laundry. The staff member sitting there told me the laundry room rules. Everyone had a laundry day according to their room. My assigned day wasn't until next week but since I was new she would allow me to do a load. I was relieved. I didn't want anyone to smell my clothes. No matter how much I washed my natural scent was always imbedded in my clothing when I took them off. I walked back to my assign room to gather my clothes. I stuck them in the wash. On my way back to my room a dark skin black girl stood in front of me. Her smooth dark skin made the scar down the side of her face almost unnoticeable. She smiled, obviously proud of her pearly white teeth. Her entire head was bleached blonde. That was the first time I had ever seen a black girl who had done that. I was waiting for her to say something but she only smirked at me as I walked by. I got to my room to make up my bed. All of my personal hygiene things were gone. I was so proud of them. I placed them on top of my chesser draw. They were lined up by deodorants, powders, perfumes, lotions, shampoo, conditioner, and sanitary napkins. Deep down inside I knew the other girls would be jealous. Heck I wanted them to be. I was willing to share but I figured that would be a way for me to make some friends. I rushed to the staff office. I explained how I had set everything up and now they were missing. I guess my nonchalant attitude during my intake was coming back to haunt me. They dismissed me before I could even get the words to leave my mouth. My devastation was written all over my face at the dinner table. Everybody kept talking holding conversation as usual but I could tell they all knew who had my things. I ate in silence. I was fighting my inner self not to cry. I didn't want them to know how bad they had hurt me. Once again my emotions betrayed me. The tears began to stream down my face as I ate my food alone and in silence. The loneliness haunted me in a room full of people. My heart shattered, while whimpers force their way thru my throat. I hated my life this just wasn't fair. I know I left those things there for them to be envious but I also knew that if anyone would've asked I would've let them have it. Now I was down to nothing. I removed my dish and took it to the kitchen along with everyone else. I knew it probably was the blonde girl but truth be told I was scared of her. I mean she had to be crazy. Her hair was blonde and she had a scar on her face. Plus she wanted me to know that she had been responsible. The way she walked by and smirked at me. I thought my social worker told me I would be safe here. My social worker hadn't shown up all day. I was happy. That meant I could prolong the first day of school. It was no big victory but it was one more day without the hassle of the unknown. A girl came into the house. I guess she was the first one home from school. She made her way to the couch beside me. I wanted to get up and leave maybe she was the one who had stolen my things. She immediately started to engage me in a conversation. Her mindless chit-chatter seemed to have no end. I guess she wanted to know my story. She would have no idea the deep dark secret I must carry. I felt bad about the things that happened in her past but I refused to let my empathy be followed by stupidity. I mean what was I going to say my mother worked us like dogs, beat us like slaves, and at night we became the object of her sexual desire. Yeah, that would really go over well. My mind was tormenting me with faded pictures of my past I had to escape this silly girl. My life was not a show and tell type of deal. "So is there anything you can tell me that I should know about this place?" I asked unaware if she was even speaking. "You can't trust too many people around here. Look, I don't steal but some of these girls do. I know they stole your things but I don't get involved with things like that. I just basically go with the flow. You're now a part of the forgotten. They place you here when they don't have anywhere else to put you then forget about you." She said as she was walking away. "If I were you I would get my social worker to put money in my account every Friday like they are supposed to. It's not much but it helps with the activities that they schedule and this Friday is bowling. If you don't mention it they pretend like they forgot. You seem like a nice girl, just try not to talk too much." She finished. I instantly dwelled on the positive. We would get to go bowling. I'd never been bowling before this could be fun. I turned my attention back to my siblings maybe on these outings I could try and sneak to see them.

I'd gotten in trouble at school. It was very trivial behavior but I did get suspended. I walked into the group home with fear inside of me the same fear that haunted me every time I walked into Kymela's house. This time things turned out different. I just had to stay in my room all day with no television privileges, do an extra chore, and go to bed early. I finally came to a shocking realization. I had no parents which meant I had no real rules to follow. I began behaving badly in class. At every turn, I tried to find a new way to push them. I was part of the forgotten and I understood that fact. There was nothing else that they could do to me. I had nothing else to lose. The only thing that the staff worried about was fighting in the house. It was not tolerated at all. They would call the cops instantly to have you place into a detention center. It wasn't hard for the cops to be called. If you became belligerent or too mouthy it was done in an instance. I grasped the fact that my behavior was less than glowing. I knew deep down inside I wasn't raised this way. All I knew was church not how to be a good rebel even though the girls in the home were more than willing to teach me all I needed to know to be successful. I began to advise a plan on how to meet up with my sisters. I asked questions a lot. My questions were posed to various staff members. My intentions were to gain knowledge of my sister's school, homes or any information they would naively offer up. After I gained the needed knowledge I began to cut school with a purpose. I would pick a sister that I would visit for the day. I'd show up at schools, churches but never anyone homes I didn't want the social worker to know what I was up to. They had deemed me a troubled child with no provocation, I just figured I would let them think they were right. I made all of my sister's promise not to tell anyone what

I was up to. I explained to them how they would stop me from coming to see them. A lot of the times I would only get to see one of my sisters for a few minutes before they would have to take the school bus home or I would sit in church beside someone like I was a part of their family until church was over. While the adults were talking to each other my sisters knew to sneak outside or to the bathroom. We would only get a few minutes with each other but it would be worth it. School was definitely easier than church. I would find their class and walk with them when they were changing classes. We would walk the halls laughing and giggling. I would find the girl's bathroom to hide in while their class was going on. When the bell would ring I would emerge from the bathroom with the rest of the students. We always cried at the end of the day. It was an emotional scene every time but nothing beats the time we would spend with each other.

Group home life wasn't that bad for the most part except for the fact that everyone treated me like an outcast. I'd made friends with the cook so she would give me extra portions. I was in my own little world. I would cut school to see my sisters when I could, give the teachers hell because I was living in a horror picture at home. In the group home I was picked on and teased relentlessly by the dark skin, blonde, scar faced girl who I learnt to be called D'keena. Rumor had it that she hated me because I told on her that she stolen my things. I didn't understand that part, I never said a name, plus it's not like she even got in trouble! I stayed as far away from her as I could. No matter how hard I tried D'keena would make her way to my side of the group home to share an insult or a disgusted glance. I got up for another day of torment. I had accidently left all of my clothes in the dryer. I figured I would use the shower on the other side of the group home; being that my clothes were over there. I opened the dryer my clothes were still wet. I pulled the clothes out of the dryer while sucking my teeth. 'Now I have to wear damp clothes to school'. I thought. As the clothes came out of the dryer it looked like there were white patches in the wet spots. The smell was strong. I knew that aroma. Bleach! All of my clothes were mysteriously bleached in the dryer. I knew it was D'keena but it was nothing I could do about it. I was too afraid to approach her directly and going to the staff was what had gotten me into this trouble to begin with. I turned the dryer on to dry my clothes. I walked back to my room. I told the staff that I wasn't feeling well and I wasn't going to school today. They reiterated the no television rule if I didn't go to school. I nodded in agreement and tried to make it to my room before the tears could fall. I laid across my bed trying to figure out what I was going to do about clothes for school. I had left numerous messages for my social worker who never called me back. This was no surprise, I had been calling her since I was placed here and she never returned my call; not once. I dozed off with my usually grief stricken heart along with swollen eyelids from still squeezing out tears from my almost dried out tear dots. I'd awaken as the children were coming in from school. I rushed to get my clothes. I didn't know what else they were capable of. As I walked past the day room all of the girls had made their way to the couch. They were sitting there pretending to watch B.E.T. as I trotted to the dryer. I pulled my clothes out in a ball I heard giggling. I guess they were all in on it. I walked back to my room to cry and pray. I hadn't done that in a while. I asked the Lord to help me get some new clothes and to be reconnected to my family. I'd decided to stay in my room until dinner. When dinner was called I went to the table by myself. I ate dinner alone and in silence as usual. I went into my room after I had done my chore. The tears were streaming down my face. I couldn't believe this is what my life had become. I began to secretly loathe my oldest sister, why did she have to tell. Kymela was bad but not as bad as this. I needed my sisters and she took them away from me. The next morning I got up to rush to the shower before anybody else could get in there. I knew they could never smell the corn-chip smell that I carried, plus I had started getting boils under my armpits and sometimes they would pop in the shower. They were always smelly. I'd washed got dress and rushed back to my room before anyone could see me. I'd sorted through the clothes and wore the ones with the least amount of damage. They called for breakfast. I knew I had to at least leave the house because another day without television was not going to happen. I sat at my usual table alone in the corner. We were having powder eggs, pork sausage and toast. I knew I could make a sandwich. I was happy about that; I grabbed my plate off the tray. I looked into the bowel they had placed on the cart with condiments. I took out a little plastic pack of butter and grape jelly. To my delight there was a plastic pack of mixed fruit jelly directly underneath. I grabbed it right before D'keena. I was glad I had finally beaten her at something. I sat at the table with a smirk on my face. I couldn't help it. I thought maybe today was going to be a good day. D'keena looked in my direction. I instantly tried to soften my face; but I could still tell she had an attitude although she had a slight smile lingering. "Can I have the mixed fruit jelly?" D'keena asked. "No, I really like mixed fruit and they don't serve it like that." I answered, my smile was still there but it was a softer I'm sorry but I really want this type of smile. "But you have two jellies." D'keena stated seeming a bit agitated. My heart sped up being fuel solely on fear. "I'll give you my grape jelly." I managed to stammer out. "I don't want grape jelly. I want the mixed fruit." D'keena voice had slightly escalated. I opened the mixed fruit jelly and began to spread it on my toast. I'd figured she couldn't take it from me if I used it. Well she took that as me trying to be funny. "Your fat funky ass don't need no damn jelly!" She yelled. I didn't respond. I continued to make my sandwich as if she didn't say a word. That made the situation worst. "That's why your mother molested ya'll." D'keena yelled hoping that would get a rise out of me. It worked. I looked up. How did she know?! I hadn't told anyone. I was at a loss for words I didn't know what to say. I just blurted out the first thing that came to my mind. "She didn't mean it!" Was my only response. "Oh, so your sister's face just fell into your mother's pussy!" D'keena smile indicated that she knew she had just won the argument. She felt vindicated. I jumped up from the table and ran as fast I could over to her table. I wasn't even aware I was moving. As I got closer I could see the fear in her eyes. She quickly picked up a butter knife from the table. As I was passing the final table before I reached her I grabbed one of the heavy plastic plates they served our meals on. She swung the knife toward my chest. I didn't know if I was cut nor did I care. I smashed the plate on her head as hard as I could. The plate broke in two in my hands. I dropped it to the ground. I pulled her by her nasty blonde colored hair while punching her in the face. I had the upper hand being that she was still sitting down when I ignited my attack. I got her on the floor. I knelt on top of her pounding my heart out. How could she talk about my family like this? I was pulled out of my trance by the staff. There were police officers coming in the door. I knew it was a strong possibility that I would be going to a detention center tonight. The staff shocked me when they told D'keena that they had warned her and she was out of the house. I felt bad for her when they pulled out the handcuffs and placed them on her. She had nowhere to go. The other girls had a look of hatred along with dismay for me in their eyes. I didn't know who was going to come after me first but I knew someone would. The staff told us to get our things to go to the bus stop. With all the commotion I had forgotten it was a school day. The staff handed out city bus tokens. I was too afraid to walk to the bus stop I knew the other girls were plotting it was logical not to go to school that day. So I didn't. I'd spent the whole day in my room scared of what was to be that evening. I walked around the next few days on eggshells. It hadn't occurred to me that no one made any smart comments or any mean remarks to me. I walked into the living room everybody was sitting there watching television. Someone actually offered me a seat. I was reluctant to sit down but I didn't want to seem rude. As soon as the video went on commercial the same girl began asking me questions, like where did I learn how to fight like that? They gathered around me praising me for beating up D'keena. Some exclaimed their shock while others stated they knew I was going to whip her ass. I couldn't believe what was going on. I had won a fight and now I was popular. My life in the group home changed drastically. I had friends and lots of them. I walked around school being downright disrespectful then I would sneak off to see my sisters whenever I wanted to; life was great! I had no rules, no parents, plus I was only twelve years old calling my own shots. I was in complete control over my life. I was pretty book smart, witty and out of control. My world was now becoming ideal. I decided to add something new to my mischievous behavior. The other girls were planning to run-away from the group home to meet some boys at the Putt-Putt golf course. I wanted in. It seemed scary but I wanted to tag along. I wanted to have a good time. The girls had composed a plan to meet at the front door at six o'clock. I was more excited than nervous not only were we going to run-away, we were going to meet some boys. I ran to my room to get dress we had to be sneaky yet quick if we were going to be dress before the staff knew what we were up to. I changed my clothes numerous of times. I'd known for some time that I had no sense of fashion. Not like them. They knew all of the latest styles. I kept running into their rooms so they could judge my outfits until they had made a decision on what I should wear. I mean they understood my clothes were limited with the bleach incident. I was too afraid to go to the door alone. I waited for all the girls to finish getting dress. I trotted behind them to the front door. I didn't know if it was going to be a scene or not but I was willing to help them if they had to fight the staff. As we got closer to the door my heart began thumping damn near out of my chest. The ring leader just merely opened the front door. I shot a look of fear towards the staff member that was sitting at the front desk. The staff member put a devilish grin on her face and requested for another staff member to call the cops. The cops I thought. Oh, Lord we were going to jail. All of us took off running in the middle of the street until we got to the furthest bus stop. I stopped with my heart pumping inside of my throat. I stood their gasping for air. Then they told me we had to walk or catch a ride to Putt-Putt. I didn't know what catch a ride meant but I knew I was not walking all the way to Norfolk. We were all the way in Portsmouth for Pete's sake. That had to be a two hour walk. We walked along the side of the road. The cool night air giving us the much deserved refreshing sting of coolness across our tired bodies. As we walked we told jokes, laughed while stopping to play a couple of games of slap boxing. When a car would zoom by we all yelled. "HEY!" Our hopes of them stopping were futile. We alerted them of our dismay by yelling profanity to the cars that wouldn't stop. Some of the girls started to get pretty annoyed with the snails paste that I had adapted and intended on keeping. One of the girls began sticking up for me and the arguments were growing the more exhausted we became. I began to pray for a ride. I was starting to become frighten. I didn't want them to leave me in the middle of nowhere. Oh' God how would I get home. Please lord I thought. Please! Send us a ride. We yelled at a car that was going by to our surprise this car actually stop. We took off running up to the car. We began piling in the car. We knew we were on our way. I thanked God for sending us a ride. I was praying for a ride because I could tell that even though we had a rule no one left anyone they were well on their way to leaving me. Plus I knew God was the only one who could help me. As the thanks went out to the man who was gracious enough to give us a ride everyone rushed to the doors of Putt-Putt. Finally I could play games. I found an arcade game that I was kinda good at. Whenever I would run out of coins I would walk around begging mothers who seemed nice. I would tell them I was from the group home and my counselor wouldn't give me anymore tokens it worked every time. My sob story was worth at least a couple of free games I thought. I stayed playing games until the girls found me. They had these stupid grins on their faces. I noticed why when I'd seen the boys that they were obviously going there to meet. They were not like any boys that I had ever seen. They had on tight jeans that showed off their thing. Nice sweaters complimented with a gold chain. "We about to hit up the hotel." A girl said. I was scared again. I knew I shouldn't have came with them. I didn't want to go to a hotel but I didn't want people to know how scared I really was. I managed to release a closed mouth half of smile. I walked out slowly asking God to protect me. I knew it was wrong but I had no idea how to get out of this mess that I had created for myself. All the girls were smiling from ear to ear. I stood in front of Putt-Putt waiting for the boys to pull their cars in front. I secretly was hoping they wouldn't come. As the cars pulled up, I thought about their ages. They were too young to have cars like this. The three boys got out of the driver seat of their cars and walked into the front of the selected hotel. All of the girls followed. I was too afraid to speak up but I didn't want to go with them. The boys had gotten us adjourning rooms. The girls didn't want it any other way. The boys ordered pizza my absolute favorite. I sat there while everybody else ate. I didn't want them to stare at the fat girl while she was eating. One of the boys noticed and ensured me that I could eat if I wanted to. I shook my head no. I added a smile to indicate that I was fine. As they sat there eating pizza, one of the boys began to yell. "Yo, roll up!" The excitement in his voice made me think we were about to do something super fun. One of the three boys pulled out a plastic zip lock bagged filled with what seemed to be dirt and grass; perhaps it was a special herb that they put on their pizza. I dismissed whatever they were about to do. I really wanted a piece of pizza. I finally convinced myself to go to the bathroom and take a quick bird bath before my corn chip effloresce entered the room. I grabbed a wash cloth washed up then threw the washcloth away. I didn't want anybody to know what I was doing. I flushed the toilet and left the bathroom. I opened the bathroom door only to find smoke rushing into the bathroom. The whole atmosphere in the room had changed. Everyone was smiling, laughing and telling jokes. At first glance I thought the boys were smoking cigarettes when I saw the white from the paper go up to their mouths. As one of the boys passed the paper looking substance to one of my friends my eyes bucked with disbelief. It looked like a rolled up cigarette. I began to speak. "What is that?" I tried to hide the dismay in my voice. One of the girls from the group home replied. "Gurl we getting high!" Oh no, I thought as I watched her inhaled the now apparent drug. "What?!" I shouted without a second thought. "You mean to tell me that you guys are doing illegal narcotics!" I continued with my resentment and shock trailing my response. Everybody in the room had bust out into laughter. I truly didn't find anything funny. Another girl from the group started to speak. "Listen you acting like we doing some real drugs, gurl we only smoking weed so sit your little young ass down." I was embarrassed. 'I didn't know there was an okay drug.' I thought. The look of humiliation and remorse was written over my face. The girl from the group home that had always been nice to me spoke up for me. "Look, don't talk to her like that if she don't smoke then that's a good thing maybe she won't end up like us." She turned to me as she continued to speak. "You don't have to smoke if you don't want to. Hell, I wish I had never started." I gave her a smile of gratitude. I walked over to the seat. The seat was located in between the door and a window. I didn't know if the cops were going to bust in but I wanted to at least see them when they pulled up. My friend from the group home made a declaration that I would be staying in her room. I was grateful again. I didn't trust the other girls that much especially since the drugs changed their attitude towards me. After her announcement I motion for my friend to meet me in the bathroom. Her face looked as if she was getting tired of me but she accompanied me into the bathroom anyway. As soon as the door shut I stated my case. "I do not want to sleep with any of them boys!" I said in a stern whisper. Her face was painted with the look of shock then the side of her mouth curled up as if she was beginning to smile or even perhaps laugh. "I don't think they want to sleep with you either." She whispered through her snickering. She turned around and opened the door then walked out. I stood there humiliated. I didn't want to sleep with them but why would she think they didn't want to sleep with me because I was fat. She had some nerve I thought. I was scared to go back into the room. She probably told everybody and now they were all going to make fun of me. To my surprise everybody was talking about something else. I was relieved. I walked back over to my seat by the door. I had to keep peeping out the window for the cops. I sat there not really saying much watching the guys roll-up more and more of the paper-drug, I began to nod. I tried to stay awake but I was just so tired from the walk to Putt-Putt. I looked out the window and seen that the sky was getting lighter. "It's about to be morning!" I shouted in disbelief. I had stayed up all night I was excited. The whole room engaged in another heartfelt laugh; at my expense. Then one of the boys who really didn't speak that much the whole night said something. "Yo man, why y'all got this little girl out here like this, word up." He stated in a matter-of-fact tone. I was livid who was he calling a little girl. I probably lived more of this life then he could have ever imagined seeing. The girls did not respond to his question. I just rolled my eyes at him. He stood up and spoke again. "Well Imma bout to call it a night, what room we are in." No he did not just include me in his room. Oh' Lord I began to pray. I then realized he liked my friend and was simply saying that we were in the same room because of her earlier comment. Everybody paired up and filed out of the room accordingly. I got into one of the beds. I laid there staring at the two of them while they were kissing. I had pulled the cover up to my eyes so that I could peak out. I wanted to see what else they were going to do. My plans were detoured when the boy finally said something. "Turn around little girl." He demanded. 'How did he know I was looking?' I thought as I turned around and did what I was told. I tried to stay awake but when I had woken up the boys was coming back into the room with a MacDonald's bag. He sat on his bed and handed my friend a breakfast sandwich. He turned his attention to me. "Would you like one?" He asked. "No thank you." I replied. "Come on you got to be starving. I'm not like that. It's okay if you eat." I took the sandwich and scuffed it down in two bites. I didn't mean to but I was hungry. I looked up embarrassed as usual. He just smile and handed me another sandwich. What a nice guy I thought. Everybody said their goodbyes, and then it was the adventure of getting home. I had not known that all boys had given the girls a few dollars so we hopped on the bus and went home. I guess they felt sorry for us, you know the group home and all. As we walked up to the group home my heart was skipping a beat as usual. I didn't know the outcome of our action but the girls was laughing and reminiscing all the way there as if nothing had just happened. They stood there still laughing and telling jokes as they rang the doorbell. One of the staff members opened the door and just let us walk right in. "Go take yourselves a shower, and you know the rules no television or any outings for a month." He said. I looked at him; he just shook his head as if he was disappointed in us. I walked into my room and sat on the lower bunk. I didn't want him to think I had done anything with the boys but I guess it was nothing I could do about that. After my shower I laid across my bed with relief. That was all that was going to happen; we couldn't go skating. The no television part kinda bothered me but not really. I had an epiphany in that moment I was alone and I did not have any rules. I always knew in the back of my mind but it was now starting to sink in as a new found reality. The next time I went to school they might as well been playing bad to the bone in the background. I was horrible. I was cutting all of my classes, except for the one teacher that I liked. I even went as far as to set a classroom garbage can on fire in front of the teacher. I mean what was the worst that would happen? I would get kicked of school, but they had to let me back in I was a ward of the state and everything I did was classified as acting out because of my situation. The girls and I had come up with another outing. We were going to runaway on Saturday night. We left with the same rules as the last time. We leave together we come home together. The only difference was we had a white girl with us. She was new to the group home. She had jet black hair that was cut into the Salt-n-Pepa haircut. She was very pretty. I think the black hair with her ice cold blue eyes made her look exotic. We reached the door opened it and walked out. I was still scared even though I knew they really weren't going to do anything to us. We hitched hike again to Putt-Putt but when we got there and the boys didn't show, we were lost at what to do next. The only thing that was left was for us to return to the group home. We walked along the highway for hours nobody would stop for us. Every time we would see a cop car we'd duck around a corner. The night was long and unusually hot. The aggravation started. We were yelling at each other and some girls were even cursing. A car stopped with three older men in it. It looked like they were in their thirties. We all quickly dismiss them except the white girl. She was determined to get us a ride. We were scared because it was three of them. Where were we going to fit in the car? The driver kept talking to the white girl. We started pulling on her arms telling her let's go. The driver told her he just wanted to talk to her for a minute. She stood by the car and they began conversing. As we sat there on the curb talking for about five minutes waiting for her to finish her conversation she jumped in the car and the car pulled off. I was mad. Everybody began yelling at the car. We told her how we were going to beat her up if she ever came back to the group home. As we walked she was our new topic of conversation. Everybody kept saying what they were going to do to her. I was tired, mad, and now aggravated. A cop car was driving by we all ran in the opposite direction. I decided to ask what the cops would do if they caught us. Nobody really knew. The only thing they knew was that we wouldn't go to jail for running away. I had come to the conclusion in my mind that they had to bring us back to the group home. I mean that is what they usual did with runaways on television. I convinced everybody to let me call the police. I called and stated that I was a runaway from the group home and I needed a ride back. A cop car showed up. I walked over to the car and ask the police what they were going to do to me after they confirmed that they was going to take me back to the group home, I waved my hand as a signal for the other girls to come out so that they too could get a ride back. We walked in and went into our rooms. Once back in our rooms the girls all gathered in my room. They started asking me questions about what I was going to do to the girl if she ever came back. I honestly had forgotten all of that.

I kept it going because of the attention I was getting. The next day I heard a staff member say she's back. I kept walking from my room to the bathroom on the other side of the group home. I wanted to see if it was really her. As I slow trotted back to my room upon the staff request; the door opened. To my surprise she was actually D'keena. I wanted to faint. My life was going so good and now she was going to torturer me. Oh, my goodness this could not be happening. All of these girls were bound to turn on me. It was obvious after she left that they were just as scared of her as I was. I walked into my room. My heartbeat was audible. I was going to get beat up. They called for dinner; I promise I did not want to go. When I sat down D'keena looked in my direction as her mouth opened my heart felt like it stopped. "Yo, I just wanted to say I was wrong for that whole incident, word up." She stated. I smiled at her and gave her a no problem but inside I was thanking God. The other girls begin to fill her in on our little adventures and the things she had missed. Then they told her I was going to beat up the new girl if she ever came back. Me and my big mouth I thought. Now I had to do something. A few more days went by with no excitement I had really come to the conclusion the white girl was never coming back so I had nothing to worry about life was good. As soon as the thought enter my mind the staff wanted to hold a group meeting. In the meeting we were told how we had threatened the white girl and she was afraid to come back. We were also advised never to say anything to her. If we bothered her in the house or in school we would be put into the detention center. I was beyond mad at this point. She left us in the middle of nowhere and now she calling pretending as if we were the reason she was not coming home. Now deep inside I thought perhaps she was scared but if she was that scared then why did she call at all. She could've placed that call four days ago. No it was more to this then that; they probably didn't want her behind back and she came up with a lie. They must have a choice after a certain amount of days or something. I sat there fuming trying to rationalize her action for trying to get us in more trouble especially after leaving us. I heard the front door open. The staff quickly escorted her into the main office. I guess they wanted us distracted so they could sneak her in. She briskly walked into the staff office. Is this girl serious? This is the same girl that stared at us with those ice cold blue eyes as she told that man to pull off and leave us on the side of the road. She didn't have any remorse she just wanted sympathy and they were all sucking it up. I knew I was going to get her fasho' now. They kept her in the main office for the rest of the night. She ate dinner in the office. After dinner it was time for our chores and then bed. The staff gave me the chore of emptying the office trash. It was the easiest of all the chores, but they needed someone they thought they could trust. Even though I was hanging around the wrong crowd I was still respectable; for the most part. I started to walk into the office one of the staff members asked me where I was going? I simply replied that I was doing my chore. I put on my gloves as I was entering the room to detour their suspicions. I grabbed the trash. I knew the staff could see me through the glass window. I walked inside the room to get the trash that was by the desk. I picked up the trash can as normal. I dumped it into the big trash bag I was carrying. I'd place the trash can back on the floor. As I started out of the office I grabbed her by her shoulders and began to shake her. "Why did you leave us?" I asked repeatedly. I'd seen the staff running towards the room through the window I threw one punch that connected to her face. A staff member placed me in a bear hug. I couldn't move. I didn't want to. I walked calmly to the living room and sat on the couch. Another staff member picked up the phone to call the police. I didn't care I wanted to shake some sense into her. The other girls were standing around cheering and clapping. I had the biggest smirk on my face until the police arrived. I was a little scared but not really. I mean how much trouble could I be in I only really shook her. The punch that I threw barely touched the side of her cheek. I wanted to cry when they had shown me my sleeping arrangements for the night. It was a little room with a hard bed. I laid across the bed knowing that tomorrow I would go back to the group home. I'd awaken the next morning to get ready for court. I basically took a shower and put back on my same smelly clothes. On our way to the courthouse they placed handcuffs on us and shackles on our feet. We piled into the jailhouse van. I got to court and sat in this cold little room that was the size of a cubicle. It only had a bench in it. I was alone because of my age. I was finally called into the courtroom. I was told to sit next to my lawyer. I didn't know who that was, so they had to direct me to her, by pointing their finger. I saw her. Directly behind her was my mother. She sat there with tears in her eyes. I smiled and waved at her. I didn't know what she was crying for. I thought perhaps it was the shackles. I only smiled to show her I was okay. My mother motioned for me to sit down. Just then the courtroom door opened. It was this bitch. Her eyes were red as if she had been crying all night. 'What a dramatic entrance when I get out Imma whip her ass for real. I only shook her and she sitting over there looking as if she just went ten rounds with death. Here she go; with her sympathy act.' 'I thought.' The district attorney stood there talking about how I have been removed from foster home to foster home because of my attitude. How violent I have been in the past, the constant fighting I have been doing over the course of a year. How I was removed from numerous foster homes, was because of sexual promiscuity, violent, or other deviant behavior. He included the fire I had set in the classroom and my constant running away. I was an out of control little girl with issues with authority figures. Now in his words I was just attacking innocent people. I wanted to fall out of the chair. I didn't know I was even such a menace to society. He didn't know what happened in any of those cases. He didn't know how yea, I set the fire but it was harmless fun, plus the teacher was getting on my nerves. He could care less about how my foster parents were allowed to beat me, girls trying to impress somebody snaked me and boys who realized how naïve I was took advantage of me and I only ran away twice to Putt-Putt Golf. He didn't know any of that nor did he care. It was on paper so it must have been true. The judge sentenced me to a month in a juvenile detention center. I had to go to jail behind this bitch. I wanted blood. I stood up in the courtroom with the intention to attack but I felt defeated I followed the bailiff out of the courtroom. He made a comment. "I bet you wish you would've listened to the staff now, don't you?" He said in a mocking tone. "Shut the fuck up." I stated my voice was cold as ice. I went back inside of my little cell until it was time for me to be transported to the detention center. I walked into the detention center with an attitude. I was wronged, this was wrong, that was wrong, my life was just wrong. The staff was barking orders at me. The rules of what would not be tolerated. I was hungry with a headache I wanted something to eat. They had given us a cheese sandwich with a choice of mayonnaise or mustard, along with warm milk. I wanted real food. A nice hot meal and a cot to sleep on. They told us that we would have to go through a full body inspection to make sure that we did not have any weapons in our possession. I didn't think about anything as they escorted us one by one into the room for our inspection. Once I was in the room I was told to strip; bra and panties included. The horror, I didn't want anyone to see me naked and more importantly I hadn't had a real shower in about a day and a half I know I smelled horrible. So I stood there and refused to comply with their demands. I just simply said no. I mean what are they really going to do wrestle me down to the ground and tear off my clothes. I should have known something was up because when I said no everybody in the room started to smile. Someone even shouted this is your last chance. I stood very calmly and firm while I stated my no again. They pulled out a fire hose turned it on and sprayed me with ice cold water. I kept yelling "Okay! Okay!", but they were laughing too hard to hear me or they really didn't care I couldn't tell at that point I started peeling off my clothes as quickly as possible. They handed me a towel and some clothes to put on. I walked out shivering from the cold water and it was cold in the facility. I didn't complain though I didn't want them to do anything else to me. I was shown to my room. It was much like the other cell I had spent the night in. It was a single size bed with a toilet in the corner. There were no bars like I expected it was just a heavy metal door that had a magnetic lock. The door also had square window in it made out of plexiglass. I asked about dinner but they told me dinner was over and I could have a sandwich. I said okay and requested mustard this time. I figured I would change it up a little bit. I fell asleep hungry. The next day at five o'clock we were awaken for breakfast. We had one hour to shower and dress. I jumped into the shower I was not going to miss breakfast. They did a head count of everyone and walked us into the dining room. My plate was eggs, toast, and bacon. We also could add cereal and milk if we wanted. I had everything. At lunch time I was told we could go to the salad bar in addition to the food they served. I found out we could do that for lunch and dinner. I barely spoke to anyone. I loved our meals so I didn't complain much I would just wait for lunch and dinner so that I could get a salad. I would sit there and dream about which dressing I would use. I'd read a lot of books and played spades a lot. The month seemed to sail by. I went to court. I sat there and waited for them to send me wherever. My social worker along with my lawyer had decided that maybe I needed professional help. They suggested a residential treatment program. My social worker explained to me that I would only have to be there for seventy-two hours if the judge agreed too it and then I would be released. She couldn't help but to add that it was my choice but it would be better than going back to the detention center or the group home. I only had to agree to it. That after seventy two hours she would have found placement for me. I agreed. The judge informed me that I would be placed into a psychiatric facility in order to be evaluated. I would return to the group home for one week to collect my things and then my social worker would take me to a residential facility. I arrived back to the group home that evening. I didn't understand what was going on. I was more upset about the fact that I didn't see Kymela at court this time. I thought that maybe she couldn't make it because of her finances. I knew we were poor when she was receiving welfare for us; with us removed from the home she must not have had an income. I felt bad I knew she would have been there if she could. I walked around the group home with a new added chip on my shoulder. I had a couple of minor conversations but I spent most of my time in my room. I packed what little I had within the first day. I only left out clothes that needed to be washed. I did not speak; someone in this house was a snake who sent all of those lies into the courthouse. I couldn't figure out who it was but the bailiffs words echoed in my mind. "I bet you wish you would've listened to the staff now, don't you." Someone here sent that information in to make me look bad. They wanted to get back at me, I guess because I was the nice one who also listened so when I had defied them they wanted to show me. I never spoke again in that house. That was horrific lesson to teach someone just because you have the power to do so. I'd been to the group sessions. They knew the truth behind all of those things but they wanted to hurt me and they had succeeded. A couple of the girls figured out the "commonwealth of Virginia" plans for me, a day before I was scheduled to leave. They crowded around me at the dinner table telling me to runaway. I would have but I didn't have anywhere to go. I sat there defeated. The tears strolled down my face. I told the stories that was said in court. They shook their heads in disbelief. They begin to speculate who could have sent them that information. They all agreed that they thought I was coming back home that day. I told them how they escorted her in as if she was a battered women rushed her to her seat the whole scenario. The girls shook their heads again. "See at first I thought you was just over here playing the victim for sympathy but that right there just took the cake. They never bring anybody to court, they claim it's because we have school. Did they bring you to court for me?" D'keena asked I just shook my head no while she continued to talk. "Look little girl I'm sorry, I mess with you like that. This is wrong. You might like it there you are pretty nice. Just don't say too much. I wish I had somewhere for you to go." She finished. D'keena got up and walked into the living room and stood in front of the desk. "It probably was your fat ass that did that to that little girl. She don't say nothing to nobody and now y'all are going to lock her up in a crazy house. Why you never lock me the fuck up you fat bitch! Let me go to my room before you call the cops you stinking bitch. This place makes me so fucking mad. That's a LITTLE FUCKING GIRLL!" As D'keena words trailed off she disappeared into the back. I went in my room and tried to process all that was just taught to me. The judge would have let me go whether I went to the residential treatment facility or not. That's why they came back there to get me to agree. My mind was overwhelmed with what ifs. I turned over and prayed until I fell asleep. The next morning I stayed in my room until they knocked on the door to tell me my social worker had arrived to pick me up.

CHAPTER 9

Crazy, Who Me, It Couldn't Be; Could It

I sat in my social worker's car thinking about how my life would be now. I wanted to ask her some questions about my placement, but I didn't know if I should say anything. I was relieved when we finally arrived to the psychiatric facility. I opened the car door jumped out and began grabbing my things from the back. A whole bunch of men came out and began to help me carry my things inside. I stood in the lobby trying to take in everything that I was viewing. The lobby was spacious, it had two big waiting areas both identical with love seats, couches, and coffee tables. I guess it was suppose to look like a living room. A white lady walked up to us and directed us into an office. There the "intake" was supposed to began. We did an itemize count of everything I owned. I was kinda relieved about this because nobody could steal my things and have the staff stand there and pretend that they did not know what I had when I arrived. I had just been through that and wasn't looking forward to going through that again. I was shown to my room. The room was painted in a soft pink color. The long curtains that covered the window had dark pink and purple flowers illuminating from it. The two twin beds had the same comforters as the curtain. The pale blue carpeting made the whole room seemed like it was mismatched, especially since the bed frames were wooden along with two matching wooden desk. It appeared to be a hotel room from what I had gathered equipped with a bathroom in the room and all. I absolutely loved the room. I walked through the facility being introduced to staff as well as patients. All of the "patients" however seemed to be around my age give or take a few years and none of them were drooling or talking to themselves like I thought they would be. The staff explained the disciplinary system and how write-ups work. They also told me they had a time out room. We walked over to the time out room. It was a room design much like the cell I had recently left except it had four leather handcuffs fixtures attached to all four points of the bed. The staff member began to explain that in cases of extreme out of control behavior those methods were used. I wanted to cry immediately. My social worker look of concern grew as well. The staff member quickly caught on to our dismay and assured us that all of the staff has to have extensive training in order to use this method. She even went as far as to tell us that in the training they themselves have to be restrained in order to qualify to use the system. Her theory was that a person would not be so quick to restrain someone if they knew what it felt like. I felt kind of relieved but I still thought it was barbaric. I could tell that my social worker fears were subsiding the more the women spoke. My mind wandered off into the great unknown as usual. I knew I would never be able to sneak away to see my sisters now. I had observed that every door that we entered had to be swiped by some type of badge except for my room. I was caged in like an animal, just in a different format. I laid across my bed batting back the tears that was sure to follow as my social did her usual call me if you need anything speech. I wanted to jump up and knock the taste out of her mouth. I turned my back to her. I mean lady it's obvious that your just looking for a place to put me at this point, it doesn't matter where it is or how it will affect me. I never hated anyone before but now I was starting to become all too familiar with what the definition of hate meant. I walked around in a zombie like state for two weeks. I wouldn't pay attention in group nor would I respond. All I would do was go to the cafeteria and pick out any and everything to eat. I would spend my allowed amount of time watching television, but then it was off to my room to read a book. I had nothing in common with these crazy people and there was no reason to pretend like it now. Then I was told I would have my first meeting with my psychiatrist. I was happy, she could let me out. I told her everything was fine. I explained the reason why I did not speak to anyone and how this was a big misunderstanding and how the social worker is just looking for placement for me and that's the real reason I was here. She told me that I was depressed and did not know the true extent of what my mother had done to me and how fortunate I was to be in a position to get help. My mind began to revert back into itself. 'This stupid bitch thinks she knows what she is talking about. Maybe I do need help that I'm not aware of but I could get that same help as an outpatient. I do not need to be caged in like a fucking animal. She really believe that she is trying to save me but she is assisting this lady in ruining my life and if she wasn't so damn self righteous she would realize I could get the same help from someone else in an out treatment program.' I thought. "Well our time is up. I will prescribe you some Prozac for your depression and we will meet every week to see if we can get to the bottom of this." She extended her hand with a smile at the end of the sentence. I shook her hand and returned her fake smile with another. I was starting to learn everyone who smile with you are not friendly and may mean you harm. I walked down the hall beyond upset. I went back inside of my room I had to get some sleep to formulate a plan. I laid there thinking of how my life was so far. I had been verbally, physically, sexually abused my whole childhood. I have been labeled a slut, taken advantage of, lied on, misused, misplaced, detained, and now I'm being classified as crazy! The tears soaked my pillow. Things just have to change, I prayed to God that day before I fell asleep. I thanked him for all that he had done for me and I knew somehow he would see me through even this.

When the three to eleven shift started they came in my room and woke me from my nap. The psychiatrist had given orders for me not to be allowed to stay in my room all day. I was told that I had to sit in the day room until dinner time, and that I would no longer be allowed to go to the cafeteria. I was to be placed on a strict diet, of fifteen hundred calories. Then I was handed three little pills. I asked to see the psychiatrist but they told me I'd have to wait until next week. The tears stream down my face as I realized what was happening. I was considered a kid and to make matters worse I was institutionalized. My hurt and anguish erupted from my lungs. "I wasn't hurting anybody. I stayed in my room and read my books. Now I have to take pills and be a doped up zombie for what? To fit into y'all quota!" I said. I heard someone say over the intercom "code blue phoenix girls, code blue phoenix girls!" I didn't understand what was going on. The other staff members were rushing the girls to get inside of their rooms. All of the security doors were being unlock with badges from all angles. More people were pouring into my room. I started backing up against my room wall. I was pissed off! I had planned on taking the medicine. I already felt like I had NO choice but to follow this fat bitches order but you calling people as if I'm out of control. I made up in my mind if it's a fight they want then a fight they will have. My room was cluttered with men one of the staff members spoke. "We are going to take a little walk to time out." She said calmly. "I thought you were supposed to ask someone to go to time out and then if they don't do it you call the code." I said purposely as I watch the men look at one another because they knew that the proper procedure was not followed. "Well you got so upset, and began yelling and crying I figured it would be best if we did it this way." She responded. "Oh, I see, you woke me up out of my sleep told me I could no longer sit in my room and read books, and now I have to take medication, and that this fat bitch of psychiatrist has put me on a diet and I wasn't supposed to be upset even though while I was crying and talking not yelling; however I did have tone I was walking behind you to get the medication. I didn't know I wasn't allowed to be human and display emotion when I'm upset." I continued. Now the men are letting their guards down just like I wanted them to. She was wrong and this was wrong; and I was so fed up with being wronged. I was going to get some kind of vindication today. The staff lady looked at the men and began to bark orders at them. "You take that arm and I'll take this one." She stated as if I didn't just speak. The man seemed hesitant to help her but she knew that if she walked over to me the men would have no choice but help her if I resisted. I waited until she was in arms reach the man began walking slowly up to me. I grabbed the lamp that was sitting on my desk and swung it widely and fast I only landed three hits until everyone in the room was on top of me like a football player with the ball. By the time they had stood me up they were walking her outside of the room holding her face. 'I bet you, she thinks the next time before she tries to play me, word up.' I thought. I got up and walked slowly down the hall toward the time out room. As we were getting close to her I pretended like I didn't see her in the corner. I began talking politely to the men as if I had just done nothing wrong. When the men began laughing at my jokes I knew I had them again. As soon as I was in leg reach of her I kicked her right in the back of her knees she fell forward like a ton of bricks. The men were mad for being played like that so they made their grips extra tight. I was screaming and winching in pain. They threw me on the bed in the time out room. One of the men put his knee on my back while the rest of them grab a leg or an arm a piece. One person held the limb while the other person put on the restraints. I tried to break free from the restraints; I kept yelling and screaming I am not a fucking animal until one of the nurses along with one of the men came in with a needle in her hands. The man put his knee on my back again and the nurse pulled down my pants and gave me a shot of thorazine in my butt. I begged for them to let me pull down my own pants. I didn't want this strange man to see my butt. I screamed I cursed them out until I finally fell asleep. I woke up hours later and ask them could I get out of restraints they told me that I had to explain why this all had happen and what had I'd done wrong. I wanted to tell them I was human and I expressed emotion and because the staff member was afraid of my size or whatever she read in my file she didn't follow proper procedure and if she would have asked me to go to time out I would've walked. I probably would've cried all the way there and tried to talk myself out of it, and on top of all that I'm tired of being taken advantage so I set out to whip her ass. All I said wasseen more than this bitch could "Because I didn't listen, and hit someone who didn't deserve it and I'm sorry." They let me go back to my room without any more trouble. I spent the rest of the week getting in trouble sometimes on purpose other times by accident. I wanted to see this fat bitch who felt the need to upset my life after talking to me for one hour. The scheduled day of therapy had finally arrived for me to see my psychiatrist. I walked into her office as she extended her hands to shake mine I just merely plopped down in the chair. She turned back around and reopened the door. "I think we will leave it open today." She said with that same fake smile but this time it had a little fear entangled in it. I gave her a half of smile from the side of my mouth. I wanted her to know I am only twelve years old but you will not play me for a child. I've seen more than this bitch could imagine in this last year alone. "Well would you like to talk about the incident that took place this week?" She asked. "No, not really." I responded. "Well what would you like to talk about?" She continued. "I would like to know how you are going to put me on a diet and your fat yourself." I asked. "Well after our first meeting I thought that you were unhealthy and perhaps could benefit from a diet." She answered. "Well I think that is something that we should have discussed first, and by the way I think you are bigger than me so you are far more unhealthier than me, so you too could benefit from a diet fatty." I said sarcastically. "Well I will not be called names." She said calmly with her smile fading. "But isn't that what you called me, by waiting until I left the office and writing orders for me to be place on a diet. Then having people wake me up out of my sleep and tell me I am no longer allowed to stay in my room. I figured you did that because you wanted me to be more active as well. I mean I see people in their room all the time with no problem, but because they are skinny that is okay. Now people are calling codes on me because I don't know what they are talking about and I'm trying to express myself." I responded with tears streaming down my face. She handed me a tissue and begin to speak. "I'm sorry I thought that you would not agree to a diet and that is something that can help." She stated calmly. "As my psychiatrist you should have asked me first and then if I disagreed tell me this is what is happening, at least I know what is going on in 'my own' life." I finished the psychiatrist made and attempt to smooth things over but by the end of the session she had realize I was not going to be an easy case. Every week I went into her office it was like the war of the roses. We would go back and forth with the bickering. Every time she stooped to my level, I felt like I was winning. She would spend the entire hour telling me how I should be mad at my mother. I would spend the hour telling her that I loved my mother. I didn't understand why someone would want to make a child hate their mother. She even decided to call my mother in to humiliate her I felt. She asked my mother to explain how the things she had done was wrong, and the only way that I could move on would be to acknowledge them. I wouldn't do it I sat there the whole session being defiant to her and my mother. I felt that my mother had done the best she could and nobody would ever convince me of anything different.

I spent over six months playing games with the psychiatrist. I needed to get away from the hell of being institutionalized. I had made some friends. Group was the best. I got to hear the problems of other children like me. I would never share though. I didn't want a repeat of the group home. I would tell jokes to the staff that I figured out who I could manipulate and give hell to the ones that I couldn't. I figured out that if you were on level three of your program you could walk the hall freely. I spent the next month pretending as if I was participating in group and personal therapy. I observed who left the unit. I also observed who was careless with their security badges. After I got up the courage I knew it was time to set my plan in motion. The staff was no longer watching me closely. I was no longer in time out every other day or being restrained once of a week. I had made the choice to make my move. I waited until it was time for shift change. When the last staff member came in I placed a piece of paper in the door to stop it from locking. It was the door at the end of the unit. It was mostly used for the staff comings and goings. When the staff took the rest of the children to the cafeteria from the main door; I made my move. There was only one staff member left on the floor with me. I told her I was going into the dayroom to watch television. I opened the door and began strolling the hall. I had to fight the urge to run down the hall. My heart was beating irately as I told myself to keep a slow pace. I got close to the second door panic began to set in. How was I going to get the door open? The door opened. One of the male staff members was standing on the other side of the door. "Oh, I see you finally made it to level three." He said. "Yes, finally." I responded as I walked briskly through the door. I had to tell myself to slow down. I slow trotted toward the lobby. I went to the office to withdraw the money out my account. The lady was very nice. She was impressed that I had gotten to level three as well. I signed the receipt and headed toward the front door just then I heard the code being called for phoenix girls. I ran to the door and started down the street. I had no idea where the bus stop was plus I didn't have any change. There was a busy street I had to cross as well. I'd seen the staff come flooding out of the front door. The chase was on. I ran as fast as I could. There was a graveyard coming up it was now or never. I had to cross the street. I placed one foot off the curb then I felt the strength of the person behind me as they grabbed my shoulder. The man had both of my arms in a tight grip. I jumped up and used his body to balance me. I was trying to flip over his head but I end up kicking him in the face. I heard the rest of the staff yell Ooooo as the blood squirted from his nose. I felt so bad I didn't mean to hurt him, although I pretended like that was my intent all along. The man tried to drop me but the other staff had my legs and two of them grab my arms, so I didn't hit the ground. As the staff tried to carry me back the facility I kicked, bucked and screamed. I'd seen the cars slowing down. I wanted to yell rape or something to make people help me but then I thought that the staff would have to tell them that I am an escapee from a mental institution. I had no choice but to go back. I cried and I pleaded for them to let me go. They restrained me and gave me a shot of thorazine. When I woke up I was still out of control. I was still yelling and screaming I told them I couldn't take being there anymore. I could hear the impressed tone of the staff as they told one another how far I had gotten and that I had the common sense enough to withdraw money. The staff finally let me out the room I hit the first person I saw on the way down the hall. I was placed back into restraints. My psychiatrist came into the room to try to calm me down. I turned my head as soon as she walked in. I did not respond to her at all. When she left the room I heard her tell them to give me some more medication. I knew that if I didn't calm down that they would have me walking around like a zombie. When they came to give me the medication I begged them to ask my therapist if I could be released and that I would behave. They came back and let me out of the room. I walked into my room. I threw myself across the bed. I felt as though all my efforts were useless, my life was useless. I was only living to endure pain. I came up with a new plan. The plan was not to live at all. I took pencil from our in-school class. I tried to think of a way to kill myself with the pencil. I couldn't stab my wrist that seemed too gruesome. So I decided to use the eraser to rub the skin away from my wrist hoping I would bleed to death. My roommate thought the idea wouldn't work at first until she started to see my flesh. She went and got the staff. They took me back to time out kicking and screaming. I got my shot of thorazine and fell asleep. This time when I woke up my psychiatrist was sitting there staring at me. "Why would you want to die?" she asked. 'Is this lady serious? I'm in a mental facility, separated from my family, and the only thing she keep telling me is that if I don't hate my mother then I'm not dealing with my problems.' I thought. "I don't know." I stated. She stood up and left the room. I laid there crying for hours. I was taken to my room and was put on suicide watch. There was someone sitting in my doorway for days. All I would do is cry. They gave me all of these pills to perk me up or make me feel better but there was no pill for defeat. This was my life, this was all I get. While I was sitting there contemplating what to do next I came to the conclusion that I would never hurt myself in the future I would hurt others.

I had finally come up with a plan to escape this institution. I was going to do exactly what they asked of me. I attended group and went along with anything they said. I participated in any and every plan they had for me. I even started to comply with my dietary arrangements. This was not going to be life. I had to do whatever it took to leave this place. I never wanted a time out to be on my file again. I knew I only had three months until my review. I did a complete 360. I even began to tell my psychiatrist that I hated my mother. I wanted her to understand that I was working the program and possibly could be released as an outpatient. As my evaluation date neared I began dropping hints about how good I was behaving. I wanted them to know that I was ready to go back into the real world. I began to realize that no one ever replied when I spoke about my evaluation. The inception of an eerie feeling was gnawing at me. In my therapy session I decided to ask about my evaluation. "So, do you think I am ready to go back into the real world?" I asked. "What do you think?" she asked. 'Just like her to answer a question with a question' I thought. "Well I think that there are a lot of things that I have sorted out. I'm sure there are some more things that could be worked on but nothing to be in here over?" I responded. I thought that would be the best answer for that question. It made her aware that there are some things that I needed to work on but I do not feel like I should remain in the hospital. I couldn't go wrong with that answer she would have to see that I had matured enough to be released. "Well, we will see." She responded with a smile. That was not the answer I was looking for. I knew she was about to escort me out of her office because she had just pushed her chair away from the desk as if she was about to stand up and walk me to the door. I'd figure I'd only have a few minutes to sneak the next question in. As I stood up from my chair I decided to go for it. "Did you get a chance to do my evaluation?" I'd asked. Her whole demeanor changed as if I had said something inappropriate. "I do not think that is something we should be discussing." She said. "I don't see why not. I just was asking if it was complete." I said innocently. "There are some things that are just for officials, if you would like to discuss this we can in our next session. But to answer your question yes, it is complete." She added. At this time we were at the door I had to see if I could get just a little more information. "I hope it is just as glamorous as I am!" I said with a giggle. "We will talk about it next time." She said as I was being scooted out the door. I walked down the long hallway to my room. That answer did not sit well with me. She had a smile on her face when she said it but it still was something that was chipping away at me. I'd decided to shake it off until my next therapy session. I continued to follow the program and smile. I actually was starting to enjoy being around everyone. I had made some friends that was always telling jokes and making my day. I had really forgotten about the whole thing with the evaluation; that is until I entered her office for my therapy session. When I walked in she was not there. My mind just jumped onto the evaluation. I had to see if it just was sitting on top of her desk. I walked quickly to her desk and to my surprise there it was underneath a couple of papers; just sitting there. I opened the review and begin to read: 'In this year Ms. Taylor has made minor progress. She displays a disregard for authority figures. She does not face reality nor has she dealt with her family issues. She spends most of her time in a fantasy state about life. I would strongly advise against her release at this time. I recommend that she stay in this facility for the next six months to a year. 'I could feel her staring at me in the doorway. When I looked up my eyes filled with tears. The look of fear on her face when we made eye contact told me this would not end well for me. She backed out the room and rushed down the hallway. I knew I was in trouble for reading my report. I just walked to the time out room. I sat on the bed in the room. With both of my hands over my face I had let the tears spill. I sobbed silently until I heard the code being called. I shook my head as I seen the staff run past the time out room heading to the nurses' station. Once they all got to the psychiatrist office I could hear the commotion about where I had gone. Then I heard the second code. I guess now I was considered on the run. I cried out to the Lord in my mind. 'Lord, I do not know why I have to stay here. You said you would help me but now I am stuck in this place with these people treating me like I'm crazy. I just don't understand.' "I found her!" a male voice said. I looked up to my buddy standing there. He had long forgiven me for using him to run and playing him when I kicked that lady. "What are you doing in here?" he asked, with a smile. "Well I read my report and it said that I should stay here for another year. I knew that I was in trouble when she walked away from the door so I thought that I'd save everybody sometime and just come in. I didn't know they was going to call a code or I just would have waited. They are always pretending I'm out of control but she didn't even ask me to walk to time out I just went. They do not follow the rules yet they are trying to teach me how to follow the rules. Then they wonder why I don't listen to them." I finished. My mind could not grasp the idea of being institutionalized for another year. I laid on the bed and turned my back to the door. I knew it would only be moments before my psychiatrist would be standing in the doorway; I had no desire to see her lying face! "Do you know why you have been put in time out?" She questioned. "Because I walked here, but you would want me to say because I read my report." I answered sarcastically. "Well I would appreciate it if you would turn around and look at me." Her tone was smooth and calm as usual. I had come to the realization it was not to soothe you it was to help you let your guard down so that she could go in with the attack. "I do not want to turn around right now and I hope I do not get into trouble for that. I just want to lay here and just think for a little while." I responded. "Well when you're ready to talk let me know." She finished. I laid in the time out room for hours. The staff would stop by periodically and ask if I was ready to come out each time I would tell them no. I knew that this was it. I went from having no rules and doing whatever I wanted, to being completely controlled. My life was not so bad I'd begun to think. I mean I did get food to eat and I had heat and hot water. My bed was comfortable I liked my room, plus Kymela was not hitting me upside my head every other minute. Yea, I have had worse days in life so I thought perhaps it was time to be thankful. I mean I did ask God to remove from Kymela and he did, plus I wanted to leave the foster homes and I did, then I asked him to remove from the group home and he did that as well. In each place I was miserable in some way but I was taken care of and I was in a better situation than the last place. How could I even imagine blaming God for anything when he had done so much for me already. I asked and he provided I just never followed through with my request. I'd just assume he knew where I wanted to be and then I'd become disappointed when it was not everything I'd hoped it would be. Yes God was good to me, and I am truly blessed. I was just being spoiled right now I thought. With that moment of clarity I asked to be let out of the time out room. I walked around the facility with a new found joy. I followed the program without trying to scheme or find an escape. It was pointless anyway and plus it must've been something I had to experience.

I'd awaken with my everyday joy and laughter. I got dressed went to the eatery for breakfast. Soon after breakfast I went to our in-house school system. I was playing around in class as usual. I was turned around in my chair telling a joke to the girl behind me. The teacher had just motion with the swirl of her finger for me to turn around. Just as I was sitting properly in my chair, I'd seen a staff member at the door. This time my teacher motion with her finger for me to come to her. I got up, I was so nervous. "They need you." She said looking at the doorway. I looked over to the staff member standing there. I was preparing to try and talk myself out of timeout. I was really having fun and wanted to go back to class. I was surprised when we walked past the time out room. I was quiet until we got to the eatery. I became happy inside, perhaps it was Kymela. This was the room that we would have our visits in. My smile began to radiate the room; as I rounded the corner through the threshold into the next room. I was puzzled by the image of a slender women that I did not know. She seemed well dress but she was no one I had ever seen before. In trying to figure out who she was I paused at the door without realizing. "Come in, and have a seat." She stated with a smile. I waltzed to the nearest chair. "Hello, my name is Brena Bronner. I will be your new social worker. Can you tell me a little bit about yourself?" she said still smiling. 'Oh another social worker I thought.' "Well there is not much to tell except I am funny and lovable!" I said in a jovial manner. "Oh, well I can see that can you tell me a little bit more about yourself." She continued her smile seemed genuine this time. "Well I don't know exactly what you want me to say." I asked still smiling abundantly. "Just tell me how you feel?" she commented. "Feel about what?" I asked, still in my playful voice. "How do you feel about here, being in here?" she continued. "Oh, girl you don't have that kind of time!" I said laughing. "Sike naw, it's alright in here. They keep telling me there are issues that I am not handling. I don't see them. It's like my therapist wants me to say I hate my mother but I don't hate her. She is my mother I know what she did to us was wrong but she gave me life. It's like that is the wrong answer. So I just try not to say anything about her so now my therapist thinks I'm in denial. I just try to avoid the topic because I'm not going to say I hate my mother." I explained in a nonchalant manner. "Oh, I see. Do you feel like this place is helping you?" she asked. "I can't think of a thing this place has helped me with. They said there helping me by placing me on a diet for a whole year, but I haven't lost an ounce of weight!" I told her followed by laughter. "Have you been following the diet?" she asked still smirking from my last joke. "I break that diet every chance I get!" I was so thrilled with myself at that point I couldn't stop snickering if I wanted to. "Then how do you expect the diet to work if you always cheating?" she asked. "Well I'm cheating but its only but so much I can get my hands on maybe an extra milk or if someone is on punishment and they have to eat in here with me then I'll ask for anything they don't want, which don't happen that often, so I should have lost something by now." I continued. "So why do you think you haven't lost weight?" she inquired. "Oh because I was meant to be big I guess or else I am eating the same amount of calories I'd been eating." I answered. "So if this place is not working for you where do you think you should go?"

was her response. "Well I was thinking about becoming an emancipated minor." I answered seriously. "Do you believe that you could take care of yourself on that level?" she kept going. "Well I know I'd have to get a job. It'll probably be at McDonald's or something like that just to pay my rent. I know I would have to live in the projects because that would be the only place I could afford. I'd have to do that until I graduate from high school then I'd go to college. I would live on campus that way I could mature a little bit more. The rest I haven't figured out yet. I just know I wouldn't really talk to anyone because I wouldn't want them to know that I live alone because sometimes people like to take advantage of children or girls and I just happened to be both." I answered not really thinking, I just said everything that I had thought of over the course of the year I was institutionalized. "Well it was a pleasure to meet you Miss Andrea, I'll be in touch." She stated extending her hand for me to shake it. "I told you I was funny and lovable!" I said jokingly while shaking her hand. I walked down the hallway towards the in house school. To my surprise school had been let out. I hadn't notice how much time I'd spent talking with my new social worker. I went along with my day without a second thought of my "meeting". I'd had enough of self loathing I was going to just enjoy myself while I was here. I continued on my everyday routine of school, group, and personal therapy sessions. However this was not a routine therapy session. I could tell that my therapist was uneasy about something. I didn't really get myself all excited; I assumed that she would tell me what I had done wrong. "So I have some good news for you." Her voice sounded unenthused. "Wow, what is it?" I asked trying to avoid her obvious dismay. "It seems that you will be leaving us soon." Her face forcing a smile. I could feel my eyes light up and widen. This had to be a joke of some kind. I could only manage to get one word out. "Huh." I said. "Yes, it seems that your grandmother wants you to come to Brooklyn to live with her." She said plainly, with a smile. "Oh wow, which one?" I asked with my excitement written on my face. "it's your mother's mother. How do you feel about that?" she continued. "Well I had thought that perhaps I would become an emancipated minor but I guess my grandmother would be the best way for me to go. My sisters are already there. I guess I'm happy. I mean it's a lot to take in all at once." I answered.

123

"Well if it becomes too much you can always come back, but you will be leaving tomorrow so you have to get your things together." She said in a dismissive tone. I couldn't have been happier about the news. I felt as if I was gliding down the hallway to my room. I told everyone of the exciting news on the way to my room. Once inside my room packing was alluring. I had to get everything together all at once in my head. I began doing laundry on my dirty belongings. I walked back and forth singing in my head. I was on an emotional high. I only had the knitted laundry bags to put my clothes in. I didn't care. I was leaving! I stuffed all I could into the bags, the rest I tried to see who in the facility wanted it. Was I sleeping, it seemed like a dream. I was so excited that I couldn't sleep. It didn't matter I was going to sleep on the Greyhound bus. I aroused early with my things packed and placed my bedding in the wash. I wiped down my bed I didn't want them to talk about me after I'd left. My social worker was there promptly in the morning. I had barely had breakfast when I'd seen her coming through the door. She waved at me and then I was escorted into my therapist office. I couldn't wait to leave. My heart was racing with excitement until one of my friends came around the corner. My feelings were replaced with sudden grief. I wasn't going to see the friends that I had lived with for a year anymore. Heck I was never going to see them again. I cried and extended hugs. It seemed like the more people I hugged the more that were coming out of their room surrounding me. The staff began to join in on the hugging. My social worker came out of my therapist office looking kinda upset. She walked to me and forced a smile. I was taken to the bus station. I hugged her and waved goodbye. I was on my way, nervous and scared but on my way.

CHAPTER 10

Where Brooklyn At?

The bus ride to New York City was uneventful. I only got off at one rest stop to get some food. I ran inside scared that I was going to be left. I ran back to the bus with my food. I sat down and let out a sigh of relief. I didn't speak to anyone while on the bus I wouldn't smile in anyone's direction either. I heard the bus driver announce Newark, New Jersey. I was confused was this my stop. I knew I was supposed to be going to New York City but perhaps that was the proper name or maybe I was saying the name wrong. I sat there agonizing on whether or not I should get off. I decided to stay on bus. I was so relieved when the lights were turned on and the bus driver announced over the intercom "Welcome to New York City!" Oh boy I'm in the "big city"! We were going over a bridge. The lights were illuminating. Everything was so bright and busy. The night sky, and the tall buildings. There were lights that were on sporadically throughout businesses and apartments. The lights appeared to be dancing off the dark blue water. It was as if the city itself was inviting you and welcoming you to stay for a while. The image made you think you were going to have the best adventures here. I couldn't have imagined that this place would be so beautiful. I was entrapped within the beauty. The bus pulled into this place called the Port Authority and stopped. Wow, they even had an underground bus station. I grabbed my things from the over head. I took another glance and checked the seat to make sure I didn't leave anything. My social worker said someone will be there to pick me up. My nerves were starting to get the best of me as I walked down the aisle. I got to the doorway I'd saw Ramon's thick framed glasses. I was more excited than ever. I had no idea he was going to be there. I poetically jumped off the bus into his arms. "Hey, hey, hey, baby girl!" Ramon said through giggles and smiles. He quickly found my suitcase with the description I'd gave him. He walked thru the Port Authority so fast I had to do a two step trot just to keep up with him. I'd began to think that I might be better off skipping, I mean I did that faster anyway. We got to the cab. Ramon got in the front seat to drive. "Daddy I didn't know you drove a cab." I said impressed. "Well, I own this cab." He replied. I sat in the car listening to him trying to explain to me how much a mandolin cost. I kept pretending like I knew what I was talking about but that seem to agitate Ramon just a little bit, so I spent the rest of the ride listening to a lecture on how I should not speak about things that I didn't know about. We pulled up to my grandmother's building. I remembered it from previous visits. Ramon grabbed my things out of the trunk and walked me into the building. He stood there pressing the button repeatedly. When the elevator door opened he motion with his hand for me to go in before him. I walked in the elevator and stood there silently in what I believed to be urine. Ugh! I held my breath to escape the stench. The aroma instantly changed on my grandmothers' floor. It smelled like fried chicken. I walked down the hall towards her door. My father hit the door knocker really loud and rapidly. Karin opened the door with a big smile. I couldn't believe it was her. It had been years since I'd seen her. I gave her a hug and a kiss. Ramon rushed passed my grandmother dropped my luggage off inside the house. He'd spoken to my grandmother quickly. He said hello to my sisters, told me he had to go back to work. He walked back out the door within a matter of seconds. I turned back around to see India face she looked as if she was disgusted by me. I had forgotten all of the weight I had put on while being in the institution. I could feel her reluctance in even hugging me. My grandmother just began to talk and order me to sit down so she could make me a plate. I was just happy that someone was happy to see me. I was shown my room which I had to share with India. I quickly learnt that Karin and India had their own life in this city. I would wake up every day with nothing to do. I knew school was almost out. They had to wait for my records to be transferred. My grandmother was concerned about my weight. She hand feed me my anti-depressant pills every day. I would spend the majority of my time in my room watching television or talking to my grandmother while she cooked. I guess I must've started getting on her nerves because she began yelling at me anytime I would go into the kitchen while she was cooking. I also noticed that Karin and India had no curfew. They would come into the house all times of night. I'd find myself staying up all hours of the night trying to make sure they got in safely. They had their own keys but I'd still be worried anyway. Plus sometimes my grandmother would get an attitude about their all night ventures and put the chain on the door to make sure that they didn't get in. I didn't like this fact at all. I'd had to put a stop to this ridiculous behavior of theirs. Being out all times of night worrying my grandmother and myself. At first I tried to reason with them by talking politely to them. Then I'd tried fighting them to get them to come in at a decent hour but that would just go for rounds and they would still stay out until the wee hours of the night. Finally my grandmother had a talk with me. She told me that I was not the mother of anyone in that house and she could handle my siblings with no interference from me. I understood, I'd probably was doing more harm than good. I was just surprise that she knew why I was fighting with them so frequently. After I got my talk and put in my place I felt there were a lot of things that they did around the house that my grandmother was unaware of. So I continued to tell them what they couldn't or shouldn't do, and if they said anything I would beat them up. I'd been afraid that my grandmother was too old to handle us and we were going to be separated again. I couldn't have that happen to us. Not again, I mean we had already been through soo much. If she got fed up with us she could send us back. Or even worse we could be placed into foster care in New York City. I knew that there would be no way to find them in a city so big, These two did not understand what was at stake here. I didn't see how they couldn't see what was at stake. We had already been through a storm. Why would they knock our only blessing so far.

I had spent my entire day lounging around the house. We all had made breakfast that morning at separate times so the sink was full of dishes. The living room was disheveled a little bit as well from sitting in there watching television. I knew it was almost time for my grandmother to get home from work. I'd begun straighten up the living room. I fluffed the pillows, wiped down the coffee table and swept the floor. I moved to the kitchen to wash all the dishes. I'd empty the ice tray in the old Country Crock butter tub. I'd filled them back up so by the time dinner was done it would be ice; grandma would go crazy over that. I was just about to sweep the floor when I heard loud rapid bang coming from the usually delicately tapped door knocker. I'd knew something was wrong. I ran to the door and yelled at the same time "Who?!" "KARIN!" The panic voice replied. I could hear other girls in the background, perhaps she was being jumped or something. I'd swung the door open to watch Karin speed past me to the bathroom leaving a trail of blood along the way. There were so many girls standing in the hallway. I walked away from the door without a thought to lock or close it. I had to find out where all the blood was coming from. Karin starting screaming "My fingers, my fingers!" My walk turn into a slow jog. As I was scurrying down the hall I started asking questions. "What happened to her?" "She tried to blow off Miss Lucy door with an M80." One of the girls replied. "What is a M80?" I asked scared and confused. "It's a quarter stick of dynamite." The same girl said. I turned around with my eyes bucked open from shock. That is when I noticed all the girls were in the house; and the one who was talking had the nerve to be smiling. I couldn't even ask the question I wanted to from the anger swelling up inside of me. What was funny about this situation? I'd reach the bathroom door to see Karin missing fingers. I ran out the bathroom to the kitchen and got the butter bucket of ice. I grabbed a dish towel and filled it as much as I could. I walked back to the bathroom with the ice filled towel and told Karin to keep it on her hand. I'd also instructed her to keep her hand elevated. My voice was escaping me but I couldn't understand how I was speaking. "Someone call 911!" I said as I grabbed the ice bucket off the table. I'd open the house door and enter the staircase door. I ran down the steps two at a time. I exited the staircase door and ran down to Miss Lucy door. I could see the blood dripping down the staircase door also on the hallway floor. I followed the trail of blood as if it was telling exactly what steps had been taken by my sister in this saga. As I followed the trail of blood I found her fingertips along the way. I would pick each fingertip up and place it into the ice bucket after I found the fourth finger I turned back around and hit the stairwell exit again this time it was leading me to my home. "Karin, let's go!" I yelled. I pressed for the elevator. Karin was screaming "My fingers, my fingers!" Once we were inside of the elevator the other girls stated they were going to take the steps. As soon as the elevator doors opened the paramedic was standing in front of us. I handed him the bucket of ice and finger tips. In the few minutes it took us to get to the ambulance my grandmother was getting out of a dollar cab. Everything was happening so fast but in slow motion. All these girls were standing there telling the story of how she had tried to put the dynamite out with her mouth just seconds before and how they were grateful she pulled it out of her mouth. I went upstairs after I smacked India for jumping in some strange man's arms screaming my sister. I didn't care what had happened it was no cause to try being fresh. After that whole incident I was upstairs and overwhelmed. I'd begun to clean up the house while doing that I'd prayed for my sister fingers; that they would be whole again. I wanted to go get in the bed it was just too much for me to handle at that time. I'd awaken to find my grandmother home and my sister in her room sleep. I'd awaken Karin and asked to look at her fingers. With Karin sleepy eyes she managed to pull her hand that was propped up on a pillow underneath the cover up and gently place it in my face. I'd thank God that they had sewn all of her fingertips back on. I rubbed Karin hair and told her how much I loved her and how grateful I was that she was alright. I'd offer to do something heck anything for her. She declined and turned back over and went back to sleep. I was just so grateful to God that everything was looking like it was going to be okay. I helped grandma tend to Karin for the rest of the day. India had spent the evening at her friends house down stairs they were a bunch of chocolate girls. They were the only people I knew in the entire projects whom had a mother and father living together. The mother was a preschool teacher and the father was a school bus driver. He also drove the charter bus on the weekend. They seemed nice enough and I'd known India was probably upset that I'd put my hands on her last night. I was going to apologize when she got up stairs. I believe she was safe for the time being. They seemed like a pretty normal family. My mind began to wonder what kinda people they really were. I'd thought perhaps I could be friends with the little girls as well. Because of my size I was afraid to even suggest such a thing. I'd never had friends before not real friends. I'd experience one or two people who were willing to help me and took pity on me so therefore they were kind but just having all out friends; that had never happened. I heard the door knocker, my heart began to race again it seemed as if it was an instant reminder of the incident last night. "Who?" I yelled on the way down the hall to the door. "India!" I heard my sister say. "Is grandma mad?" India asked on her way inside of the door. "No, I covered for you. I told her you were downstairs at your friends' house and the mother and father were home." I replied. I didn't know how to apologize to India. "Why you slapped me?" India asked. "Because I had seen it on movies. People panic and then somebody slap them; then they calm down." I answered in a joking manner. I tried to make light of the situation but that really was the reason. Plus she had to have lost her doggone mind hugging up with some strange grown man in my face, she better been hysterical. India didn't seem to be to please with the event but she accepted my apology anyway. I guess the whole thing was traumatic for everyone so she couldn't hold a grudge, like I could tell she really wanted to. We began talking about all the fun she had last night while at her friend's house. I told her how I wanted to be friends with them and did she think they would want to be my friend as well. She informed me how she had already asked them and they told her no, my feelings were hurt. I hadn't done anything to them I guess they just was disgusted by size. The next couple of weeks were spent in the house without my grandmother approval. My health was a constant concern of hers and how I would never go outside. She had quit her job because of the whole finger incident. I guess she came to the realization that we needed constant supervision. She came around the corner and told me that my father had arranged for me to go to his sister house for the rest of the summer. She lived in Albany, New York. I didn't care. I mean it wasn't like I had anything else to do. I packed my clothes and waited for my father to pick me up. I was just excited to be going somewhere. My father blew the car horn, I ran to the window and waved my hand out to signal I had seen him. My grandmother had given me a couple pieces of fried chicken and some bread for the bus trip. I kissed her on the cheek and ran towards the elevator. I arrived to the car. Ramon jumped out the car and helped me with my bag. After he put my bag in the trunk we were off to the Port Authority. Ramon informed me that his sister would be at the bus depot waiting for me. Once we were over the bridge I ate my chicken and fell asleep. The trip to Albany was short by the time I had awoken from my nap the bus pulled into the terminal. I'd seen my Aunt waiting outside the bus stop. It was Ramon's pudgy sister Diamond with honey brown eyes and the lovely dimples that I so wished for. She was a doctor and had no children of her own. My Uncle Poe was standing beside her. That was one of Ramon's younger brothers he was fair skinned like his sister and he had hazel eyes. In the car were my three little cousins. They had been in the car giggling. I figured it was at my size but when I got in the car I realized they were just laughing about one of their brothers passing gas. I was allowed to sit in the front sit because of my size. I was embarrassed by that, but nobody seemed to even have notice. On our way home we stop by the grocery store. I ran through the store with my little cousins until my uncle instructed us to get inside the car. I remember the serenity of my Aunt's neighborhood as we pulled up. The boys raced out the car into the house. I helped bring the groceries in the house. As I was being shown to my room the boys ran past me outside. My Aunt asked me if I owned a bathing suit, I told her no. She left the room and came back with one. "Here I think this one will fit you." She said with a radiant smile. "We will be out by the pool." She continued as she walked out the room. The pool, I thought with excitement. I hurried to put on my swimwear. I walked slowly outside I thought everybody was going to make fun of me because my bathing suit did not have a skirt to cover my stomach. To my surprise no one looked at me funny. I took the first step inside the pool while my cousins eagerly waited for me so that we could play together. The water was so cold I removed my foot instantly and shook it off. My Aunt was sitting there with her juice beside the pool. I looked over to her. She smiled with a look of approval. My cousins began to splash me for taking too long but my Aunt quickly told them to stop. I knew I was going to have a good summer. After that day I'd spend my days and nights trying to get back into the pool. My uncle cooked hot dogs and hamburgers everyday on the grill unless it rained. My Aunt would sit there with her Harlequin Romance novels. I'd admire her. She moved away from the projects and built something for her whole family to come and enjoy. I wanted to do that. I had too, for me and my sisters. Summer was soon approaching its end and my Aunt was so funny and nice I didn't want to leave, but Ramon had called for me to come home. He said I had to go school clothes shopping with Aunt Da'keena. So Auntie Diamond dropped me off to the bus station where I slept until the lights came on and the driver was announcing the Port Authority. I jumped off the bus looking for Ramon but it was Da'keena who was standing there. She seemed to smile but she was in a big rush to leave. I arrived to grandma's building. I grabbed my bags out of the trunk. I had to pass all of these girls that India hung with. They were staring at me. I knew they were blinded by my size. One of the girls lifted her hand to say hi to me. I returned the wave quickly still keeping my head down. I sped up the pace and got into the elevator. I was so relieved no one laughed directly at me this time. They had never done it before but kids had in the past. When I walked out of the elevator I could smell the chicken aroma that seeping from under grandma's door down the hall. Oh' yeah! I rapidly tapped the door with it's attached knocker. I could hear grandma calling. I was happy to be home. I spent the evening eating dinner and watching television as I told India about all of the fun I had at our Aunt's house. Grandma was listening even though she was pretending as if she wasn't. Plus now we were going shopping with Aunt Da'keena next week. I probably should have thanked God for my blessings I mean I was grateful but I guess it kinda escaped me at the time. I just knew I was happy. For the first time in a long time I was happy when I fell asleep.

"Ring, Ring, Ring!" The sound of the phone made me jump out of my sleep. It was Aunt Da'keena telling me that me and my sisters better be ready in an hour. I jumped up out of bed and ran to take a shower. Everybody else was already up. I got dressed. I wanted to be ready on time because Da'keena had already threaten to leave anybody who was not ready. India and Karin was not too impressed by her threat but it made me move a little faster. She picked us up without incident. I got everything I could fit. Then we walked around for hours while everybody else picked out their clothes. It seemed like we walked through Albee Square Mall for an eternity. Aunt Da'keena got mad at me because I told her I didn't know how to take an escalator. So she left me at the top of the escalator. I kept trying to put my foot on the escalator but it kept moving. My father must have made her come back for me. I was sorry for not knowing how to take the escalator and for being afraid but I didn't say anything. I just let her vent while we drove home. When I got to the house my sisters were going through their clothes. I quickly joined them. I didn't know if my clothes were the latest style or not but I felt like they were nice. I began dreading the first day of school. India had friends and people that she knew and so did Karin I didn't have anybody to talk to on the first day of school. Even when I lived with Kymela at least I knew everybody. I was tired of being the new kid all the time. I asked India if she thought I would have friends she told me probably. I didn't like that answered at all. When it was all said and done I went to bed feeling unsure of what the next day would bring so I called on God and asked him if I could please have a wonderful first day of school. I was even more afraid because I found out I had to take the city bus, plus they had placed me in my right grade which mean that I had skipped two grades. Hopefully God would answer my prayers. I got dressed early in the morning, before my sisters even got up. My grandmother told me that the bus driver would let us on the bus for free today. I stood at the bus stop waiting for an early bus. I figured it would be a couple of kids out there with me, but I would ultimately avoid all the crowds. One of the dark skin girls from the building came across the street. I managed a slight smile. I didn't want to wave because I knew she didn't like me but I still wanted to speak. Surprisingly she spoke to me. "Hello you going to Lafayette High School too?" she asked with a winning smile. "Uh, yes." I answered in a small whisper. "Oooh, shoot! My name is Stella. That's good I'll have somebody from the building to catch the bus with. You're India sister right?" She asked still smiling. "Yes." I answered smiling. I didn't know if she was trying to play me and when we got on the bus she was going to talk about me or what. "Is this your first year?" she questioned. I nodded in agreement. "Mine too." She said. My grandmother yelled out the window; the bus is coming. This was it the moment of truth. I was about find out if I was going to have a good year or not. The bus door opened and it was filled with kids. Oh no, I thought as I walked past the aisle. To my surprise the chocolate girl looked just as scared as I was while riding on the bus. We didn't say anything to each other all the way to school. We just sat there quietly together and watch the other children laugh and play with each other. I walked as fast as I could to keep up with her. I think she noticed my panting so she slowed down. I was grateful, even though I didn't mention it. We got into school and walked around looking for our first period class. We had decided to meet back up at the end of the day. Once I got into my class I realized nobody made fun of me. It looked like people were actually being nice to me. At the end of the day I was scared that she had left me but when I finally found her she looked as if she was scared that I left her. We walked to the bus stop talking about our first day of school. We were quiet on the bus ride home like we were that morning. Once we had reached the front of our building she invited me to play cards. I made a look of dismay. "Okay, why do you keep looking at me like that?" She asked. "Because India told me that you guys didn't like me and now I'm confused about why you are being so nice to me." I said in a puzzled tone. "Let's go." She said. "Where?" I asked uncertain where all this was going. "To my house for a minute." She continued. I didn't want to say no, I didn't know what to do. I didn't know what they were capable of in New York City. I was too much of punk to say anything, so I just followed her. "Is India in here?" She asked "Yes" one of her little sisters responded. "India! Your sister is here for you." The little brown skin girl continued. India came to the door with a different personality. "What's up?" She said with a hint of arrogance. ""Why you lie to her like that?" Stella asked India. India shrugged her shoulders and looked embarrassed I still didn't know, what was going on? "We had been asking India to invite you down stairs to play cards with us for the longest she would tell us that you didn't want to come." Stella finished. Oh now I get it. I didn't say any anything I just let out a little smile. I tried to look for an excuse to leave. "Oh, she probably thought I wouldn't come. Well let me go upstairs to let my grandmother know that I'm home from school." I said I knew they could tell my feelings were hurt and that I was embarrassed, but that was the only thing I could come up with. "Well you wanna come down later to play cards." She asked "Okay let me see what my grandmother say first." I said just trying to make my way out the door. I couldn't understand why India would tell a lie like that. When India came upstairs she told me that she was embarrassed by my weight and she didn't want me to be around her friends. I was devastated I couldn't believe the hurt that I felt in that moment. I had made my mind up that she could have her own friends and I would just go out and find me some friends. I kinda liked the girls from the fifth floor anyway. They were the ones who had brought Karin to the door when her fingers had gotten blown off. I would just make them my friends. Karin was friends with the oldest sister though. I didn't want her to feel like I took her friend so I started talking to the girl that was close to my age. They had a lot of children in their house like the chocolate girls but they were honey brown. On my first day there I realized that they were not like the chocolate girls they were bad. They could do whatever they wanted in front of their mother. Plus my new friend would spend hours talking about the chocolate girls telling me that I should not be their friend and how they were going to snake me. I would go to school with the thought of how they were going to do something to me but they were the only ones I went to school with. The light-skin girl would do the most irrational things. She would steal boys cars and drive them into brick walls, or set white people hair on fire while we were riding the train. I was beginning to become afraid that she was going to get me arrested just for being around her. I started to stay to myself again. I didn't need any more problems coming to my grandmother house, she had enough to deal with. Karin still would stay out all times of the night and it seemed as if India was following her. I continued to discipline them as much as possible with fights but they did not seem to care. In their mind I should have minded my business. I couldn't afford for us to be split up again. They were so stupid not to recognize that our grandmother could get rid of us at anytime. I'd thought once I'd gotten India in check then grandmother wouldn't think that we were all bad and she would have some lency in her for Karin. However India felt I was only her older sister and had no right to tell her what to do. I would ride the train with Stella to school and back but I was reluctant to hold much of a conversation with her. The school year was uneventful and I actually had some friends. Once school was coming to an end I was looking forward to spending the summer in Albany with my aunt and cousins. It appeared that my grandmother had other plans. I had to get a summer job. I knew that the chocolate sisters were going to be working this year so it didn't seem that bad. I had obtained a job with the free lunch program. I had to work with a different chocolate sister. This one seemed nicer. She had dimples but was not as pretty as the other sister. Her heart was better by a landslide. We would wake up early for work and walk home together. It was a lot of girls that worked in the school. There was another girl named Laneisha there. She lived in Gravesend projects with us but she was not that fond of me. I would often get into verbal spats about me not doing any work. Even though I knew it was unfair of me but I was out of shape, I couldn't help that I would often become tired and took many breaks. I wanted to explain it to her but I was just too embarrassed. Towards the end of the summer we all had brought things for school. I knew Ramon was going to buy our school clothes so I brought some jewelry. I'd spent every ounce of money all summer long buying rings and earrings I couldn't wait for school to start so everybody could see the new me. I had more gold then Mr. T. and I was so proud of that. I still didn't have a real fashion sense so all of my clothes came from Lane Bryant and they only seemed to have ugly cotton sets for older big people. On the first day of school I grabbed the least of the ugly outfits in order to get dressed. I had my gold and a pair of name brand sneakers so I figured people would not talk that bad about me. I found myself waiting at the bus stop for Stella. Once she crossed the street we got on the bus this year however I had joined in the bus shenanigans. I was play fighting laughing and joking. Stella met a boy that was very attractive. He went to a different school so we found ourselves cutting school so she could spend time with him. On our cut days we rode the train all day and would go to McDonald's or Burger King for lunch. I felt like I had it all. I would walk through the halls as if I owned it. I had no problem with getting in trouble. I knew my grandmother was not coming up to the school and my father worked too much to come up to the school. I spent more time on the train then I did in school. While running the streets I found something else I had become good at. Being hospitalized for all that time and fighting adults so that I wouldn't be put in time out I found out that I was good at fighting. I would fight any and every one that dared test me. I easily became enraged; when it had anything to do with my friends or family. I was starting to be well known for my fighting skills. I never became a bully though, honestly I never had a fight with anyone over anything that they had done to me. I was no longer afraid of living in New York City. I had become New York City. I eventually dropped out of school and enrolled into a GED program that I later dropped out of. My grandmother was becoming increasingly disappointed with me and my sisters. I decided once I had turned eighteen that I would move out of her house. I deviously brought things for my apartment, without my grandmother knowledge. I had my drawer filled with all sorts of toiletries. Once I had enough to start my life I packed my bags and went to Greyhound bus terminal. I was going to make a life for myself somewhere. Anywhere away from people telling me what to do. Away from Kymela who had decided to come back to New York City to be close to her children. Kymela had suffered a nervous breakdown from all of the stress of being back in the mother house who despised her, also living three blocks away from the love of her life that was now in a healthy happy relationship, not to mention the children whom had lost all respect for her and the fact that she couldn't look them in the eyes, nor did they want her to. They were filled with secrets and pain. Pain from keeping secrets, yet the secrets had to be concealed, or we would endure more pain from the ridicule of harboring such an evil dark secret. People would always seemed to be understanding, at first. They would give the whole spiel about how it was not our fault but then that same person would shy away from us. It would be even more hurtful to watch a mother run around the corner once they have realized who is alone with their child. I guess they figure history might repeat itself or perhaps we were as sick as Kymela. Either way no parent was willing to take a chance on what could perhaps be a tragedy which in hindsight who can blame them. But now I was free from my pass, free from my pain. I could be anything and everything my heart wanted to be. I really had a chance. No secrets.

CHAPTER 11

Hi-Ho Syracuse Flow

"Um, I would like to go to 1809 E. Fayette Street." I had spoken to the cab driver in a voice barely above a whisper. I had told Karin that I was coming to her house. She just had a beautiful baby and some girl had stepped to her while she was holding my new born niece in her hands. So this was a situation that I had to control and not only that; Karin had also told me how easy it was to get an apartment in Syracuse. Not like in New York City. In New York City there was a waiting list. I paid the cab driver and watched as Lana and Karin ran out the big green door to greet me. Lana was our friend from Brooklyn her babyfather name got mixed up in some stuff. So Lana had moved to Syracuse a month before me. They were greeting me with laughter and open arms. We took the elevator to the fourth floor. I stepped inside Karin's apartment and dropped all my bags on the floor. I grabbed my niece and began to smother her with kisses. I glanced around. I loved Karin's apartment. It had wall to wall carpet and a garbage disposal. It also had central heating and air conditioners. The rooms were spacious and there was a balcony attached to living room. It was considered a lower income housing project but it appeared to be a bit high class from what I was use to. In Brooklyn projects the floors were hard and cold, the heat was controlled, and we definitely did not have a garbage disposal. I just knew I was going to love this town.

I had awaken early in the morning to apply for my apartment Lana stated it only took her two weeks to get her apartment. Karin said it took her the same amount of time to get her apartment. I was happy to hear that I was only going to be in Karin's house for a little bit of time. I headed out to the rental office as happy as a clam. However as soon as I got to the rental office I instantly hit a problem. The lady explained how grandmother had an income for me, so technically I had an income which meant I could not go and get welfare. This meant that I did not qualify for rental assistance. Also I had no children so I did not qualify for food stamps or any other programs that would help me with rent, food, or any other living expense. I felt so disappointed. I didn't want to go back to grandma's house. I left the office trying to fight back tears. Karin and Lana were trying to be supportive but they knew I was stuck in a hard place. I thought about how to fix the situation. I went out on job interviews but I had no other experience except for summer youth or other youth employment programs. Once Karin realize she had the upper hand she began treating me mean. I became afraid of when and if I was going to be put out. I found a way to scurry up the security deposit. I told them to place me on my income which mean I had to pay rent. It was subsidized but unlike the rest of the tenants who received a monthly stipend for the electric bill I received bills, bills, and more bills.

I'd finally received my apartment keys. They placed me in a two bedroom in 1815. I was excited about my address 1815 E. Fayette St. apt 2J Syracuse, NY 13210. I repeated my address in my mind and out loud. I wanted to remember my address but I also couldn't believe I had my own! The first night I slept on the floor with my duffle bag as my pillow. I was surprised to find myself crying again. This time I was crying because the sad truth of my life set in once again I was alone. I was afraid of how I was going to handle taking care of myself. How would I provide for myself. I still couldn't find a job and grandma still received my SSI check. There was no food, phone, cable, or furniture. But in the back of my mind was the rewarding thought that it was all mine. I had a home. It had took 19 years but I finally had a place that was mine. I was no longer a visitor or guest it was mine. I fell asleep as the tears of misgivings rolled silently into the cold hard surface of my duffle bag. I awoken to the sound of knocking and laughter at the door. I jumped up running to the door. My first guest. I invited Lana and Karin in with jokes of having them into my new home. Although the day seemed to be filled with laughter my thoughts were dark. I had doubt and discouragement in the back of my mind. I had to call my grandmother. I didn't know how to bring about the conversation of money. Even though it was rightfully mine. She had struggled so much to take care of us. I knew that the money would come in handy around the house. How could I burden her with the trouble of forfeiting my income. I patiently waited for my sister and Lana to leave. I took my last little bit of money and went to the store and bought a calling card along with a phone. I knew I could use the dial tone along with the calling card to call my grandmother. When she answered the phone I was hesitant at first. Once the conversation began I was relieved at her willingness to help. She told me that since my rent was only fifty dollars a month and I had to pay my light bill and I'd smoke cigarettes she would send me one hundred and fifty dollars out of my check a month. I was kinda disappointed in the amount but I understood where she was coming from. I agreed and was happier than I let on to be. I knew with the money she gave me I would be able to survive even if I had to eat oodles & noodles with hot dogs, it was still manageable.

The first month of the money agreement with my grandmother went as planned. The next month I was fifty dollars short and the third month I'd received no money at all. I'd called my grandmother to see what happened to the money. As the phone was ringing I didn't know how or what to say. "Hello." my grandmother said above the static on the phone. "Um....hi grandma." I muttered. "Who is this?" My grandmother asked. "Taylor." I stated with my cowardice persona seeping through the phone. "Yeah, well what do you want?" She continued. A small part of me began to hope that something had happen to the mail; and she had sent the money. "I um.. well I umm..." I replied. "What you didn't get any money. Well you just can't up and leave me high and dry. Your uncle came over here for some money or they were going to get evicted. Plus they going to shut the cable off." Her voice was harsh and cold as it trailed off to a halt. "Um, well grandma, what am I supposed to do for money?" I asked in my same cowardice tone. "Beats me honey, you better find your way back here." She stated. The dial tone was immediately followed. I sat down I had no money. Karin was so mean to me the last time I really didn't want to have to go to her. Lana barely had anything herself. I walked over to Lana's house. I sat there and cried trying to explain how my grandmother wasn't a bad person. Lana couldn't understand why I was defending her, even though she never said it her eyes spoke volumes. I ate dinner at Lana's house and bunked on her floor for a couple of days. I stayed because she had cable, food, plus she was nice to me. I knew that was a temporary fix. I went home to try and figure out my next plan. I awaken to the feel of a draft in my house. It was a thermostat in each room. I walked around the house to each thermostat and turned the heat up. I walked toward the bathroom. As I entered the door I slipped my hand on the wall to flick the light on. To my surprise the light didn't come on. I flicked it a couple of times and my reality set in. The lights had been turned off. I instantly began to pray as I grabbed my clothes to get dress. I needed to find change around the house to catch the bus. I was going downtown to social service to see if there was someone there to help me. It took a little digging but I found the change I needed. I'd caught the bus to the Civic Center. Apparently that was the name of the welfare building. I walked around and was sent from floor to floor. I was eligible but since my SSI check was not in my name it tied their hands. I almost gave up but before I did I'd said another prayer in my mind. 'Most heavenly father I need your help, you have always helped me in the past can you please help me again. PLEASE!' The desperation in the tone in my head, made me want to cry. I went to the last floor feeling overwhelmed. I stood there waiting to speak with this unknown person. It started off as the other interviews about how their hands were tied. I needed to go down to SSI and try to take ownership of my check since I no longer lived with my grandmother. She began to tell me how my grandmother could get in trouble for what she was doing even be placed into jail for theft if I so desired. Then something seemed to change in her heart as I batted back the tears. "Well here is what I can do for you. I can give you what is called a HEAP loan. You will be responsible to pay the money back. Or they may take the money from your check. There's also this place call case management downtown. They can become the payee for your social security checks. They pay all your bills, it's a pretty nice program. Here's the number I'd go there if I was you." The lady explained. I was so grateful to God for helping me through that situation. I thanked the lady and raced home to call Niagara Mohawk so they could restore my services. To my surprise they had twenty-four hours restore policy so I had to spend another night with the lights turned off. When I awaken the next day I tried waiting around for my lights to come back on but I knew that I had to go to case management. I told them what had happened and they ensured me that they would take the check from my grandmother. I was adamant that no action should be taken on my grandmother. They tried to persuade me. However they could tell the talk of her being place in a legal bind would be the deal breaker and I would find some other way to get my check. I left the office feeling comfortable about my decision. They took my check away from grandma with ease, the very next month. All was well when it came to money with a little ups and downs here and there. Meanwhile my life was fairly looking up I'd spent so much time with Lana she was slowly becoming my secondary best friend. Plus Karin had her daughters dad living downstairs with his sister staying down the hall. After Lana's children's dad came to stay with her they moved into a different part of the little town. I felt so alone. I'd began hanging around Karin's sister in law she was fun. She kept a lot of male company but she was good to me, so I never judged her. She would supply large amounts of alcohol along with music and laughter. I couldn't stand to drink but I kinda started taking a liking in the feeling of freedom. I was free from problems stress and all worries. Time slowly ticked away. My best friend and one of her sisters moved to Syracuse but then they moved back Karin was pregnant with her second child. Her children's father was now engaged to the women down the hall. Life was happening all around me and fast. I had signed up for college and dropped out due to financial trouble. I had become such a permanent fixture in Lamuziga's life that we were almost completing each others' sentences. I'd felt as though she was too pretty to be a "whore". She had a butter pecan complexion, big dark brown eyes, thick long luxurious hair, and a kick ass body. She had one major flaw her teeth stuck out like a beaver working hard on his next meal. I tried to talk her out of her lifestyle but she loved her life just the way it was. She was the most popular women throughout the whole neighborhood.

Sometimes guys would try and hold a brief conversation with me while they were awaiting their turn; but I didn't even know how to respond. I guess they were feeling me out sort of speak. I didn't know how to tell them that other then the foster home and the doctor's office I was still a virgin. I didn't even know what to say to a boy and these were grown man. I couldn't tell them I was inexperienced. I'd felt as though they would laugh at me so I just stayed to myself. I started to notice her son. When we first moved to Syracuse he was a pudgy little disrespectful boy, but then one day he woke up with a deepen voice, nice abs, and a killer smile. He was so intelligent, mouthy and humble. Unlike his older brother who needed the most expensive choice of every and anything. With his mother's coaching we began flirting. She would say little things like "don't make me tell Taylor to take you in the room and show you a thing or two." We'd glance at each other and smile. It was a very innocent mutual attraction.

CHAPTER 12

My First Love

I stood on the terrace of 1809 E. Fayette. St. I looked up the hill to see if I knew anyone walking down it. It was pretty peaceful outside. No sign of anyone except for people sitting on the benches around the corner so I really couldn't see who they were. That's the moment I realized that time was moving forward. I had actually knew quite a few people. My mind began to reflect on a conversation I had with Ramon. He was asking me when I was going to lose my virginity. He told me if I didn't lose it soon I'd be one of those women who would always find a problem with every man she encounters out of fear. To be my dad, Ramon was often inappropriate but he was always honest. I didn't want to be some weirdo who never lost their virginity. My thoughts were interrupted by the sound of this God awful person. I'd looked down and to my surprise there stood one of the most attractive man that I had seen in a long time. He had the cutest cheeks ever. They were pudgy like Arnolds from Different Strokes. He was a little too dark for my taste but overall he was a good looking man. He looked up and waved. I yelled down to him a hello. In an angelic voice I didn't even know I possessed "How you doing?" He yelled back up. Maybe he got something caught in his throat, I thought. "I'm fine" I replied with a smile. He walked in the building and I walked back inside the house. I had decided he was the one that was going to take my virginity. I knew he would agree. I mean what man wouldn't, no matter how big I was; getting a girls virginity was a big deal. Plus Ramon was right I was about to be twenty-one years old what was I waiting for really. I just knew I had to find the right time to tell him that he was the one to take my virginity. The days went by with the same ole everyday interactions but I would make it my business to flirt with the boy who I affectionately named cheeks. The nickname was in my mind of course. The summer was slowly leaving with autumn leaves falling, I'd become pretty close to Cheeks, by now I knew his real name but I still didn't know how to make the move from harmless flirting to I think you should be my first. So one day I just blurted it out. "Your going to be my first." Cheeks turned around with barely any emotion being portrayed "Okay, but let's wait a little while, it will make it better." He replied. "Okay, how about my twenty-first birthday." I suggested. "Whens that?" He asked "In February." I replied. "Alright." He said in agreeance. There were other boys sitting in the green windowsill of the lobby with a blank stare on their faces. I simply turned around and walked towards the elevator leading up to Lamuziga's house. I knew my actions were pretty brazen but I had to go for it. I sat down on Lamuziga's black leather couch and popped open a beer as if nothing had just happened. Yup it was a done deal, I was going to lose my virginity; and I got pissy drunk to that fact!

It seemed like just yesterday I was plotting on my virginity therefore how did I get here. Lying on the floor between the living room and terrace door. The room was spinning and I'm about to throw up. I tried to look around but it was hard for me to keep my eyes open. It's my birthday! There are three guys lined up to do the honors of deflowering me. Then there was a knock at the door. Lucky number four. These pillars of the community had come to do me this great service, yeah right! In my mind I started thinking perhaps I should open the bidding for these low down dirty rotten scoundrels. Lana and Karin started looking a little nervous when the fourth guy entered. Up unto this point it was three guys and three girls they all knew it was my birthday but none of them knew they were all there for the glorious occasion of taking my virginity. I knew if they figured it out I was going to get cursed out and perhaps even fucked up. The cool breeze hit me in my face. 'Awe, I needed that.' I thought. 'How in the hell did this happen' my thoughts continued, it ended with the slamming of the front door. 'Oh, by george I think he got it!' Making jokes in my head was the only way to deal with this pressure. At first I just wanted a backup plan just in case Cheeks backed out. Then somebody told somebody who told somebody else. Plus the boys who were in the hallway that day. I couldn't quite figure it out but I knew I was screwed. "Yo' shorty you okay?" a male voice asked. I managed to open my eyes long enough to see who actually cared enough to ask about me maybe it was his night. "I'm fine, thank you." I answered. 'Oh this the boy I met in the hallway, why is he even here.' I thought in an annoyed tone. With that another slamming of the door. Shit I wonder who that was. Lana and Karin started making excuses to clear the house because the last two didn't seem like they were leaving and one of them had the nerve to be from the hallway. So I guess the process of elimination was working. Just then it was another knock at the door. I sucked my teeth so loud it was definitely clear what I was thinking. 'Who the hell is that?' The sweet annoying sound of Cheeks voice filled the room. "Why yall got her laying on the floor like that?" He asked. I smiled with my eyes partially opened. "Come on." He said while helping me off the floor. He walked me into the second bedroom of Karin's house. I laid on the bed. "I'm ready!" I yelled, followed by a giggle. "Naw, not like this shorty." He said as he turned to leave the room I managed to lunge after him while grabbing his wrist. "Please don't go! I have to do this tonight or I'll never do it. I'm scared and I choose you so please don't reject me it will hurt me too bad. Plus if I wait the next time I will be just as drunk, so why not tonight on my birthday." I asked in the same angelic voice as our first hello. He turned around and began kissing me with passion and endearment. I could tell he cared. I think he cared more than he was letting on. I slowly began pulling off my griddle like that shit was sexy. I laid across the bed and closed my eyes really tight. I knew it was going to hurt. I could feel him enter me slowly I winced in pain but not to the degree that should have been there. Little did I know I had lost my virginity to that doctor years ago this was just a formality. It was finally happening and five to ten minutes later it was over. The act itself was magnificent though I couldn't figure out what took me so long to do this. I couldn't wait to get up the next morning and dish about my night. I heard Cheeks leave then I fell asleep. The next day Lana was banging on the front door bright and early. "What happened?" She asked as she pushed her toddlers stroller into the house. "Dang come in, let me close the door first." I answered while giggling. Karin made her way down the hall to see who was at the door. "I did it." I said with a smile of pride. Lana screamed "I knew it!" "You lying." Karin stated. "What happened?" Karin asked "How was it?" Lana asked. " Well a lady never tells, but I tell you what. I'd be doing it again." I replied "That's some bullshit." Karin stated. Lana just turned her head but I was pretty sure their first time was not next day news but I did like being the center of attention. I walked home feeling like a whole new person. I took a shower smiling. I got dressed and turned on the television. I heard three taps at the door. I opened it to my surprise Cheeks was standing there. I almost ran. I knew he probably wanted to do it again but this time I wasn't drunk. "Why you look scared?" He asked "Cause I am" I replied "Why?" He asked again. "Oh, because I didn't think you knew where I lived." I lied. "I been knew." He answered. He sat down on the couch and opened a St. Ides beer. "You want one?" He asked. "Um, no thank you." I replied. He picked up the remote and started flickering through channels. I sat on the couch and tried to act normal but that was not working. I kept fidgeting. He finally patted the seat beside him. I got up from the love seat and walked over to sofa and sat down beside him. I sat there while he kept flickering through the channels with one hand and he began gently massaging my shoulder with his other hand. I offered him dinner but he declined. I knew the dreadful moment was coming. He would want to go into my bedroom. I didn't have my liquid courage to my surprise I didn't even have the courage to drink my liquid courage in front of him. Once he stood up and started walking towards the bedroom I knew it would be something disastrous. I went to take off my clothes but he shook his head no. He sat on the side of the bed slowly removing his timberlands. I climbed on the other side of the bed by the wall. I stuffed my feet under the covers. My heart began palpitating out of control he began to slide the covers back. He laid beside me with all of his clothes on. I felt his hand slowly moving across my stomach. "Turn over on you side." He whispered. I wanted to run in the bathroom. What the hell could we do on our side. If we could do something on our side then I wasn't ready for it. Nor did I ever think I would be. His arms was still around my stomach. "Are you comfortable?" He asked. "Mmm, hmm." I responded. I was paralyzed with fear until I heard him snoring. He fell asleep! I didn't know if I should be infuriated or flattered. How could he lay beside me without touching me? Was I that horrible the last time? Or perhaps he was just being nice. I chose to be flattered. I could feel the tension leaving my body as I drifted off to sleep. This was kind of a nice feeling. It was different. It was like I felt safe for the first time. I awaken to my heart racing and my lower half pulsating. I could feel him inside of me and I loved every minute of it. I was doing everything I had seen in the prono's. It look like I was pleasing him. It was over and it was better than the first time, for me anyway. I wasn't sure how it was for him. He sat on the edge of the bed and got dressed; while I laid in the bed I was looking for some kind of sign. 'Was he pleased with me? Was he done with me? Was I so terrible that he just wasn't speaking to me?' He was quiet the whole time and so was I. He leaned over and poked his lips out. I sat up and leaned in for the kiss. "I'll see you later." He said as he stood up and walked away. I heard the front door closed. I laid back on the bed and kicked my feet up and down violently while laughing. I have a man! Yes! I fell asleep for the first time feeling that everything was wonderful in my life. My furniture was just delivered later that day. My color theme was gold and black. I'd picked out brand new leather couch and loveseats with gold trim. I also brought the matching coffee and end glass table tops that were gold and black on the bottom. I also had purchased a matching dining room set. The table was black with a gold trim that had a gold base. The chairs had black leather backs with a gold trim. I had already painted the house what I believed to be a gold color but it turned out to be what I called a sunrise surprise. I had to be creative so I placed black broader going from one end of the house to the other in the middle of the wall. To my surprise it took away from the brightness. I sat on the couch and looked around my house. It seemed that everything in my life was coming together beautifully. After watching television for a little while I went to take a shower. I didn't want my new MAN to come to the house and I was sitting around stinking like a wild boar. I climb out of the shower. I dried off and put on some lotion. I pushed my little bit of hair into a ponytail. Once I felt like I had done enough prep work for his arrival I went back to the living room to watch television. I began to get sleepy so I went and got a pretty comforter out of the closet and stretch out on the couch. Every time I heard the loud slam of the metal staircase door my heart would skip a beat. I anxiously anticipated his knock. As my eyes grew heavy, my heart grew weary. I began to think he was not going to show. I'd started to feel real used. I had gave him my virginity and he wasn't coming back. I laid across the couch trying not to cry but the embarrassment that I felt fell from my eyes anyway. I didn't leave the house for a couple of days. I didn't want to look in his face.I knew he would be standing outside or in 1809's lobby. I had this image of everybody snickering when I walked in the building. I just knew he probably told everybody the way he had used me. I had decided that I had stayed in the house long enough. I took a shower, went and got dressed. I'd left my building and walked the three buildings down the hill to 1809. As I began to cut across the parking lot I could see him sitting in the windowsill of the lobby. His back was to me. My first instance was to turn around and walk back home but I figured we was going to have to face each other sooner or later. As I got close to the lobby door he turned around and looked at me. I tried to hide my disgust and hurt but for some reason my eyes rolled on their own as I reached for the door handle. When I walked in I could see the bewilder look on his face as I strutted past him without saying a word. "Um, hello miss lady; I know damn well you not about to walk past me without speaking?" He asked in a joking tone. I turned around with a bright smile on my face and spoke. I got on the elevator to go to Karin's house. I began walking down the hall to the house feeling flattered and bewilderment. I didn't know if he liked me or just used me. I drunk a couple of wine coolers and I was feeling kinda tipsy. I left Lamuziga's house and began my journey home. It was less than a half a block I told myself as I swayed from side to side up the hill to 1815. Once I was at my building I'd felt some relief. I had looked for "my new man" in the building but he wasn't there. I walked up the two flights of stairs and entered my house. I was grateful for being safe. I sat on the couch trying to think of what I had to eat in the kitchen. I got up and walked into the kitchen. I heard a knock at the door. I took the two steps from the kitchen to the door. I looked out the peephole and seen his face. I'd unlocked the door and walked back to the kitchen. I opened the refrigerator as he locked the door. I looked up from the refrigerator to see his eyes piercing at me. "What's wrong with you?" I asked. "Nothing, why are you mad?" He answered my question with a question. "Because you said you'd be back later and you never came back." I answered. "I was coming back." He replied. "So what happened?" I asked "No, see, I meant that I was coming back not that I was coming back that night." He answered. "Oh." Was all I could managed to say. I didn't know if he was telling the truth or not. I just knew I was happy he was there now. "Would you like something to eat?" I asked "Like what?" He asked. "I could fry us up some chicken." I replied. "Naw, I'm straight." He answered as he moved in for the kiss. I new what time it was as soon as he moved to my neck. He kissed me softly on the cheek and whispered in my ear. "Let's go in the room." His voice was so seductive, that I had forgot I was even hungry. I'd awaken to him sitting on the bed with his back to me again. He was putting on his Timberland boots. I sat up in the bed. "When will I see you again?" I asked "I'll be back." He answered "I don't know exactly when, but I know I'm definitely coming back." He added. I wanted to badger him and tell him; that wasn't good enough. I needed and exact time but I was too afraid he would never come back again so when he leaned in for the kiss I just poked my lips out to receive it. When he left I still was happy but I didn't like not knowing. Was I his girlfriend or not? I couldn't tell. I didn't even know the signs to be able to tell. I went up to Lamuziga's apartment to get drunk and ask her a couple of questions. I needed to know if there were signs to be able to tell if someone really liked you or if they were using you. I told her the ins and outs of this new relationship and I couldn't tell from her evasive answers what to do. Soon after that my sister Karin told me she had seen Cheeks in his boxers walking around Lamuziga's house. I didn't know what to do. I confronted him with her accusation but he denied it and told me she was jealous of me and that I should stay away from her. In my mind that was the most absurd thing I had ever heard. Why would my own sister be jealous of me, and more importantly why would the man that I gave something so precious to treat me so bad? That was the real question. I'd acted unaffected by their act of betrayal. I knew he slept with her and I would deal with that at a later time. At this time I needed to appear to be comfortable so that is what I did. I spent my entire day over there with them telling jokes to one another and giggling while I sat on the couch just sipping my drinks and telling my own jokes. As the night went on I left them on couch talking. Again I left drunk and could barely make it home but this time I knew there would be no knock at the door. I knew I had given my virginity to someone who was not worth it. I was just being so fast, that's what I got. I knew all of that but I was still mad. I made it up in my mind that I was going to sleep with Lamuziga's son. We'd flirt often and I kinda liked him but I was going to use him to hurt her. I knew she would be hurt if I slept with her son. My intentions were devilish and evil I was going to hurt him to hurt her worst than she ever hurt me. My plan was very easy to incorporate. I'd just continue to flirt with him. I mean I was already curious so what the heck, why not make this whole situation work out to my advantage. When I met him he was some pudgy little boy but now he is a tall slender tender roni. Our flirting began to intensify. Day to day he would find me make his pecs jump because he knew I liked that. Then we progressed to kissing. He would start kissing me and sucking on my neck. This went on for months and I had gotten quite comfortable with that. This was how our relationship would stay. With some minor petting and heavy kissing. However one night everything changed. We were sitting on the couch watching television with Lamuziga and she fell asleep we started out kissing and petting. I moved up closer he put his hand up my night gown and seen that I hadn't on any panties underneath. With my eyes closed and enjoying our usual kissing and dry humping I felt the sharp pain of him entering me. My eyes popped open I wanted to scream but I couldn't wake up his mother sleeping on the next couch. I'd shot a look over to the other couch. What in the world was he thinking? What if she wake up? I was in pain but enjoying the feeling at the same time, while staring at his mother to see if she would wake up. The experience was an emotional roller coaster. In my mind I thought Lamuziga was up. She turned over and then I closed my eyes and began to enjoy each thrust. My body did something it never did before from intercourse. It tensed up and I began to tremble uncontrollably. It felt so good. His let out a soft grunt and climbed off of me. He walked towards the bathroom. I'd turned over to face the couch. I heard the bathroom door open then he walked into his room. After his room door closed Lamuziga got up and walked into her room. In my mind she was awake the whole time. Her room door closed. I fell asleep, while anticipating the uncomfortable conversation to come in the morning. I awaken to her son sitting at the foot of the couch. I looked at him puzzled, he returned my look with a smile. I got up went to the restroom then to his mother room. I'd sat on her bed and waited to hear what she had to say. To my surprise she acted as if she really didn't know what was going on. I kept seeing him with no intention on loving him. Our relationship began to progress in a way I hadn't anticipated I started to really like him. I guess it was there all along. Then one night Lamuziga and I was getting drunk. She began to confide in me. First she apologized for sleeping with my first then she looked at me with an expression of softness and concern. "Please don't hurt my son. He really like you and he is too young to deal with heartbreak. You have the ability to ruin his life and make him hate all women." she said abruptly. I was astonished by her remark. Had she known all of this time. But I'd also had to process something more devastating. How can I intentionally hurt another human being? What gave me the right to think what I was doing was okay? I quietly walked away with no response. I couldn't entertain her at the moment. She was blowing my drunken high with her revelation. I sat on the couch as if she didn't speak to me at all and began singing the song on the radio. "Did you hear me?" she asked. "Yes." I responded flatly while continuing singing. She walked in her room and slammed the door. What she didn't know was that her conversation changed my entire mindset. I was wrong and I wasn't going to move forward with my plan plus I knew he was a senior in high school. I didn't want my plan to backfire, she could put me in jail for my actions. As the room began to spin I knew that I was not going to intentionally hurt him. The next day I viewed his and our relationship differently. I began to be as accommodating as possible. I didn't know that with the intent of not hurting him, I began to lose myself. Our relationship started to be one-sided. The years rolled by and I realized his ultimate pleasure was hurting me. I'd walk in the house to his name calling and degrading comments. I wouldn't respond because his mother's words always rang in my ears. 'You can ruin him for all women.' I couldn't bare the thought of my actions being the end of someone's happiness. He loved me in his own way, I needed to believe that. I came into the house with the intent on getting drunk and having sex with my baby. I drank so that I could be uninhibited during sex. I didn't keep count of my drinks and the room began to spin. I walked into his room where the stereo was to listen to my song and await his arrival. I played Jon B. They don't know about this. The room wouldn't stop spinning enough for me to enjoy my high. I tried to lay across the floor seductively but I flopped down, skinning my arms on the carpet. With my forearm burning I knew it was going to happen. It was going to come up. Everything I ate and drank within the last twenty-four hours was looking for a quick exit. I was too drunk to move. Vomit spewed from my mouth. I didn't want to do this in his room plus I didn't want him to see me like that. I tried crawling into the bathroom but only made it to the doorway. His mother came to the door. "Lay down!" she yelled. I kept crawling as if I didn't hear her. What she didn't understand was that my man was going to be home soon and he was going to be mad at the way I left his room. I had to pull myself together and clean this mess up. I tried to will myself sober as she continued to yell. "Taylor, lay down! Don't worry about the mess, we'll take care of that in the morning!" My thoughts were scattered was she still yelling or was I just drunk. Either way she needed to shut up. I'd succumb to her demands along with the pleading of my body to lay on the floor. I could feel her step across my motionless body to the window. "You need some air Taylor, that'll make you feel better." she said as she opened the window. She stepped back accrossed me and turned off the radio that was still blasting through all of this. "Goodnight." She said while closing the room door. Sometimes she could be so sweet to me. I love my friend. As soon as I began to doze I heard the creaking of the bedroom door. Oh, no he's here. I laid there with not much more energy but deep down inside I wanted to get up kinda. I heard him suck his teeth. He walked out the room grabbed a towel and placed it over the vomit. He then got a washcloth and wiped my face chest and neck off. He kiss me gently. I wanted to open my eyes smile or anything to show him that I was appreciative for his kind gesture but my body wouldn't let me move. He kept kissing me with each passing kiss it became more enduring and he added more passion until I could tell he was fully aroused. I tried to respond but I was just to weak. I felt him enter me while kissing me gently. For the first time I could tell he was concerned for me and that he possibly really could love me. I laid there enjoying every thrust but I was unable to respond except for a small moan or a whispered I love you. He dressed me and climbed onto his bed. Just then Lamuziga opened his room door. "Be patient with her tonight son, she had a little too much. Okay." She instructed him. "I wasn't even going to say nothing to her MOM." He answered. She closed the door and I drifted off to sleep. The next morning I awoken to children laughter and birds chirping. Today was going to be a beautiful day. My baby pleased me last night. Everyone in the house was generally smiling, laughing, and playing who could ask for anything more except perhaps a do over from last night of course without the vomiting. I showered cleaned my mess up in the room. I'd watched him leave, I lounged around all day with Lamuziga's. We laughed joked and enjoyed our buzzed plus we ate leftovers from the night before. We started drinking a little late which I was glad about because I wanted him to come in and service me again. I sat on the floor playing music but this time I wasn't as drunk. I laid across the floor to go to sleep. I could hear him walk in. "Yo, get out of my room?!" He shouted. I didn't respond. I wanted him to think I was sleep. "I said get outta of my room!" He stated again. I thought that if I didn't say anything and kept pretending I was asleep he would leave me alone at least. I mean at this point I was too embarrassed to show everyone I had been pretending, by leaving the room this time. I didn't want to take that walk of shame into the living room; I'll pass I thought. He began to become enraged. He grabbed my arms and pulled them above my head so he could drag me out of the room then when that didn't work he started stomping me in my back as hard as he could multiple times. I just laid there speechless I didn't know what else to do. This had turned terribly wrong. He was so loving just last night and now he's trying to injuror me prementantly. He walked over to his bed and laid across it and called me a fat bitch before turning over and going to sleep. It was no possible way he could have known that I was up or whether or not I was drunk he just didn't care. He wanted me out of his room by any means. I laid there with my back throbbing from the sting of each kick he distributed to me. The tears kept rolling down my face how could he hurt me in such a manner. I thought he loved me. Perhaps he knew I was awake the whole time. It didn't matter none of that was necessary. When I got up off the floor the next morning it was a terrible creak in my back. 'It still comes and goes till this day.' I walked back to my house. I'd limped into the bathroom for my morning ritual. I tried to work the creak out of my back. It didn't seem to work. I left the bathroom walking with a limp and misty eyed. He didn't have to do me like that I thought. I went home to stretch out on my bed and relax my back. Despite the pain I was in I kept thinking about the love we had made the previous night and I knew deep down inside he was just mad because despite himself, he loved me soo much. I fell asleep while reminiscing. I opened my eyes to the throbbing pain in my back. It seemed to be getting worse. I limped to the bathroom and back to bed, about three days later I was back to my normal self and headed back to Lamuziga's house. I'd miss my love, her other children, and her. I needed to be next to him, even from a distance. I sat there I didn't speak I just caught subtle glances when I could. I'd drank my alcohol. I didn't want him to notice me or get mad at me again. I left that night drunk and wobbling back up the hill to my building. I heard the key in the door. My baby was here. I heard the television come on but I didn't move, I fell asleep waiting for him to come to bed. Upon daybreak I sat up and realized my lover didn't come in the room to please me. I walked out my room and could hear the television playing. He was slumped over on the couch asleep with the remote in his hand. 'Oh, no he stayed the night out. His mother is going to be mad. Oh, she is probably worried sick.' I thought. I didn't want him to leave though. I reached for the remote out of his hand. He flinched from the unknown touch. Once he realized it was me I could see his whole body relax. Then his eyes widen once he recognized the daylight. I knew what he was thinking. Lamuziga was going to kill him. He glanced at me and got up and walked to the door. In the unspoken words I could have sworn I heard sorry even though he never said it. I wasn't going to speak about again. That day I took my shower and got dressed only to walk back down to his house. Lamuziga was not letting on to any feelings she was holding on the whole situation. I sat got tipsy but not drunk however after that day I had lost my friend. I don't know if it was the realization of what she had suspected to be true or the fact that after her coaching the relationship in the beginning it was still going. After that I'd find myself constantly defending myself from her antics. She would do anything from lie on me in my face to down right disrespect me. I didn't know how to handle the situation. I just knew you couldn't disrespect someone you loved mother and expect to still be in a relationship with them. I just kept my mouth shut until the day I thought I was pregnant. I went to Karin and told her the whole story how it started off with harmless flirting that Lamuziga kept eggin on. Plus now I'm pregnant. Fifteen minutes after Karin left my house I received a phone call. "Hello." I answered "Hey come down to my house for a minute." Lamuziga responded. Before I could respond I could hear her son "No, don't come!" He yelled in the distance then the phone call dropped. I didn't understand what was going on, unless Karin had told her what I had just said. I couldn't phantom my own sister betraying me in that manner. I sat there not sure of what to do. Lamuziga had never called me in all the years I had known her. I thought it would be best to just sit down and wait to see what was going on. The next couple of days I didn't see him so I went to her house. I mean I had to see my man. Plus I wasn't sure about the phone call it could have just been my guilty conscience. She could've been drunk and was just arguing or playing around and he just didn't want to see me. I walked in without leading to any indication of my possible pregnancy. I started drinking with Lamuziga as usual. Once I got good and tipsy I could see Lamuziga cutting her eyes at me. I finally had enough of ignoring her smart mouth antics all night; if it was going to happen it needed to pop off now. As soon as she cut her eyes at me I went for it. "What's wrong with you?" I asked calmly. "What?!" Lamuziga responded with a slight attitude. I maintained my composure because if she had heard about my suspected pregnancy, she had every right to be mad about this whole situation. "What's wrong with you? You been cutting your eyes at me all night." I politely inquired. "Well you know what my problem is, don't you?" She replied. My heart sank with that comment I knew she knew everything. I didn't know how to respond or if I wanted to respond at all. "You pregnant with my grandchild?!" She asked harshly. I sat there staring not really knowing how to respond to this entire situation. I was beginning to get mad at myself for even bringing the whole thing up. "Karin came over here and told us. She told us everything." I could hear the malice in her voice. 'Why the hell did Karin do this?' I thought. "So you pregnant with my grandbaby or what?" Her questioning continued. "I-I-I don't know." I manage to get out over my nerves. "So you keeping it or what?" Lamuziga asked. I knew she was always proud of her fifteen abortions and spoke of them like a badge of honor but I thought it was just murder. She knew that's how my sister and I felt about the situation. My sister and I had spoken to her in detail about this topic. I couldn't bare to go through this conversation any more. "I don't know." I answered "I don't know what you did to my son but he kept protecting you. My sister and I wanted to bring it to your fat ass but he kept arguing with us. He told us to mind our business! He's brother told him, he know how your family is." She stated. "Ya'll just trying to get this family name so bad. I'm not going to say anything because of my son but I'll tell you this, if that's my grandbaby, uh you'll see." Lamuziga said spitting toxins after every word. I stood my drunken butt up and headed toward the door. I couldn't take any more of this. I mean she had the right to defend her son. It was her motherly instincts that were kicking in. What could I say I was older than him. This is just a bad situation all the way around. "Taylor!" She shouted. I turned around with no fight in me. I didn't want to argue with her. "It would be a cute baby and all but I can't allow that, I just can't." I turned the door knob with no words and exited. The sad part was I had made up the whole story. I don't know why I guess it was my way of telling my older sister about my relationship without just blurting it out. I was in love and I wanted the whole world to know. The whole idea was a big ole' stupid mistake. I was too deep into the lie at this point I had to keep it going, for a little while at least. I walked into the house just to hear the key in the front door. I looked in his face without expression, I thought. "Don't worry about it." He said. I guessed I looked sad to him by the look of concern in his eyes.

But it wasn't sadness he saw, it actually was guilt. The guilt of starting all of this nonsense, for what; some attention from my sister. Just to tell her something I would've been better off keeping to myself. He sat on the edge of the bed and smiled at me. He was happy. I could see it in his eyes. He was actually happy. The thoughts of my deceit was getting the best of me. So I just began to kiss him. I just wanted to feel him inside of me. To take away the pain of the ugly truth. I could tell he wanted to make love to me. That was not what I wanted. I wanted him to fuck me. I wanted him to pound out every lie. I wanted him to punish me with his sex. He returned my kiss gently while smiling and rubbing my stomach. ' I shouldn't have done this.' I thought. I began aggressively kissing on his neck. Everytime he would touch my stomach I would smack his hand away. I grabbed the top of his box fade and snatch his head to the side. I licked along the nape of his neck so seductively. He still was kissing me softly. I'd had enough of this. I wrestled him down to the floor and jumped on top of him. While straddling him I could see the lust grow in his eyes. I wanted the lust to grow into animalistic passion. I knew the only way I could get him to do that is by making him prove his manhood. I forced his hands above his head as I grind on top of him licking his ears and sucking on his neck. He tried to move his hand, the moment I had been waiting for. I'd thrust his hands back down like I was in control. With that he flipped me over. Finally I thought. He started pulling my hair sucking my neck. I needed this. He entered my without restraint. The force made me let out a yelp. I could see the pride in his eyes from my reaction. He tightened his hand around my neck and began pulverizing my vagina. The harder he thrust the more I threw it back. The more I move the tighter he squeezed my neck. I couldn't take it anymore I was trying to hold out but my body began to tremble from within. "Oh, Oh!" I yelled out. However it came out sweet, soft and a little above a whisper. He collapsed on top of me. "Dang, what was that about?" He asked before he could finish the sentence I was all over him again. After the third time I finally was exhausted. I laid next to him panting trying to catch my breath. "That baby got you going." He said while smiling. I did a half smile and fell asleep. The next morning I woke up expecting him to be gone. I went into the bathroom. I heard the television but I went back to bed. Before I could go back to sleep he walked into my room. 'Guess he had fun last night.' I thought. "You know you can't keep this baby right." He said easily. I looked up from underneath the cover. Is he serious? "Huh?" I asked. "The baby, you can't keep it." He said again. I didn't like the conversation. I didn't like the way it started, I can't stand the direction in which it was headed, and I think I know where it is going to end up. I know I lied but what gives him the right to think he could tell me what to do. First his mother threaten me and now he is on his little rampage. And a worst thought entered my mind. What if last night was just to get the result that he wanted. So now he is manipulating and playing me. "Look let's just see what's going on first okay." I answered. "What is there to see?" He asked. "Please I don't feel well. " I said as I pulled the covers over my face. I mean it wasn't a complete lie. I didn't like the way this whole incident was playing out. "Ok, I'mma leave you alone for now but we going to have to discuss this." He walked out the room. I expected to hear the door close but I just heard the television again. 'Son- of-a-, he still didn't leave.' I thought. I fell back asleep. When I woke up he was sitting on the couch eating some left over chicken. It was mid day. "You feel better" He asked "A little." I answered. "I'm not going to start with you. Are you hungry?" He asked. I shook my head no. He glanced at me out the corner of his eyes. I could see the concern. What he didn't know was that I was sleeping off my hangover like I usually did. Plus I like the attention he was giving me. I sat on the couch. He moved from the loveseat to sit on the couch next to me. He fell asleep with his head on my lap while watching television. I must've fell asleep as well because I opened my eyes just as the front door was closing. I was starving I stood up and went to the kitchen to grab something to eat. I knew I was going to have to fake a miscarriage really soon. He was staying out all night catering to me. I felt lousy. I didn't come around for a couple of weeks. I had to make it look good. Thank goodness he came just like I had scheduled in my mind. I had just started my period. He walked in, I looked at him and pretended as if I was fighting back tears. "I lost the baby." I said above a whisper. He spun around I could see the disappointment in his eyes. "When?" He asked. "The other day." I replied. He sat down and looked like he might cry for second. I sat on the couch beside him not breaking character. I thought I might actually cry. Probably because I was so disgusted with myself. He sat beside me and started rubbing my back. "You alright." He asked. "Yea." I answered. He took my short responses as me hiding my hurt. What he didn't know was that I couldn't say too much because I was afraid he was going to figure out my lies. He sat on the couch and I curled up beside him. I pretended to fall asleep. I heard him get up and leave. I was so happy that was over. I'd vow to never do that again. I eased my way back to Lamuziga house and thought I had eased my way back into her good graces. Time went on and I began to notice the big difference in Lamuziga's attitude. She never told me I couldn't come over but I knew things would never be the same. I guess I was the one to blame. Plus this unethical relationship was getting rocky. The whole family knew about the relationship which was becoming somewhat of a hardship for him. He was constantly defending himself in front of his friends and others for being in love with this oversized girl. I knew it was hard for him. I just wanted him to come to me and we could work things out together but instead he began to alienate me. He treated me as if he was in love with the enemy. We would have sex and soon thereafter he would call me names like fat bitch, slow, or anything else degrading that would come to his mind. I had enough of his behavior and decided to call it quits. Once I did that I found out how unhappy I was without him. I knew that one day he could love me the way I wanted him too. I could see it in his eyes but it wasn't today. Once I had broken all ties from him I started my first year at Onondaga Community College. I was an official college student. I needed that, to be doing something with my time other than drinking all the time. One day after school I walked down to his building. I stood in 1809's lobby talking and watching whatever ghetto movie that was playing outside. It was always some sort of show going on. Either they were fighting, arguing, or dancing but either way I was always thoroughly entertained. This tall chocolate guy walked in. He was easy on the eyes but not up my alley. I mean the brother was too dark for me. He always walked the street with his significantly shorter, lighter and younger counterpart. These two were the best of friends and inseparable. I stood there looking to see what these two were going to bring to the buildings entertainment for the night. They stood there watching me as I told jokes. I thought perhaps Lamuziga was bedding one of them but it wasn't my business. They watched as I told jokes all night. I glanced upward to catch the chocolate one smiling. He had the stellar dimples that I love soo much. I always thought people with dimples were that much pretty than other people. It's like God left a permanent kiss on both cheeks before they left heaven which they get to carry the rest of their life. I may have mentioned that before. Plus his hair was braided back and he had a chest to die for. I turned my attention back to my task of being a clown. "Yo, is those pictures?" He asked "Um, yea." I answered a bit startled by the question. "Can I see them?" He asked. I started to hand the pictures over with my heart racing. I did not want to be the butt of anyone's jokes tonight. As he was taking the pictures out of my hands he began to speak. "These pictures are of your baby or something?" "No, of me." I answered as he pulled the pictures out of their Wal-mart packets. He flipped through each set of pictures without a word. As he was handing them back he began to speak again. " What, are you a model or something?" He asked. "No, I just figured my sisters was taking pictures of their kids, so why not take pictures of myself while I was there." I answered. After handing the pictures back he stood up as he was about to push the big metal door that was painted green he turned around to speak again. "They nice. My name is Conor by the way." He stated. I smiled as he and the younger boy headed out the building and up the hill. "Thanks." I spat out right before the door closed. I was so happy he didn't start making fun of my pictures. I continued with life as usual until I got a knock at the door. "Who!" I yelled running towards the door. I wanted it to be my baby. I had missed him so much. I still continued to go to Lamuziga house but I would never even look in his direction. I figured things was best the way that they were. "Young Skizz." The voice replied. "Who?!" I asked again. "Young Skizz." I looked through the peephole to see a small child about nine years old standing in the hallway. I knew he ran with the chocolate boy Conor. I opened the door. I could see that one day he would be an attractive young man he had natural hazel eyes along with a joyous smile. "Yes." I said "Well, I like you but my dick is small; but I'd be good to you." He responded. I stuck my head out the door to look towards the staircase leading to the front of the building. Was this some type of joke? "What?" I asked baffled. "I want to be with you." He replied. I grabbed my house keys off the black dining room table. "Let's go." I said in a motherly tone. I walked downstairs out the building. I searched every lobby to find the two boys. I'd finally seen one of them in 1809. "Come on." I yelled to the little boy still in my motherly voice. I walked inside the building and stood in front of the light skin boy that be with Conor. " What's your name?" I asked. "Chingy." he stated."Ok, hi I'm Taylor. Tell him what you just knocked on my door and said to me." I instructed Young Skizz. The little boy put his head down with embarrassment. "Well he told me that his dick is little but he like me and would like to fuck me." I responded without skipping a beat. "Ewe Skizz you did that shit!" He asked in amazement. "Ewe! Why you said ewe. I'm beautiful. By the way y'all better put that little motherfucker on a lease or something." I said while walking out the building. I could hear Chingy laughing uncontrollably as I trotted back up the hill. Once I got in the house I had to chuckle just a little bit at the situation. I had cooked dinner and got in the bed I had school in the morning. I'd awaken with my day going the same way it always did. I barely had enough money for bus fare and there was no food in the house. By the time I made it home I knew I would enjoy my pack of Ramen Noodles and hot dogs. I was about to put a pot of water on the stove when I heard a knock at the door. I just knew it was my baby. I looked through the peephole. Nope I was wrong again this time it was Chingy. I wasn't in the mood for their nonsense tonight. I opened my door but before I could ask him what he wanted he proceeded into the house. "May I help you?" I asked. "You smoke?" He asked. I had just picked up the habit of smoking weed. "Yea." I said. "Well I came to spark you up." He stated. "Why?" I asked. "Because I want you to make me laugh." He responded. "What I look like some type of clown to you?" I asked in joking tone. He sat on the couch and began to break up the weed on the coffee table. We sat there laughed and joked all night. He fell asleep on the couch. I went to the linen closet and got him a sheet. I threw the sheet over him. I walked into my room closed the door and went to sleep. I got up took a shower and headed off to school. I left him a little note that asked him to make sure the slam lock was on when he left. When I got home from school I was pleased to see that I could trust him. Nothing was missing or out of place. As the day grew into night I heard the familiar tap at the door it was Chingy again. We got high and told jokes. This time he got up and left before he fell asleep. On the third night I couldn't wait for the knock. This time it was Chingy, Conor, and Young Skizz. Conor walked in as if he was surveillaning his surroundings. After he did a mental inventory of his environment he began to speak. " I just wanted to see where my man was spending so much time." He said. I was a little nervous about the whole situation. It just seemed weird. "He's just trying to figure out why I spend so much time up here that's all Taylor." Chingy said. I guess he could see the fear on my face. I didn't wanna refuse to smoke so I took a pull. I began to relax after a while. I began telling my normal jokes by the end of the night we were all sitting there telling jokes on each other. By the way Conor stood up, I could tell he was the one in charge. "Yo, we'll be back." He said through giggles. The door closed behind them. I sat on the couch still slightly giggling to myself until I fell asleep. I had stopped going to school regularly. I was just having too much fun. I had meet a couple of girls at school who all smoked weed. They knocked on the door early enough in the day to jump start me with a massive high. We sat around smoking all day. As they walked out the door I couldn't help but to vow to return to school the next day. As soon as I sat down, the knock came. Yea, it was my buddies. I opened the door as they piled into the house. They started to roll up as I sat there really too high to ingest any more weed but they kept me company. I told jokes until I fell asleep on the leather loveseat. I'd turned over sticking to the couch. Oh how I hated sleeping on leather. Just then a thought popped in my head. I had left those three boys in my house. My body jerked up right. I could see through the flickering light from the low sounding television. All three of them were sleep on the couch. I had to laugh because Wren foot was dag-gone in Conor's mouth. The only thing he had to do was turn his head ever so slightly. I got up to take a string and run it across Conors face so he could turn around and eat Chingy foot, but I opted against it. I continued into my room. I laid across my bed. I was still kinda concern about leaving them in the living room but they seemed like good boys. I awaken to laughter in the living room. I grabbed my watch to see what time it was. Almost one o'clock in the afternoon. I know they not still here. I couldn't help but to be happy. I had company at least for a little while I thought. I walked into the bathroom took a shower. Once I entered into the living room it was all types of fast food containers on the coffee table. 'They left and came back.' I thought. Someone passed me the weed. We started our normal joke routine. After a while I was hungry. I didn't want to eat in front of them. I was so happy when Conor stood up and told them they had to go get this money. I wasn't quite sure what that meant. I was beginning to think they sold drugs. I mean they always had money. None of them had a job. I figure it was a safe assumption. As soon as they left I made some cheese eggs and toast. By the time my meal was done there was a knock at the door. They had returned. Our routine repeated itself for days, then the days turned into weeks. The next thing I had known it was a whole month. One day I stood in the kitchen and came to the realization that I had drug dealers living with me. Soon came the knocks at the door. It was all their "licks". Licks were crackheads coming to retrieve drugs. This scared me. I didn't want the cops to come and knock on my door. Or worst kick my door in. I didn't know how to handle this, it was all so new to me. Plus things had started to heat back up between me and my little boo. Lamuziga didn't mind all of the boys being in my house because her and her sister was entertaining them on a personal level. As I was sitting in Lamuziga's house my baby walked up to me spitting some rap song he personally wrote. "I thought you were the shit but my friends told me otherwise, then I found out you was messing with those other guys." He recited. I couldn't have him believing I was involved with them on that level. The whole situation was getting out of hand. I needed an escape. I enjoyed their company. They made my days shorter and my nights filled with laughter but they were sleeping with all my friends. Which made no difference to me but I knew everyone would question my loyalty when they found out about the other girls. Plus I just couldn't get over the "licks" knocking on the door all day and all times of the night. I was growing increasingly concerned. I began to pray. 'Lord please help me.' I'd think often. I didn't want them to be mad at me but at the same time

I could see my whole life spiraling out of control. I went to school. I'd taken a test that I thought was pretty easy. I'd thought I'd done good and got a D-. Wait, what. I was always good in school. I reviewed the test of other classmates. They test answers was not as in-depth as mine. After the class quieted down, I raised my hand immediately. "Yes." Mrs. Coaster responded. "I would like to discuss my grade please." I responded. "We can address any issues after class." She answered. I sat there impatiently waiting. When class was over I walked over to her desk. "I think my grade is unfair." I spat out, not withholding my contempt. "Well you think you can get through school with your charisma and Brandon thinks he can get through on his charm and good looks. Well not in this class!" She stated matching my contemptment. "Well did you know that Brandon was in the Air Force and was topped ranked. So he is using that scholarship along with his basketball scholarship in order to get an education to help raise his daughter. By the way I have bust my butt to remain on the honor roll. I have achieved this except for in your class. I have very little money and I hardly ever have food but I take what little I have in order to obtain a bus pass just to come to school. Every since I have had the misfortune of taking your class my GPA has dropped considerably. I know that the classes you teach is mandatory because of my major but you have no right to just screw me over because you don't like my "charisma"". With that I went to my guidance counselors' office to complain. I brought along the other test scores that were higher than mine but answers was lacking content. At first they tried to find problems with my work but they had to admit there was something a miss with the papers. After they heard what she had to say about me and Brandon they started making her grade on a curve. She no longer was allowed to look at the names of the students before the grade was handed out. This was the only way the school would be able to know she was being impartial. I was no longer as hyped about getting an education. Plus I had bigger things to worry about like when will the police come a knocking. I needed a miracle. 'Lord, please help me' I thought as I had done many times before. The next week Conor came into the house with someone new. It was another young boy. I expressed my concern about the new random guy, but Conor thought I was just jealous of the new addition to "the family". I tried to assure him that I was not like that he just didn't strike me as a good person. I would later be proven right. The next week I heard a banging at the door. I jumped up off the couch my clothes were half way off. I screamed for the person at the door to come in. I wanted whoever it was to see this disrespectful little boy in action of pulling up his pants. I opened the door. Young Skizz was standing there. "What's going on, in here?" He asked slightly amused by the scene. My response did not have a hint of humor. "Why don't you ask him?" I yelled. Young Skizz looked at my face and could tell I was upset. "Tell Conor y'all have to go!" I shouted as I walked into my room. My house phone rang. "Hello." I stated. "Taylor, what happened?" Conor asked. When I heard Conor voice my heart began skipping numerous beats. I didn't want to deal with this. Plus I didn't want to deal with any repercussion of my decision. "Look y'all have to go." I managed to blurt out. "What! What happened?" He asked again. "You know what happened." I said then I slammed the phone down. My thoughts began to race. I know when they left the girl house down the street they had destroyed her apartment according to ghetto gossip wheel. I didn't want that. I hurried up and called Lamuziga. I awaited the knock at the door. I knew they respected her and plus one of them was sleeping with her so they would be less likely to act up with her there. Lamuziga walked in seconds before they came. I opened the door and sat on the couch beside her. "Yea, you better had called her." Conor walked in and said. I heard them in the front bedroom tearing up the furniture. I sat on the couch as if I didn't hear anything. I knew Conor was waiting for me to come and see what was going on but I pretended like I couldn't hear anything. I felt bad really I did but I just couldn't have people selling drugs from my house and now with these new boys anything was possible. As Conor was walking to the front door he stopped by the table and deliberately knocked down a chair. I just looked at him. I was hurt by his actions but I knew he was hurt by mines. We weren't around each other that long but we were all close. It was like I was putting my brother and his friend out. I had secretly grew a crush on Conor. My actions just made everything better this way. I knew they were going to be okay. Once the front door slammed Lamuziga and I ran into the front room to see the damage. The bed was flipped and the wicker chairs were turned upside down. It wasn't that bad. I guess that's when I heard Chingy telling Conor not to do that. He probably jumped on his back, wrapped his arms around his neck and started wrestling with him, to make him stop. He was good for doing things like that. I closed the room door, then Lamuziga headed back to the couch. She offered to help me clean up the mess but I was too hurt to deal with anymore of this today. We walked to A-Plus gas station to grabbed our St. Ides 22oz cans of beer. I got drunk. Lamuziga and I talked about the whole situation extensively. She was so upset at the way they did the first bedroom. I wouldn't reply at all. I kinda felt as though I deserved it in some way. I mean I knew we could work everything out if I just had a conversation, but it was just too much riding on our friendship. Plus I was going to miss the dogs they had at my house. I sat there reminiscing on the day they walked in with all of these pitbulls. I ran to the bathroom and locked myself in there. Conor was turning the knob demanding that I come out and meet the animals. I had no intentions on that whatsoever. I kept yelling through the door. "I can stay in here all day!" They laughed so hard until Chingy finally suggested bringing the dogs in one at a time. On different days of course. I waited until I could hear no sounds or whimpering, howling, or barking then I exited the bathroom. I sat on the couch watching television when Conor walked in with the cutest black and white puppy. "He's yours if you want him." he stated as he sat on the couch beside me. My first instinct was no until he looked at me with those big ole' soft puppy dog eyes. I just shook my head yes. I'd named him little shit, because he was the runt of the litter. Conor named him something like annihilator. That dog followed me all through the house. I would let him sit on the couch and eat whatever I ate. I didn't know that was not a good idea. I always seen kids on television feed their dogs food off their plate. He got worms and had to be put to sleep, They snuck in when I was sleeping and took the sick dog to have him put to sleep. As I glossed over our days and nights in my mind. My baby walked over to me with concern in his eyes. "You alright." He asked with empathy. I just shook my head yes. I saw Conor standing on top of the hill by my house but I wasn't going to deal with them today. I took the long way home through the parking lot. Young Skizz seen me walking around the building to the front door. My heart almost stopped. I just knew he was going to alert them of my presence. To my delight he turned back around as if he didn't see me. I walked in the building and up the stairs. I could see this may be a bigger problem than I had anticipated. I put the key in the door hurriedly as if they were walking up the steps behind me. I pushed the door open with speed and force. I slammed it immediately behind me. I let out a sigh of relief as I hit the couch. The moment I sat down I heard the knock at the door. My heart was racing. I stood up to creep to the peephole. I glance through the peephole. I'd seen my baby standing on the other side of the door. I opened it quickly. From the moment he walked in I felt protected. I knew he wasn't a fighter like that but at least he was there. I could see the hurt in his eyes. Even though he had come to protect me he felt as though I had really been sleeping with them. I kissed him as passionately as I could. I wasn't sure if he could tell whether or not I had been with anyone since him but I was sure going to try and show him. As the sweat beaded off my face in the throes of passion I heard a knock at the door. I kept going as if I didn't hear anything. He must've heard it too because he stopped in mid stroke and I could see the hurt in his eyes reappear. He began inserting himself so hard I wanted to scream. I could tell he was trying to hurt me. I could see the rage in his eyes with each thrust. Once he was done he got up, dressed himself and walked out the door. I didn't know how to fix it. I didn't know if he was going to let me. I cried at the thought of losing him. I cried myself to sleep. I'd spent the next couple of weeks trying not to be face to face with Conor. Screaming I love you to Chingy and Young Skizz whenever I had seen them alone. Every time Conor would see me it would be seconds after I was close enough to be in his reach which meant he could only yell obscenities to me. I'd made my way to school finally. I guess things were back to normal. I'd have my secret rendezvous with my baby. Now graduation was approaching. Lana had started college with me this year. I still had to take Mrs. Coaster class to finish my degree being that she was the only one who taught what I was matriculated in. I just walked in did my class work and accepted whatever grade she issued me. When Mrs. Coaster walked in the classroom I immediately took my seat looked at the front of the class with anticipation of learning. The guy next to me asked if I had gotten my cap and gown already. I told him no not yet, I'd go today. I was feeling great! By the time I had gotten to my final class I received a note stating I should report to the guidance counselor's office. I left the classroom scared. The last time I was asked to come to the office it was because my favorite cousin had died. Plus I had nothing but bad memories about any school office. I walked over to my guidance counselor's door. "Oh hi, Mrs. Coaster requested to be your guidance counselor. I hope you didn't mind I turned you over to her." She stated. "When did she do this?" I inquired. "Today, she really wanted to talk to you about something." She replied. 'What does she want?' I thought as I walked over to her door. I knocked and entered upon her command. "Well hello there." She said with enthusiasm. "Hi." I responded puzzled. "Well I couldn't help but overhear your conversation in class today." She continued. "I'm sorry; I'd only answered his question because I didn't want to seem rude." I said defensively. I mean really where the hell was this going? "No, that's alright. I understand. You have become a good student as far as not talking in class." She said. "Thank you." I replied. "Whelp, it seems we have a little problem here. From my understanding you think you are graduating this year that is not the case." She stated. I was confused by her statement. "Huh." was all I could manage to get out. "For the human service field you have to do two field studies and you have not done that yet." She continued. "What is a field study?" I asked worriedly. "That is when you work in a social work setting as a volunteer in order to learn, what we cannot teach in a classroom. Things like empathy, compassion etc." She stated. "Well I have that already but I can do both of them next semester." I added. "I'm not saying that you do not have those qualities Taylor, but it is something that some people need help with. However there is a problem. You can only do one field study a semester. Being that you are full time student they will not allow you to even try to do two field studies in one semester. You have to do a certain amount of credited hours in order to complete each course study. It is just too much. Unfortunately you would have to do one field study next semester and the other one the following semester. So you won't be able to graduate until after the January semester." She finished. I stood up from the desk and walked out of her office. She tried to follow me to tell me that she was just concerned about me. What she didn't know was that I had just figured out how she manipulated my guidance counselor in order to be the one to tell me this horrible news. My guidance counselor didn't know about me going to Mrs. Coaster superiors in the past so it was easy to pass the buck on some bad news like that. This woman was taking pleasure in my defeat. I left school that day never to return again. I knew I would have to take her class at least two more times in order to complete my degree. I also knew I would break her fucking neck if I ever encounter her again. I got off the bus just in time to see Conor. 'Just my luck I thought'. Surprisingly he let me walk past him without much taunting or torment. I walked right back out my house to Lamuziga's house. It seemed she wasn't feeling me all that much. I was about to leave when I heard the key in her front door. I was hoping it was my baby. He walked in then a girl from his school followed him. She sat on the couch and spoke to me. Was I in the fucking twilight zone? My hands were tied I wasn't going to be able to say anything without exposing us. He positioned himself on the couch leaning behind her, with his arm extended around her to start playing his playstation game. She was giggling at his gesture. I mean she had every right to be gitty; he was practically playing the game with her sitting on his lap. I tried my best to bat-back the tears as I left the house. I walked up the hill with tears streaming from eyes. I didn't care who seen me crying. By the time I got to the front of my building I was distraught. I walked in the house fell face first on the couch and cried myself to sleep. I awoken to see that someone had placed some type of notice under my door. I received a pay or vacate notice from the rental office. I had three days to pay my rent or vacate the premises. I looked at the time. It wasn't five o'clock yet maybe I had time to get to the rental office. I walked to the rental office to talk to them. They were unsympathetic to the fact that I was just asking for an extension. They stated they had already started the court proceedings. I would have to pay the lawyer fees along with back rent. They also told me if I could work out something with the lawyer then that's fine with them but at this point it was out of their hands. I went to court and spoke with the lawyer. He agreed to help me of course if I paid his fees and the late fee along with whatever rent I owed. I had to give almost all of my next month check in order to stay in the apartment. The phone went off and the lights had gone off when Conor and them was here. The cable probably was going to go off next but I wasn't going to complain I didn't have the energy to. The man that I loved had a new girl; that was my main focus. I brought myself a new outfit from Label Shoppers got dressed and headed to Lamuziga's house. I couldn't stay in the house by myself any longer. I wanted my baby back but I wasn't going to push the issue. He was young and deserved to be with someone closer to his age. I knew that fact, but my heart just wouldn't let me stop loving him. I tried to avoid all eye contact with him. Then I kept my distance as much as possible. I laid on the other side of Lamuzinga. I had fell asleep watching television. I felt the familiar pulsating wetness that I had become accustomed too. I opened my eyes and felt someone inside of me. My vision finally focused on him. Was he fucking crazy? I could hear Lamuzinga snoring beside me. My whole body froze. He had lost every bit of his damn mind. I just layed there silent. I was trying to even soften the thump of my heart beat. Lamuziga was still snoring. He pulled up his shorts and climbed off me. As soon as he made it to his feet Lamuziga turned over opened her eyes slightly and asked him was he going to bed. I thought I was going to die. She was sleep again in seconds. I fell asleep bewildered and happy. I had my baby back! When I woke up the next morning he walked passed me as if nothing had happened. He had the phone glued to his face laughing and giggling with the girl from his school. I felt hurt and used. I left and walked up the hill to my house. I wasn't going back down there again. I had it in my mind, that the next time he came over I was going to ask for my key back. If he ever came over again. My girlfriends from school came over often and we would have smoking sessions. One day finally it all came to a head. I'd cut back on the smoking being that I no longer attended school. All of my smoking buddies stop coming by. Except for one person. I guess they felt as though they didn't want to be a dropout like me. I'd been in my bedroom watching television. I heard the key in the door. 'I wasn't going to have this' I'd thought. My conversation left me when he began touching me. I had so much I wanted to say. I had it all planned out. I was supposed to let him have it. However what I found out was that he was not giving me up. Not from the trail of kisses he was leaving all over my body. My lust stifled my common sense. I couldn't stop it nor did I want to. By the time he left I was in love like I had been for all the years prior. That was a mistake. His infidelity was now something that I was very much aware of. It seem like whenever he got mad he threw all of his cheating in my face, by calling girls in front of me. Parading them around me whenever he could via pictures, letters, or any things else he could come up with. I was humiliated daily by his words, thoughts, and deeds but I dare not mention it. I felt as though, it was my fault had I not been cooped up in the house with those boys he would have never had the image of me cheating on him seared in his head. If I had to guess in time he would see that I am not that kind of female, but it didn't work out that way. The relationship was going from bad to worst. I kept thinking the more sex we had, that he had to love me deep down inside. I came up with the plan to get pregnant. This way we would never break up. I walked up to him and began lying immediately. "I'm pregnant." I said with fear draining from my voice. I knew he thought the fear would be in anticipation of his reaction, but in reality the fear was from him seeing through my lie and leaving me for good. "No you not." Was his only reply as he walked away. He said it with so much confidence that I knew he knew the truth. However I kept the lie going for about two months. One day while his mother was at work we started up. The passion was intensified. At that point I had come the realization that perhaps I really was pregnant. After our sex session was over he turned around and said nonchalantly "In nine months you'll be a mother." I turned around. I couldn't believe it I had won. He gave me my baby. I also thought this could work out because he would be eighteen in a couple of months. 'Yes, yes, yes!' I thought as I went to the bathroom to wash up. I fell asleep on the bed only to be awaken by his sweet familiar touch. Again I thought. This time was better than the first time. His mother was walking in just as we finished up. I could hear the outside door downstairs. He and I ran across the room straighten everything up as best we could in the few seconds we had. It took everything in us to keep our hands off each other that night. As soon as his mother hit the door for work it was go time. We were all over each other again. The entire day we commensurated our love. It felt as though he was insatiable. This time however he timed when his mother was coming home. At our designated cut off time I could still see the passion in his eyes. I woke up the next morning feeling nausea but I didn't pay that any mind. It was Saturday! Time to get my drink on with my girl. I'd spent the entire night drinking even though the first sip made me queasy. He was sitting up under me all night. I really wasn't in the mood for all that, for the first time in our relationship. I actually didn't want him near me; at all. Everytime he would speak I would suck my teeth. I kept glancing at him from the side of my eyes but the usually sensation of admiration wasn't there I wanted to walk over and slap him. The next day I'd awaken with a little more tolerance for him. I was still drunk from the night before. I started my usual playing around. I jumped on his little twin brother bike and took off in the middle of the street. I dropped the bike when I felt a sharp pain in my side. I almost fell over. I stumbled but I caught myself. I could hear him laughing but I let out a big yelp! "Owe!" I could see his face change. I screamed again "Ooowww!, Fuck Ooowww!" I sat down on the step next to his mother. Now the look of concern was on both of their faces. Sweat starting pouring from my face. My heart was beating fast. I sat there trying to regain my composure. I was embarrassed. I could hear them both asking me was I alright. Even though I was shaking my head yes, I felt like I was going to pass out at any moment. The pain subsided. I stayed over there for a while. But I was beginning to hate him. Even his breathing was aggravating. It hit me all of sudden. I had originally taken my foul attitude towards him as me about to start my period but it hadn't come last month and I was late this month. I rushed home immediately. I lived right across the street from the health center. I knew I had to make a doctor's appointment. I couldn't wait. I went into walk in care. I told my primary care physician that I was pregnant. She took a urine sample but it came back negative. I walked out feeling disappointed. She had told me that if I had just become pregnant it wouldn't show up on a urine test and to come back in a couple of weeks. I looked for my period for the next two weeks. It never came. I walked into the doctor's office excited. I took another urine test. It came back negative. My doctor told me that I was not pregnant and by now it would have shown up, but I could come back in two more weeks. The next two weeks was torture. His little brother and sister birthday was coming. Since I was their Godmother I had to do something nice for them. I had been lollygagging all day. I was looking for the perfect decorations and gift. I realize they would be home from school really soon. I left Shop City and rushed to their house. I rang the buzzer but he didn't answer. So I leaned on the buzzer and didn't stop until he ran down the steps to answer the door. As I walked up the steps I was disappointed because he didn't offer to help me with the bags. As I walked up the stairs his rants became more audible and profound. I didn't understand why he was so mad. I knew it was because I was laying on the bell but I only did that because I thought he was sleep and I was in a rush. I tried to calm him down by asking him to help me with the decoration. He started slamming things and rolling his eyes at me. I knew I had to get away from him. I cleared the dining room table and placed the decorative tablecloth on the table. I added the matching plates and cups along with the children gifts. I placed the cake in the middle as the centerpiece. I was moving as fast as I could. I just had to get away from him. He was working my last nerve with his mouth. Once I got everything set up I grabbed my things to walk out the door. He came out his room still talking smack. "Fat bitch!" He said loud enough for me to hear. I turned around in my ghetto stand with attitude to match. "What!" I yelled sarcastically. "You heard me! Fat BITCH!" He yelled back. I started to go off yelling all types of irrational shit. I knew I had hit him below the belt and that was exactly what I was looking for. I turned around to gloat in my moment of triumph. I heard the palm of his hand connecting to my back. The smack was loud and intended to harm. I turned around and fell out laughing. I knew he had hit me with all of his might but it didn't hurt. The absence of pain tickled me. He grabbed me and tossed me on the couch. I could see it in his eyes that he wanted to hit me. I was laughing so hard that he just shook his head and walked away. "You're CRAZY, you know that right!" Was his reply as he walked in his room. At that point I was laughing so hard tears was streaming from my eyes. I'd stood at the bus stop still laughing at him. Once I got home I felt a slight stinging in my back. I stood up and walked over to a mirror. As I stood in front of the bathroom mirror I turned my body slightly so I could see my back. I slowly pulled up my shirt. The black and blue bruise on my back was no laughing matter. It seemed that the hit was really all that it had sounded to be. I kept turning from side to side to see the whole bruise. I had come to the realization that I was pregnant and the doctor didn't know what she was talking about a long time ago, but I hadn't banked on the fact that I could no longer feel physical pain with this pregnancy. I wanted to put my theory to the test. I walked down Genessee St by Syracuse University Campus. I entered the tattoo parlor. I'd told them I wanted a tattoo. They let me see a book of tattoos that they had done. I knew that wasn't going to work. I didn't want a tattoo that someone else had. So the man sent me to the wall. There were many symbols of tattoos they could perform. I didn't see anything I liked so I just picked out a heart with a rose through it. I thought it was too common but I had to see if my theory was correct. I mean from the bruise on my back I should've crumbled in pain when he hit me. And it did sound that bad, so why was I unaffected. I sat down in the waiting area with the image I wanted embedded in my mind. I picked up the magazines on the table in the waiting area. I began flipping through impatiently. In one magazine was a beautiful picture of a comic. There was a sexy girl holding a gun. I told the tattoo artist my reasoning for getting the tattoo. He was reluctant to do it. He kept asking me that if I'm getting a tattoo to piss my boyfriend off that it was not a good idea. I was so frustrated with his lecturing. I had to explain to him that if I was getting my boyfriends name then try to talk me out of it, but this is just something I always wanted and never had the balls to do. I sat there getting the tattoo without even flinching. The punk that I am for pain I couldn't believe none of these many different needles affected me at all. I left the tattoo parlor feeling excited about this new no pain thing. I went back the next week to get a tongue ring. I'd always wanted a tongue ring because people told me that it enhanced oral sex for men. I sat there twitching. I was nervous about the pain I should be feeling but it was over within minutes with not much pain attached. I'd been doing so much ripping and running after my last confrontation with my boyfriend. I was done with him. I had a life to live and he was not going to be a part of it, and if he was, he was going to have to fly right. No cheating, lying, verbal, mental, or emotional abuse. As I sat on the bus gathering a game plan over my life it dawned on me that I had not gotten my period. I couldn't wait to go to the doctor. I jumped off the bus I was on and took the next bus to the health center. Once in walk-in care I told them I needed a pregnancy test. My doctor was willing to see me, so they said it shouldn't be a problem. They gave me a urine test that came back negative as I sat and waited to talk to the doctor I was a bundle of nerves. "Hello there." She stated with a smile. "Hi" I replied still nervous. "Well you're not pregnant." She repeated not knowing the nurse had already spilled the beans. "I haven't gotten my period this month." I replied. "Well it could be stress, are you under a lot pressure?" She asked. "No." I responded disappointedly. I guess she could hear the disappointment in my voice. She interjected with a positive spin on things. "Or perhaps it is just too early to tell." She added. I nodded to keep from her hearing the crackle in my voice. I went home and weighed the pro's and con's of the situation. I never had to deal with him again. I could tell him I'd had a miscarriage. I would go back in two weeks like she suggested just to make sure. I walked around for two weeks in anticipation of my future doctor's appointment. Every morning I jumped up to check for my cycle it still hadn't come. As I walked into the doctor's office I was confident that they were going to tell me that I was pregnant. The doctor walked in and informed me again that I was not pregnant and maybe it was still too early to detect the pregnancy. I left feeling as though she was wrong. I knew I was pregnant but I'd made the appointment for two weeks later as suggested by her once again. I went thru the same thing for the next two weeks. Checking for my menstruation, pacing, and being impatient. The night before my doctor's appointment my boyfriend came in with his key. I looked at him with disgust. He walked over and sat on the couch. I went in my room as if he was not even there. I heard my front door soon after. I wondered if he left my key. So I hopped off the bed and walked into the living room to see. I'd glanced on the table and kitchen counters but it wasn't there. He could throw it away for all that I care. His leaving was a bonus because I didn't have to tell him about my doctor's appointment. I could just get up and get ready for my appointment and be out the house without incident. I'd awaken with nothing on my mind but finally finding out that I am pregnant. I got to the doctor's office in record timing. I didn't want anybody to see me going inside. Only because it was a little town and somebody would have started asking me questions. I felt as though I had evaded enemy territory once I got inside the health center. I signed in for my appointment sat down and waited for my name to be called. Once I was in the examination room I waited for my doctor to enter with my test results. When the door opened I looked up with anticipated glee. "Well sorry Taylor, you are not pregnant. Are you trying to get pregnant?" She asked. "Um, no I actually haven't had sex in a couple of months." I stated. "Well why do you think your pregnant?" She wondered. "Because I haven't had my period in two or three months and we planned it. I replied knowing I was lying about the last part. "Have you ever heard of something called a psychosomatic pregnancy?" She asked calmly. 'Did this bitch just call me crazy!' I thought. "Yes, I am fully aware of a psychosomatic pregnancy." I answered with as much patience I could mustard. "What is it?" She asked still with the smile on her face that I used to think was a term of endearment now I know it's condescending intent. 'Not only is this bitch calling you crazy, she is also calling you a liar and stupid.' I pushed those thoughts to the back of my mind and answered the question. "It's when you think you're pregnant but you're not, it's all in your mind." I answered. "Yes, sometimes we can want something so bad our mind just tricks our body into developing the symptoms. It can seem very real, but it is a part of our imagination." She explained. I hopped off the examination table and grab my clothes to begin getting dress. "Listen I'm not crazy, there is one thing that I have been able to count on my whole life and that is my period coming on time every month! If I'm not getting a period then I'm pregnant it just that simple." I continued to get dress in front of her with no regards of her seeing my anatomy. "There could be other medical problems that could cause this as well." She stated. I rolled my eyes and walked out the examination room down the hall, out the building, across the street. 'Other medical problems I thought. humph. Why didn't she say that before she automatically assumed I was crazy. Who the hell did this woman think she was. I mean really.' My thoughts trailed off as I began approaching my building. I needed to speak as minimum as possible to these people and keep it moving. I got up the stairs and sat down on the couch. I heard the key go inside the lock. The door opened. 'What was he doing here. He should be in school.' I thought. I really wasn't in the mood for any of this. Not right now. He walked in the kitchen open the refrigerator. I heard the refrigerator door close back. He came and sat on the couch beside me. I went to stand up. I wanted to go in my room. I just didn't have the energy. "So you just going to keep leaving every time I come around." He asked. "No" I replied softly. He didn't know I was weaken. My fight for us was dwindling. I tried to love him. I tried to be what he needed, but perhaps he was just too young for this type of commitment. That's why they have laws against the shit. He wasn't ready and being that I was young and naive mentally, I thought we were on the same level. However he couldn't be the man I wanted him to be because he was not yet a man."Well I had a talk with one of the brothers today and they told me it's my job as a man to teach my son the mathematics. So you are going to have to learn them too." He interjected. I wasn't smart enough to learn the five percent way of life. Those people were so intelligent, I thought at the time. But I was happy to please him. I was happy he was showing me a part of his world that I never had been allowed to be introduced to. "How do you know its a boy. It could be a girl?" I said with a bright smile. "I just know." He replied. I sat there listening to him talk for hours some of the information I retained but a lot of it went in one ear and out the other. Until he told me that he was aware that I wasn't paying attention. I eventually fell asleep while he was still talking. I awaken to him sleeping on the bed beside me. It was late I woke him up so that he could go home. To my surprise he got up and asked what I was cooking for dinner. I began to cook. I told him I needed to get a job for the baby. We had to be good parents. I didn't expect much from him because of his age. I knew I would have to carry this family on my back. Time was creeping by slowly; and that I was thankful for. I had found a job in a factory. It didn't pay much but it was something to put on my resume. He began spending more and more time drilling me. Teaching the mathematics for the day. The number one through seven were the most important. I had to acknowledge the man, he was the head of household. That the women was wisdom and children brought on understanding. It was number seven that I had a problem swallowing. It stated that the black man was godbody. That the black man was the original being. It was a bunch of racist talk against multiple religions or races. I didn't want to be hatred filled but I wanted him to love me. I wanted him to know that I would support anything that he laid before me. How could I forget the one true living God, my precious Lord and savior Jesus Christ who died on the cross for me. I began to rationalize the things I was being taught. Some things I would internalized other things I would just dismissed. He set there day in and day out teaching how to hate. How to dislike or distrust different races, cultures, and unbeknownst to me God. The real God. The same God that I knew personally, the one who had saved me and helped me time and time again. I knew what I was feeling was wrong but I needed him to love me. Even though I already had the greatest love of all from my Lord and Savior Jesus Christ. One day I was off of work and decided to go to my mother's house. I went to the bathroom. I'd seen bright pink blood. I knew something was wrong with my baby. I asked my little sister to accompany me to the hospital. I'd told her I was pregnant on the way to the hospital while I was in the ambulance. Once I was inside of the hospital I knew better than to tell them that my primary care doctor said I was having a psychosomatic pregnancy. I just lied and told them I was pregnant and bleeding they took blood work and came back into the room to take me to have an ultrasound. Once I was in the room to get the sonogram Rose told me that I would see a big head and they were going to tell me that was normal. I'd seen the radiology technician come into the room. They were pointing to certain pictures that should be taken but I did not see a baby. I turned to Rose and told her something was wrong with my baby. Everyone in the room looked at me with sadness in their eyes. Rose didn't believe me, she left to go tell the whole family I was pregnant. I knew it was bad when a group of technicians came into the room to take me back to radiology. This time they were just snapping picture after picture, but nobody was telling me anything. I looked up with mist filled eyes and began to talk for the first time. "Can someone please tell me what is wrong with my baby?" I asked with tone. "Well Mrs., you have to wait for the doctor to come and talk to you." One of the technicians replied. They wheeled me back down the hall to my room. Upon my arrival a group of doctors formed outside the room. I was scared. I was too scared to even think to pray. Something was wrong, terribly wrong. I'd strained to listen to what the doctors were saying. "Who do they got on this?" One male doctor said. A female responded but her voice was inaudible. I could barely hear past her tone. "Do they think that's a good idea being that he just lost that mother in childbirth?" The male doctor said again. I could hear her mumble something else, but I still couldn't make out what she was saying. Then everyone was quite. A doctor walked in the room with a team of physicians behind him. "Hi, I'm your doctor. It seems your baby is in your tubes." He stated calmly. "We can give you some medicine so that you can push it out, but it will be very painful. Or we can get you to surgery and take the baby out of your tube. It depends on the damage to the tube but we might have to remove the tube as well." He continued. I sat there not knowing what he was actually saying. I thought I was going to have to push the baby out of my vagina. I didn't want to see my deceased child. I didn't know he meant he could push the baby out of my tube into my uterus. 'Why would I go through all of that pain and not have a baby to show for it.' I thought. "Ok, let's do the surgery." I responded. They all exited the room. I sat there and looked around the hospital room. I'd spotted a children's book on a little yellow chair. I hopped off the examination table. I picked up the book and climbed back on the examination table. I began to read the book to my belly. I knew that my baby would hear my voice. 'Well they say that they could anyway.' I thought. I finished the book. "I love you and thank you for choosing me. I hope I will see you again." I said a loud. I just wanted my baby to know that. I batted back the tears and continued the conversation with my belly. "I'm not going to cry, I going to be strong. I want you to be strong too." I finished. A nurse walked in the room to check on me. "How are we doing?" she asked with sympathy in her voice as she checked my vitals. "I'm fine. My IV hurts, I know I need it but do you think you can take it out and redo it." I asked barely audible. "No you would have to wait for someone from the IV team to do that." She said. I pressed the call bell. Someone from the nurse's station answered.

"Yes." the voice said through the intercom. "Hi, I was wondering if I could have someone come from the IV team to redo my IV it hurts." I stated. "I'm in here!" The nursed yelled to the intercom. "No, no! You do not press the call bell when a nurse is standing right here!" she yelled. "Well Mrs, I asked you to do it, you told me they had to get someone from the IV team. I just was askin--" I couldn't finished my sentence before she interrupted. "Well it is not our fault you have little veins! You are going to just have to wait!" she yelled again. "But Mrs, you are acting like I said you did something wrong I just wanted someone to help me." I said in a soft voice. The curtain flung open and two more nurses were standing in the doorway. "What's going on?" The heavy set nurse said. "Nothing she have to wait for the IV team. She has very small veins and she is just going to have to wait that's all." The nurse barked. "Well all I did was ring the call bell and she started yelling at me. I just want someone to take this out of my arm. I told her I was willing to let them stick me again." I said still holding my composure. "No, she has to wait for the IV team!" she ordered again. "Look Mrs, I do not need to wait for the IV team to have this removed. I just want someone to take it out while we wait for the IV team. I don't even know why you are so mad. You didn't even put the IV in. Can someone please remove this IV?" I asked the two nurses in the doorway. Neither one of them responded. I began taking the tape off my arm to pull the IV out myself. One of the nurses walked over from the doorway to the bed. She snatched the IV out of my arm. I looked in Aw. I stood up and started gathering my clothes. The same nurse that had been yelling stood in front of the door. "You can't leave, you need surgery! she was yelling again. I was fighting back the tears as I put on my clothes. I couldn't believe she was carrying on like this. And these other two was just sitting there watching. "Call security!" she yelled to the other two nurses. They began running down the hall. They were acting like I was the villain. All I wanted was a stupid IV out of my arm. I wasn't rude or nasty. I just wanted it out because it hurt. Now they are treating me like a criminal. I finished getting dress and walked down the hall towards the door. "Stop that lady!" She yelled. I just stopped in my tracks. Security was blocking the exit door. I had enough of her and this whole scene. "Ma'am what's going on?" he asked. I didn't know if he was talking to me or the nurse but she responded. "she needs a life-threatening surgery and she is trying to leave." she said with tone. "Ma'am why are you trying to leave." he asked with concern. "Look, I asked her to remove an IV and all hell broke loose. I am going to another hospital. They are surrounding me yelling at me like I'm subhuman. I have the right to go to a different hospital. You have no cause or authority to keep me here. I'm leaving excuse me." I stated with tone. "But ma'am why don't we have a seat and try to talk about this." The security guard stated. The nursing supervisor was running down the hall towards me. "Miss, wait, Miss! She was yelling to the top of her lungs. 'This is crazy I thought.' "Oh my God I can't take this anymore I'm leaving! I'm going to a different hospital. Crouse employees' must've gotten their license from Ronald McDonald's school of medicine. Listen I have the right to refuse medical assistance at this hospital. I am going to a DIFFERENT hospital. You can call an ambulance to escort me if you want to but I am leaving. You are all standing around me like I have committed some type of crime with animosity in your eyes. Like I would ever let you cut on me with all this hostility." I yelled. The nursing supervisor nodded her head to the security guard for him to let me past. "Well I'll stop her then!" The nurse yelled. "Look if he detained me it would be unlawful imprisonment, but if you touch me it would be assault and I'm going to whoop your ass!" I yelled. She stepped aside. "Well I just want you to know that if you walk out that door you're going to die! You hear me, you're going to die!" She continued to yell as the automatic doors closed behind me. I walked to Kennedy Squares to my mother's house. The door was locked and everybody was asleep. I knocked on one of the neighbor girls door. I knew she was up. I hadn't realized how the time had slipped by while I was in the emergency room. She opened the door and I explained the whole situation. I asked her to call an ambulance so I could be taken to a different hospital. She was eager to oblige and she even volunteered to come along for moral support. I got in the ambulance with my heart still racing. I was going to have major surgery and I hadn't even told my mother. I figured it would be better than sitting around worrying waiting for me to come out of surgery. I arrived at Community General Hospital. I explained the whole scenario again. I was getting tired of repeating the story. I was scared and I'd felt all alone. I didn't want to communicate with anyone. I was losing my first child. The doctor walked into the emergency room he explained how they were going to do more test just to verify the information I had given them. I wasn't too happy about having to go through all of those test again and I voiced that to the doctor but he assured me that I would never want to see a doctor that goes on the word of someone else. I thought it made sense so I shut my mouth. The resident came in the room a little while later. "Well it seems there is a baby in your tubes. According to the other hospital you decided you don't want to push it out right?" The resident doctor asked while shaking his head no. I took that to mean that was something I didn't want to do. This made me believe that I had made the right choice. So I shook my head in agreement with his statement. The doctor walked in behind the resident. "I'm finding it hard to believe that you have an ectopic pregnancy. Women with ectopic pregnancy usually come in double over in pain. And you keep making jokes and asking when can you eat something. However all of the test are stating that you definitely have a baby in your left tube. So I am going to perform the surgery but I just wanted to let you know my concern." He informed me. I shook my head up and down to acknowledge what he was saying. "Well if the baby is not in my tube will it be okay if you perform the surgery?" I asked. "No, unfortunately then it will be too late, but you want to go through with the surgery correct?" He asked, not knowing that no one had fully explained the other options to me. "Yes." I responded ignorantly. They wheeled me into surgery and the tears began streaming. "What's wrong why are you crying?" The anesthesiologist asked. "Because I'm scared I won't wake up." I responded through my sobs. "Don't worry I'mma make sure you wake up. Just look for my face okay." He replied. I shook my head in agreement. I started to count backwards from ninety-nine and then there was darkness. I woke up kicking and screaming. "Hold her down!" The doctor yelled. "I can't believe this I gave her a strong dosage." The anesthesiologist yelled in a panic voice. I could seen bloody instruments in the doctor's hand. The doctor took his forearm and forcibly mashed it into my chest. My back hit the hard cold iron table. I'd seen the anesthesiologist walk over to my IV and injected something then I met the blackness again. I was being brought out of anesthesia. I couldn't make out what they were saying or doing I began swinging violently again. "Stop hitting me!" The anesthesiologist yelled as he slammed my back against the cold hard operating table. His image started to materialize and I began to calm down the nurses' faces was in shock when they realized that I was not doing it on purpose. For at that very moment everyone came to the same conclusion I was fighting for my life. Perhaps they figured someone who was fighting this hard must've been through some things. "Sorry." I said as I faded back out of consciousness. I awaken in the recovery room. "Mrs, I'm in pain." I said to the nurses as they sat there talking. "Mrs., Mrs. I'm in pain." I said again a little louder this time. I thought perhaps she couldn't hear me before being that she didn't respond. The nurse began to speak from the nursing station. "The doctor has you on pain medication. You see that IV over there it is releasing pain medication into your IV every thirty minutes." She responded. "But miss I am in pain." I exclaimed again. "I can call the doctor to see if he is going to increase your medication. I doubt it though you are on a high dosage as is." She finished. I was mad at this point I was in pain and I needed some medication. "Well look around you everyone in here is asleep because they just came out of surgery I am up and holding a conversation with you. That should tell you something, perhaps that my dosage isn't high enough. I mean I am a big girl maybe I need some more medication." I said while turning over. I was cold and in pain. My breast were hurting and on one of the worst days of my life I have to argue with a nurse. I'd forced myself to go to sleep. That was they only way I could see to alleviate my pain. I was awaken by the nurse's touch. "The doctor allowed me to put this button here so that you can just press it when you are in pain." She said. I turned around and pushed the button multiple times. I heard her gasp as I turned over to go back to sleep. I didn't care even though I knew what I had done was mean and life threatening I just wanted her to know that she had gotten on my last nerve. I awaken a few hours later in less pain, I was able to hold a conversation. I asked what happened to my nurse. Another nurse told me she had went home and how she worked very hard to keep me comfortable. I felt bad after her comment, although I didn't let it show. I asked the nurse for something to eat she told me the doctor had me on a liquid diet. I was so hungry I just wanted something to eat I asked them to call the doctor and tell him he promised me a meal. The nurse did as I asked. They told me I had a couple more hours in the recovery room. I'd awaken on the floor with the same agenda of a meal. They called the doctor and he took me off the liquid diet. I received my food and I was in fat girl heaven I ate my cheese burger with glee. The nurse kept trying to warn me that I didn't want to do that but I was hard headed as usual. I ate every bit of my burger and drank my soda. I'd began to sweat profusely. I rang for the nurse. She came in the room to ask me what was going on. I told her my insides were on fire. I had this bubble of pain and something was wrong. The nurse put on a sly smile when she alerted me it was gas. The pain was worse than that of having the tube removed, it seemed like every few minutes I either had to belch or pass gas. I guess from the soda. The cesarean incision that I had; made it hard for me to move from end of the bed to the other so I was upset when they told me I had to get up and walk. At this point I had learned to listen to the doctors and nurses it was for my own good. I got out of the bed and took slow steps down the hallway. I heard babies crying. I walked in that direction. I stood in the window and looked at all the pretty little multi-colored faces, their precious innocence. It was as close to God as any human being was ever going to get. I had the sweetest smirk on my face until I heard my nurse. "Oh No! What are you doing down here? We didn't have any rooms on the floor you were supposed to be placed on so we had to put you on the maternity ward." I could hear the panic in her explanation. "It's okay, I love babies." I responded. "No you don't need to see this right now." She continued while ushering me towards my room. I'd saw the person I needed to see the most walking down the hall, Carlos and his sister D'keena. I smiled as wide as my emotions would allow me to. I was so happy they had came. I mean my sisters had come up one at time plus my would've been baby father called to say he was coming but never showed. It was something about having your parent there to show their love and support at a time like this. It just made me feel grateful and joyous. Especially with a nurse who was acting like I would or should be having some sort of emotional crisis. I was losing everything and I knew it. I just didn't want to deal with it. I wanted to look around and tell jokes to mask the pain. I knew when my love didn't show up to the hospital it was no way I could forgive him. I mean despite it all I did lose our child didn't that mean anything to him. I was discharged after a week. I put on my best outfit and went to Kennedy Square housing complex. I didn't want to see that boy; not right now. I sat there playing spades all night; with my sisters. My niece walked up to me crying. I didn't know what was wrong so I asked her. She simply replied "I wished your baby would have lived." I consoled her through her sobs. I knew at that moment my stay at my sister house was ending I needed to go home. Everyone could see through my mask especially if a five year old just exposed me. I left that day to deal with whatever life had to offer me on the hill. I walked around the apartment complex better known as "the hill" in a daze. How could I get through this. I thought the best way to handle the situation is to just pretend like nothing was wrong. I listened to the key enter slowly into the lock. Finally my so-called boyfriend decided to show up. Perhaps this was all my karma coming back to haunt me. My intentions were so impure when I first started our relationship, but I knew it was over. I just couldn't muster up the words to express my inner thoughts so I sat on the bed watching television and reading a book on commercials. My favorite episode of a different world was rerunning that day. I loved the part when Whitley has to make a decision to marry Dwayne or Byron. As the show progressed I began hearing slight sighs coming from the background. I glanced up to see my boyfriend sitting on the edge of the bed staring at what appeared to be a picture. Throughout the show and especially on commercials his sighs would escalate. I'd decided to ignore him. However my favorite part was coming up and I did not want to hear all of the noise he was making. He was intentionally trying to get under my skin sighing and smiling at this picture awaiting for me to purpose the ultimate question. So I obliged him. "What are you looking at?" I asked trying to ignore the increase of my heart palpitations. I didn't know why my heart was racing so fast more than likely because I knew the answer to the question before he'd spoken it. "Sandy." He said leaving a hint of glee in the air. Sandy was one of the many girls that he had cheated on me with but I had assumed she was cut off with the rest of his tribe. "How did you get a picture of her?" I asked with an agonizing feeling of defeat creeping over my spirit. "She gave it to me!" He replied with a hint of sarcasm and a devious smile. "When did she give it to you?" I was trying to give him an out. Really I was looking for an out. I knew it was over but I didn't want to come to terms with it. I didn't want what was lingering in my mind and weighing on my heart to become a reality. "Yesterday." He responded flatly. Mission complete I thought. He obviously wanted it over and I semi wanted it over, so I guess this was how it ended. The words spued from my mouth but I have no reconciliation to what they were. I remember him standing up going towards the living room and hearing his keys hit the dining room table. Seconds later my front door slammed so hard a picture had fell from the wall. I ran to the dining room to see if it was his keys that had hit the table and it was. I walked back to my bedroom and cried so hard. I'd tried to finish watching A Different World, but I would never felt the same joy or glee that I had once felt for that moment of theatrical love. I knew it was all a hoax; loved ended and that was something that I had grown accustomed to in life. I guess I loved the episode because it made me have hope that one day everything would be alright but at that moment and every time I watched that episode thereafter I relieved the pain of saying goodbye to my first love.

A few weeks went by and I was trying to adjust to single life. I didn't dare go to Lamuziga house because I knew eventually something would pop off between her son and I. If it had been good or bad thing, I no longer wanted any part of him in my life. He had done things to me that I am too embarrassed to repeat. How could I love someone who idea of love is hurting the one they loved. Screw love! I went for daily walks trying to escape this inner pain. It was unbelievable it was something that I had never felt before. It was indescribable. It was a pain so very relevant in my heart but words escaped me in my description. How could something feel catastrophic inside with no physical injury. My mind was racing on ways of how to escape this pain. But one can not escape themselves so the pain went wherever I went. And I went everywhere. I got up every morning with my Walkman and just walked. I had no real destination. At times I felt as though I wanted to walk to the ends of the earth. I would cry on my walks on certain days and other days I would try to find the joy of God in my walks. I would reach down just to smell a flower. And I would be thankful for a beautiful day. I eventually found a park that was very pleasant. No one seemed to be there very often so I would go inside the park and swing on the swings by myself listening to Destiny's Child's Survivor. I had to survive this turmoil. I had been through worst but nothing felt as painful. After a few weeks of taking these long walks to the park I began to lose weight. I hadn't notice. My intention was to come down some sizes I mean if his only problem was accepting the fact that I was big maybe I'll get married if I lost some weight. Maybe somebody would love me and just me. Maybe then I would be good enough. I began getting dressed for my daily walk to the park. I was told Ramon mother had taken ill and she would need some help once she left the hospital in a couple of days. I immediately volunteered. It would be just what I needed to distract me from my heartache. Plus I loved Ramon mom dearly she was always good to me, despite my many flaws. I felt like it was a win, win situation. I could help grandma and my heart could heal.

I arrived in Albany with my Auntie awaiting my arrival. I got to Grandma's house. She could see the fear in my eyes as I sat there listening to her healthcare instructions. Once it was bedtime she told me to sleep in the bed next to her. I declined her invitation. I wanted to sleep on a pilot made-up of pillows on the floor. I told her I would be more comfortable that way. She insisted but I was persistent. Once I had turned off the lights and I thought grandma was asleep I began to sob. I felt this breaking inside. My throat burned from muffling my cries. My face was flushed with hotness and dampen with my tears. I cried myself to sleep. I spent the next couple of days and nights with the same pattern, until one day grandma asked me why I cried at night. I didn't know how to explain it. I felt silly and embarrassed by my actions. I knew I had to say something and I certainly wasn't going to lie. She had always been kind, good, and sweet to me even when I didn't deserve it. "Um, well I broke up with my boyfriend." I said short and sweet. "There is pain in this life but it will go away it just take a little time. Plus there will be other boyfriends." She stated in her usual polite tone. I smiled in agreement. I suggested that we watch a movie. During the movie there was a funeral I looked at grandma and she was covering her eyes with both hands. I had forgotten that she had to bury five children. The horror she must feel everyday and to still be kind and patience filled with empathy and understanding made her seem like a shining star amongst a room full of mediocrity. I was ashamed of myself to say the least. How could I have been so petty? I sat reevaluating what was truly important in life. The movie was over. Grandma leaned over the bed looking down on me like a teenager in a slumber party. "You not going to cry tonight is you?" She asked. I let out the most heartfelt laugh. "No, ma'am." I managed to get out. She was cute I thought to myself. "Alright." She said as she disappeared on the bed. For the first time in awhile I went to sleep with a smile on my face.

My time was coming to an end at grandma's house. She was back to normal and she was encouraging me to get back to my own life. I didn't want to leave. I didn't want to face my reality of loneliness. I knew I had to suck it up. I arrived back to Syracuse feeling somewhat refreshed and apprehensive. I didn't know if I was strong enough to handle this phase in my life. I had settled into a routine of mundane survival. Once I had gotten comfortable with being alone there was a knock at the door. "Who?" I asked assuming it was one of my sister's. "Wayne." I heard through the door. I was startled. What part of the game was this? Did he send his brother here so I could answer the door? Perhaps he didn't know we had broken up. He was in jail when we split up. Oh shoot, what am I going to do? I don't want nothing to do with his brother. I guess I can't just ignore Way. First off I had just spoken, plus he didn't do anything to me. When he left I was a constant figure in his household. "Just a minute!" I yelled through the door. "Fuck!" I thought. I opened the door slightly. He gave me an I know you not acting funny glance. I slung the door open and extended my arms to receive my hug. The smile on his face showed he didn't give a fuck about the break-up. I had been in contact with his lawyers. I had did a lot of running around even brought his mother birthday gifts in his name. I didn't mind. He was a good kid for the most part. Everybody has to find their way and selling drugs was his, I guess. "When you get out lil nigga?" I said laughing. "Yea okay." He replied while chuckling. "Yesterday." He finished. "Oh, I see. I was an afterthought." I said teasing. "Nah, not at all. Mom threw a little dinner for just the fam in my honor so I couldn't just leave like that." He answered seriously. I didn't know what to say after that. I knew he probably was wondering where I was but I wasn't going into all that. "So what's up?" I continued. "Nothing I just came to check you. What I can't stop by?" He asked. "No I didn't say that." I answered. We sat up half of the night talking until he fell asleep on the couch. I got up turned the television off. I went to the hall closet and grabbed a clean sheet. I came back he looked so innocent sleeping there. I gently slid the sheet over his slinky body. I turned off the lights and walked into my room. I was confused about my next move. I guess I'd figure that out in the morning. I'd awaken to him sitting there watching television. "You hungry?" I asked. "Nah I'm straight. I'll be back." He finished. When he left I let out a gentle sigh. I began to think: how sweet it was of him to check up on me. I know the commentary about me in the house when he asked about my whereabouts was not flattering to say the least. People always made you into a monster when they've wronged you. Plus it was good having someone to talk to. Even though the conversation was about nothingness it was still enjoyable. As the day was turning into night there was a knock at the door. 'I know damn well…' ran across my mind as I screamed "Who!" "Wayne" He said. FUCK! I thought. He probably got his brother with him. I'm not in the mood for these games. I looked thru the peephole. I only saw him. What in the hell is going on? I opened the door with bewilderment written on my face. "What's wrong with your face, I told you I was coming back." He asked. " I thought you meant another time, not today." I answered. I let him in and repeated the same thing from the night before. He fell asleep I went and got his sheet and went to bed. The next morning when I had awaken he was gone. While folding the sheet I heard a knock "Who?" I asked even though I knew the answer. I opened the door before he could even complete his name. I saw a bookbag on his shoulder. "What's that?" I asked. "The game." He answered. Did this fool just said he brought his game to my house. That means he's planning on staying awhile. "You can't stay here. " I blurted out. "What you mean? Why not ?" He asked. "I mean it just doesn't look right. I was dating your brother now you sleeping on my couch. The shit just don't look right." I answered "Taylor I need you right now." He replied. I didn't know what was going on but he was always a very honest person. Something was up I wasn't quite sure what but I would never turn him away all that I had done to his mother she had never turned me away ever. So I guess it's my turn to return the favor. "Okay, listen you can stay here until I get a man." I stated firmly. "What- why, how you sound??" He asked. "Because men like to have dick swinging contest and I don't want my MAAAANN to feel compromised at any point in our relationship." I responded in my normal cheerful tone. "Yea,ok!" He stated thru laughter. "Sooo you going to teach me how to play the game or what?" I asked. "Yeah I'll teach you." He replied. We had set up a routine unbeknownst to us. He would wake up early in the morning rushing out the door to handle his business and I would spend the day mastering the latest game he had purchased. By dinner time he would always managed to be in the house. I'd cook us something to eat play the game and laugh until it felt like my side would split. I was generally happy that was until the day my oldest sister came running out the staircase. She literally ran into me. "Wow, what the hell is wrong with you?" I asked "Wayne up there cutting up crack!" She said. 'What!!!' I thought, hoping my face or demeanor didn't reveal my shock. "What do you mean?" I asked in a nonchalant manner. "He got mad crack on the table cutting it up in front of my fucking kids." She stated "Com'on kids!" She finished. I ran up the steps as fast as I could. Had he lost his fucking mind! I couldn't get the key in the door fast enough. I'd slung the door open. I looked at the coffee table it was covered in a hard rock like substance. 'Yup, he lost his fucking mind.' I thought. I walked in the house closed the door lightly. I sat softly on the couch. His face showed he knew something was wrong but the bewilderment in eyes showed me he had no clue what it was. I tried to find a nice way to go about the situation but the words just blurted out. "HAVE YOU LOST YOUR FUCKING MIND?!" I yelled to the top of my lungs. "What, I can't cut up in here?!" He asked genuinely. "Uh, NO YOU CAN'T!" I answered. The look in his eyes revealed his hurt. I didn't think it was because of the situation, I knew it was because of the way I was talking to him. I'd known him

since he was a child and we had built a bond and now I'm screaming at
him like he was twelve years old again. "Listen Way, this is not a spot, a
spizzy or whatever else y'all call it in the streets. This is my home that I
am sharing with you. I know what you do and how you make your living.
I've just always hoped none of that would enter into my house. And I
know I shouldn't have yelled like that but my nieces and nephews eat off
that table and I just got mad thinking about their little faces coming in
Auntie's house and seeing crack on the table. I mean com'on for real." I
stated calmly. He grabbed a saucer off the couch and placed it in a
timberland boot box. He picked up the steak knife off the table and
started scraping the crack into the timbs box. I sat there in silence
watching. My feelings was hurt. I knew he was about to walk out the
door. He had become my buddy, my confidant, my friend, but I knew I
had to let him go. Once he started packing up his game system in silence
I knew what it was. He was planning on leaving and never coming back.
I got up and walked into my room. I hadn't realized how close he was to
my heart. I closed my room door. I laid across the bed. A part of me
wanted to stop him. I had to give myself a talk like, you can not possibly
be this lonely. I heard the front door open and close slightly. I jumped up
swung opened the bedroom door. I ran down the hallway made a
shortstop in the living room. I scurried the living room for his things.
Everything was gone and the area was neatly organized the way that it
was. My heart sank with sadness. For a second I thought I might even
cry. I was alone listening to Patti Labelle in my head sing 'on my own,
this wasn't how it was supposed to be'. I hated being alone. I sat down
turned on the television and flipped through the channels. The day
slowly turned into night. My first night alone. I walked into the room
replaying the days events and giving myself a lecture. 'It's not like he was
your boyfriend or anything. You weren't intimate, so get over it.' But he
was my friend. I went to sleep misty eyed. I was sad despite all the logic.
I had to admit I was still sad. The first day was torture but by the third
day I was well on my way back to my normal jovial self. I heard a tap at
the door. His tap. Nah I thought as I walked through the door. "Who!"
I screamed. "Way." He answered. My face was puzzled as well as my
spirit. I hope everything is okay. I knew the lifestyle he lived perhaps

something happened outside. I knew he would still be in the area from the ghetto grapevine. I'd rushed to open the door. He walked in, in his eyes was fear. My heart was beating erratically. What was wrong? Was his mother okay, did something happen to his brother, the twins, oh God not my babies. "What's wrong?" I asked trying to hide my anguish. "Are you still mad at me?." He asked. Is he serious? This is too cute. He is afraid of my response. He always acted so hard. I had no idea that he was such a sweetheart. "Nah." I said with a smile on my face. He walked over to the couch to roll up the weed. We began talking like nothing happened. I wasn't going to make a big deal about the situation. I figured he overstepped his boundaries and he knew it. I knew this conversation would never had to be thought about again.

CHAPTER 13

I Thug All My Bitches

My days were mainly a blurr. I would wake up smoke. Cook something, smoke some more, clean up and smoke. Everything was a hazy fog. I had dropped at least ten sizes which meant I was no longer big as hell I was pudgy and mostly ass. I couldn't phantom life without this little nigga he was my best friend. I had forgotten about even finding a man. Between his friends and my friends it seem like my house was always full of jokes and laughter. I had been so hurt by all my life's problems weed was my new coping mechanism. Somewhere along the way I felt like God had forgotten about me, so why was I brandishing my life for him. He left me here alone. I would walk around saying the most disrespectful and distasteful things about the Lord I wanted anyone to hold a conversation about Jesus so I could laugh at them and call them foolish for believing. My feelings was hurt. My soul was damaged. I began to hate slowly. My level of anger should not be compared to no other. I lived a fuck you life. The only thing that could bring me peace was death. Since I was not about to kill myself; if someone else put me out my misery it was fine by me. But of course laying me down was not going to be an easy task. I wouldn't have tired it, because if you missed or miscalculated even by a fraction of an margine it would sure to expose the beast I had become. The lust for payback and blood that I so anxiously waited for was the arousal I needed to wake up in the morning. My best friend son had decided to become a drug dealer so he was my ultimate escape. If anything should happen to him I'd slide right in and finish the nigga before he could see it coming. He wasn't just my friend he was my out. He kept me so high I use to wake up dumber than I was the day before. I was sitting on the couch watching television when the door flew open. We had long since graduated from me getting up and getting the door. He had his own key. "What's wrong with you?" I asked. I could see the steam in eyes the vein in his forehead always popped when he was real mad. He was holding his bottom lip. 'yup he got punched in his mouth I thought.' "Man this mother fuc.." I decided to interrupt him I was too high to die that day. "Aw, let me see." I said looking at his mouth. "Calm down, I'mma get some ice." I said really feeling bad inside for him. "Now relax, take a deep breath and tell me what happened." I finished. "This mutha fu…" He continued. I cut him off again. I figured having him tell the story while he was angry was going to make him do something horrible. "Let me see." I said in my softest tone and a smile; while removing the self made ice pack which was just a washcloth with ice cubes inside. He couldn't help but to smirk. At that point I knew I had him. I knew I could soften his spirit with my words. I knew my words would penetrate his soul and ultimately help to defuse the situation. "So what happened?" I asked again. "Man, it won't about nothing really." He answered. It was no way I was going to let that anger lie and fester up in him. That just wasn't an acceptable answer. "It don't look like nothing." I replied. "What that's supposed to mean? My shit look bad or something?" He asked referring to his lip. He fast trotted down the hall to bathroom to look in the mirror. "No, I'm not even talking about your lip. I mean nobody hit nobody for no reason." I responded. I could see his body relaxing as he made his way down the hall towards me. "Well it started over some little shit. Dude had made a smart comment when I was on my way to the store" He stated. "On the way back I saw him and asked him what was that slick shit he had said; when I was going to the store. Now it's a crowd of people out there and he decided to get extra loud with me. So I snuffed him." He finished. "Oh, so you was wrong?" I asked. "How you figure?" He questioned. "Well, if it wasn't important enough for you to take action when it was just you and him then you should've let it go. He probably felt like you were being funny being that in front of the building was crowded. I would've gotten loud too." I declared in my nicest tone.

"You're probably right. Imma head home" He stated as he got up and headed to the door. "You aight?" I asked to double check his mental. "Yea, I'm good." He stated while walking out the door. I felt bad for him. His ego was bruised and he wanted revenge. I could understand where he was coming from but I wasn't going to follow him there; not today. I sat there with my heart racing and hoping he didn't come back in and tell me he did something stupid. I sat around in a panic for the majority of the day. Everytime I heard the slam of the heavy metal staircase door my heart would skip a beat. I would wait to hear the door. I was glad when day turned into night, I knew he was safe at his mother's house and I was grateful for that. I went to sleep still nervous but figured he would be okay. I was really hoping that he had listened to me. Days went by without even a phone call. I figured he had given up the street life. Perhaps he'll stay home from now on. Once I had settled into my daily routine I didn't hear the key in the door. I was in the middle of cleaning, singing and listening to music. I was hitting a high note to the best of my ability when I turned around to see him standing there smiling. My whole body jerked at the surprise of him standing directly behind me. "Boy you scared the shit outta me." I stated annoyed. "You better change your little funky attitude." He said in a stern voice. I turned around because I couldn't help the little smirk that was appearing on my face. 'Who he think he talking to. He acting like he a grown man or something.' I thought. I knew he was eighteen but he was still the little boy who loved Wu-tang clan to me. Shit he repped them so hard you woulda thought he was from shaolin. I walked in my room to regain my composure. If not I woulda fell out laughing in front of him. I walked back out the room to the sweet efforence of marijuana. I plopped down on the couch beside him. He looked at me and passed the weed. I began smoking. We laughed and joked all night. I went in my room to go to sleep even though I wanted to sleep on the couch. I figured if he wanted to leave he wouldn't feel obligated to stay just so he wouldn't hurt my feelings. I got to the bedroom and heard the front door. 'I knew it.' I thought. I assumed he just wanted to let me know there was no hard feelings. I climbed onto the bed and drifted off to sleep. I awaken in the morning with a smile on my face and a light heart. 'Such a good kid.' I thought. I went to the bathroom to handle my morning duties. I almost walked out the bathroom naked but something told me not to. As soon as I opened the bathroom door he was standing there. I jumped back in defense mode until his face materialized. "Oh, boy, you scared me. Imma put a bell or some shit around your neck so you can stop sneaking up on me." I informed him with laughter attached. "Yea, right!" He replied sharing my laughter. As he was closing the door I began to speak. "What are you about to do today?" I asked as I walked into my room. "Nothing real, why what's up?" He responded. "No reason." I answered. I walked in the living room and turned on the television. He went to the front door and turned around. "I'll be back." He stated. "Okay." I stated flatly. Since when he makes announcements, I thought. It was a dreary day. The clouds overshadowed the entire sky. Dark, dank, and gloomy is the path my life was on. Seems since the beginning of time. I walked into the bathroom to wipe the tears from my eyes. I hated when I reflected on my life even for a moment it always led to tears. I looked in the mirror and began searching for my flaws. I didn't have to look that hard. For a second I thought I heard someone coming down the hall but by the time I had wiped my face and looked down the hallway no one was there. I turned off the light and began walking down the hall. "Yo, Taylor." He shouted. I answered him as I was entering the living room. "Yes." "What you was doing?" He asked. "Nothing." I answered as I was entering the living room. "Why what's up?" I inquired. "You was crying?!" He answered my question with a question. "No!" I replied as sternly as I could. I was hoping my voice didn't crack. I was hoping my face didn't reveal the truth. "Yes you was." He exclaimed. "No I was not." I replied trying to have as much attitude as possible. I figured he might have crept up the hallway while I was in the bathroom, but I wasn't going to let him know he was right. If I did I would have to talk about my past and some things are better kept than said. To have him look down upon me in disgust, as I have seen many times in the past. I just couldn't. I wouldn't. I would just call him a liar up until a fight if I had to. "Oh, well, I'll be back." He announced as he left the house again. He wasn't gone for that long before he re-entered the house. This time he came in with a bag from the corner store, and a timberland shoe box. I looked in his face to see what he was up to. His face didn't reveal anything. He sat down and pulled chips out the bag along with a juice and handed it to me. I was puzzled but I only said a quick thank you. After that he handed me the Tim's box. I opened it leary as into what I might find. I was smiling but I was opening the box at a snail's pace. Once the box was opened it uncovered DVD movies lined up neatly in the box. I looked up somewhat relieved but still baffled. "Pick a movie." Way instructed. "Huh." I replied my confusion more apparent. "I decided to chill in the house today just eat junk food and watch movies." He stated. I bust out laughing as he pulled out the box what he believed was a good pick. He instructed me to put the movie in while he went to split the cigar down the middle and dump the tobacco in the trash. I started the movie once the weed was rolled. We began passing the marijuana back and forth in our own little cipher. As soon as I curled up on the couch good and began zoning out to the movie there was a tap at the door. He got up off the couch and slow trotted to the door. Of course my nosey self couldn't wait for the door to open to see who he was letting in. His brother! I'll be a son-of-a-bitch! Did he go get his brother? Did he think I was crying over him? Unfreakingbelievable! Ugh! I looked his brother in the eyes I wanted to get up and run in the room but I was stuck. My stupid ass was too high to move. I tried to act unimpressed with his presence. I didn't want him to think it affected me one way or the other. I watched their interaction. He grabbed his things and walked out the door. Is he foreal right now. How he just going to invite him in and leave? The nerve! My ex looked at the black leather chair at the table and pulled one out as if he was so interested in the movie. I kept my eyes on the television. I wasn't going to speak, gesture, or even look in his direction. He sat there quietly as did I. When the movie was over I got up from the couch and politely walked in my room. I climbed under the covers. I awaited to hear the slamming of the front door, but it never came. I began wondering what he was out there doing. Just then his silhouette darken the light from the hallway that was seeping through my door. My whole body stiffen with fear. What was going on in his head? He crept over to my bed. My eyes was wide with anticipation. He lean in to see if I was awake. I guess he was expecting the sleeping game; but I knew he had hurt me for the last time. I knew if I gave him another chance he would hurt me again. "Yo, Imma bout to leave, I wanted you to come lock the door." He stated with as much sincerity he could muster. "It slam locks, just make sure the bottom button is pushed in." I instructed while turning over in my bed. I heard the door closed and drifted off into a deep peaceful sleep. He showed up a couple more times revealing nastiness and insecurity with each encounter until eventually he realized he was in the previous chapter of my life. My life was cascading with blunt filled days and smoke filled nights with an alcohol chaser. I didn't need anything from anyone; especially a man. I had met a couple guys. I realized I hadn't been intimate in a while. My heart was cold. My focus was weed, alcohol, and money. Fuck love! Who needed a man. I had three boyfriends in rotion. Neither knew about the next one. I needed Gucci, Louis Vitton, Fendi, Parda and whatever other name brand item my heart desired. Now that I got my gear up I had to work on my jew-els. I wore two rings on every finger, the biggest chain in the store. I was cheating, stealing and using people. My relationship with God had long since been forgotten. I woke up on the kitchen floor with help from Way. "Why are you crying?" I asked with my normal sarcastic smirks. "Why are you unconscious?" He replied. I got off the floor with some help and went in my room to get dressed. I had to go to the emergency room. I had been under the weather for some time. I called an ambulance about three o'clock in the morning. I didn't want anyone to know I was sick. I mean at this point I stayed so clean I knew everybody was waiting for something to talk about when it came to me. I came and went; and made sure I looked good doing it. The girls was jealous and envious but I often let them know what I would, could and still will do to them on any giving Monday. Cold wasn't the word. My heart was blacken filled with rage and hate. I was in the emergency room losing my cool as usual. I began to snatch the IV out my arm. I knew I had to get back to the building before my public awaken. Because as much as the girls hated me the guys loved me. To smell my perfume as the wind blew. I'd shash shay pass them. Ever so often I'd walk over give them a conversation and walk away reassuring them they could never touch me. To be honest the Jersey boys really didn't want to fuck me. They just appreciated the fact that I matched their fly. I would give them great relationship advice, tell jokes and go home. Plus I think they respect the fact I always came with my own weed, and alcohol and I would share. They started to think of me like a little sister kinda. My thoughts were interrupted by the entrance of the doctor. "It appears you have an std." He stated calmly. A what! The impact of the news made my body thrust my back against the examination table. I had to grip the bed rails tightly just to keep my balance. I scooted my butt onto the examination table. As I exhaled and let the weight of the information sink in. My eyes began to water. I began to reflect on how I had gotten myself in this situation. I mean, I had three boyfriends but I didn't cheat on them. I really didn't even set out to have a boyfriend; yet alone three. It kinda happened accidentally. I had met one man. We dated for a little while then he did what I felt like, at the time; all men do. He began to lie and cheat. When I decided to stand up for myself he left. About six months had passed, I thought he was never coming back I began dating another man. It seemed like the minute we became intimate the first one came back apologetic. I didn't know how to tell him I had moved on so I didn't. Juggling two relationships was easier than I had thought. I just simply made sure pop-ups wasn't an option, after that it was smooth sailing. Once I convinced myself to become comfortable with the facts of my deception, both relationships were over. I had to let out a sigh of relief. I was never going through that again. Then I met someone else. It had been at least seven months since I had seen, heard, or been intimate with the other two. Those relationships had definitely ended. So when a couple more months went by I felt like it was okay to become intimate with the new man in my life. It seemed like when we became one the other two came back literally a week apart. I didn't mention anything because I knew they would leave again. Plus I felt like I owed it to myself to see if this relationship would work out. I knew they were cheating and so was I, so it made things fair but now, in this moment, I don't have anyone to blame but myself. "The good news is that it's treatable. So we are going to give you a shot of penicillin and you can go home, okay." The doctors words was entering in my ears and trailing off into sunset just like my thoughts. How could I be so careless? I sat there and beat myself up until I returned home. I had to make a change with my sexual conduct. No more sexcompades for me. Obviously I'm not good with relationships, or just casual sex. I had decided to just give up. I had chosen one sex partner. He lived in Kennedy Squares Apartments. He wasn't well known but he always had a crush on me. We had sex on and off when I was in between relationships. I felt like he wasn't the man for me. He would beg for my attention and I'd sleep with him and send him home. It was wrong but he was my sex buddy nothing more. Little did he know he had just graduated to my only sex partner. I found it hard to tell them it was over through the anger and guilt. This could have ended so much worse. Somehow I found a way.

With nothing to lose I began club hopping. I had depended on my best friend more for companionship. If I wanted to go out on a date I would ask him if we could go to the movies or out to dinner. He wasn't good with stuff like that with me. I guessed it crossed some imaginary line. I understood though. He would however lounge around the house with me all day rolling weed and telling jokes. He always declined my invitations, but he would go scoop my goddaughter and drop us off and pick us up. If it was sex that I needed I would go to my sex buddy. I owned every name brand purse, shoe, belt, jacket, sunglasses and scarves. I needed something more. I purchased my first car a maroon Mitsubishi Galant. "Um, hello, yeah, I just bought a car." I stated nonchalantly. "Yeah fucking right!" Way exclaimed his excitement oozing through the phone. I walked away from the car dealer and began to whisper. "I just have one problem." I explained. "What's that?" I could hear the aggravation in Way voice. 'It must be hard being him, people playing up to you just to see if they could get money out of you all the time.' I thought. "I don't know how to drive." I said matter of factly. "You what!?" I could hear the laughter erupt from his lungs. "Yea, well I need you to come get me and drive me home." I finished. I turned around and let out a slight smile to the car dealer who was so happy to have just closed the deal. "Where you at? I'm on my way." He said. When he walked up I casually walked over to my car. I didn't want him to say something stupid in front of the dealer. I shot him the car keys. He followed suit. I climbed in the car and he pulled out the car lot. As soon as we got to the red light he turned and looked at me then he bust out laughing. "So you just woke up and decided to buy a car today." He asked through his laughter. I was too busy touching everything trying to figure out my new toy. "So you going to teach me how to drive?" I answered his question with a question. "Yea, I gotchu'." I got out the car and walked upstairs like nothing spectacular had happened. As I was exiting the car I told him to take it for a spin. He was more than happy to oblige me. I knew he would tell me if it was a lemon or not. I had so many things on my mind that I had to accomplish. The car was the first on my list. Helping Way was my second agenda. During my investigations into this drug dealing thing I found out selling large quantities or pushing weight was where the real money was at. Days had passed. It was raining outside. I knew that Way would want to stay in the house all day. I decided to redirect his mind set. I just simply made mention of how much more money was at stake when large quantities was sold versus small amounts. I'd assured Way that I would always be there if anything was to ever go wrong. I had his back at all costs; even if it meant my life. I deliberately left out the last part. I didn't want to become an expandable part of this non existent partnership. I didn't require any money or fame but if he was going to risk his life it definitely should've been for more than some Tims and a hoodie, or perhaps some weed or sneakers. I made it very clear that if you're going to risk it all including your freedom, perhaps even your life make every second count. I knew it was wrong to push him in that direction; but how could I honestly say I was his "best friend" if I didn't let him know everything I had learnt. His life started to improve slightly. I could see the change in him. He was trying to match my fly. I knew that was a mistake. I had to grab a handle on this before things got outta hand. So I waited until we was chilling, high and ran outta shit to talk about. "Way." I said softly trying to hide the fact that I had a hidden agenda. By the look on his face I could tell I was unsuccessful. "Don't look at me like that." I snapped. "Wassup Taylor." He said barely hiding his dismay. "Ew, never-fucking-mind!" I stated while sucking my teeth. "Girl, you better talk!" He stated firmly. I couldn't help but smile. 'He swears he grown.' I thought. "Look I know you don't like me meddling in your business, but I just wanted to say you been looking real nice lately." I finished with a compliment hoping to stroke his ego and soothe his agitation at the same time. "Shza, man what do you want?" He asked firmly. 'well I guess that didn't work.' I thought. I knew I had to jump right in, he did his little I'm annoyed sound which meant any minute I was on my way to a verbal assassination. "Well, it's just that you've been keeping up with the latest fashions. Which is a good thing but..." He interrupted me be before I could finish. "But what?!" He demanded. I could see that maybe I shouldn't have started the conversation. My voice was faint as I continued. "It's just that the streets be watching and you don't want them to see that you caking before you ready. People will rob you, lie on you, set you up if they see that you have the possibility to make more money than them." I finished. "Man, you talking crazy right now." He said still in an agitated tone. I didn't know how the conversation had taken such a sour turn. I figured at that point I should just say what was on my mind. "Way, greedy gets you caught and flashy gets you kilt. I just don't want anything to happen to you. That's all." I finished as sincerely as I could. With the end of that statement he got up collected his things to leave the house. As he was gathering everything I began to speak again. "Think about it, anybody out here selling weight is not pushing a flashy car. They dress nice but not over the top. If you wannabe rich and famous it going to come at a price. If you're doing this to take care of your mom and siblings one day like you be claiming I don't understand the problem." I said nonchalantly. He glanced at me from the side of his eyes. I knew whatever he was thinking wasn't nice, considerate, or flattering. He walked over to the door and left the house. Never taking his evil eye off me. 'Shit' I thought. I didn't mean to make him mad but new money should never be show money. Not until you've reached your desired amount of money. I felt responsible for his surplus of funds thus wanted to make sure that I'd given him the tools he needed to survive and thrive out there in those streets. I knew he would come back I just didn't know if when he decided to come back whether or not he would collect the rest of his things. I'd understand either way. Time passed by slowly without my buddy. I'd guessed he had enough of my meddling with his personal affairs. So when I'd heard the key in the door my heart began to beat erratically. I didn't want the whole break-up scene. For one he wasn't my boyfriend and second of all I didn't want him to see me cry. He was a fixture in my heart. I didn't need him to see how much I really cared. I glanced at the door then back at the television. I spoke in a nonchalant manner. He sat down and talked for a little while. On the way out the door he gathered some more things. Yep, he definitely was moving out slowly. I just remained focused on the television show as if nothing had just happened. I guessed it was for the best. I thought as I switched off the t.v. and carried myself to sleep. I'd awaken to loud laughter and the smell of weed. 'What the hell is going on in here?' I thought. I got up walked into the living room. It was crowded. All of his friends were sitting on the couch. They were smoking, playing the game, and laughing at their jokes they were making on each other. "What?" Way asked from the puzzled look I had on my face. "I didn't say nothing." I responded. The whole scenario felt like deja vu. I walked to the bathroom just as puzzled as my face betrayed. I began getting myself together for the day. I went back in the living room and joined the cipher I also began kicking butt in Madden. I had gotten too high, too drunk, too early. I excused myself and went in the bedroom to lie down. I'd awaken mid-day to a pleasant aroma shrimp egg foo young. My fav. I walked straight to the kitchen and grabbed a plate. As I walked back to the living room Way let out a monstrous laugh. "Yea right!" He screamed through his laughter. "You just going to get a plate, without asking or anything." He said while laughing. "Yup, sure did! I want that one." I said pointing to the biggest piece. "How you going to say you want the biggest one?" He demanded to know. "Um because you get two and I get one." I said confidant that the piece was already mine. He always gave me the big piece. "Thanks." I said when he handed me my plate. "Can you please put on a movie?" I asked as I exited the room to retrieve my comforter. I came back A Bronx Tale was playing. Yez my favorite I thought. I had fallen asleep during the movie. I'd awaken to pounding on the door. I jumped outta my sleep and swung the door opened. "They got Way!" A girl yelled in my face. "Who?" I asked while grabbing my keys and shoes. "The police!" She responded. I tried to walk calmly but my panic had set in. I walked as calmly as could down the hill. I got there as they were putting Way into the cop car. I walked over to the officer outside of the car and began asking questions. "Hello officer I'm Taylor and I'm trying to figure out what is going on with my nephew?" I asked confidently. "Well he has no identification and he was smoking weed." The officer answered. "Perhaps you could help me with some information." The officer asked. "Is he under arrest?" I asked. "Yes, ma'am." He answered. "Then you can kiss my motherfucking fat ass." I said in protest. "And now he's going to jail!" The officer responded. "I thought you said he was under arrest." I said trying to back peddle. "I was just going to issue him a ticket; and he would've been given a citation to go to court." He replied. "Your going to jail and you can thank your little girlfriend here buddy!" The officer explained to Way after tapping on the window. "I'm not his girlfriend." I said while walking away. I couldn't look Way in the face. I had just messed up bad. I sat in the house ignoring his mother phone calls. The level of stress I was under. My phone rung again. I guess I was going have to face the music sooner or later. I didn't recognize the number but I figured Lamuziga was calling me from an unknown number to try and catch me. "Hello." I said sounding just as defeated as I felt. "Yeah, I found out why you didn't want me to search your nephew." He stated. 'I know this fucking cop just didn't call me.' I thought. "Yeah we found the crack up his ass." He said while laughing. "I don't know what you're talking about." I said still with defeat in my voice. "Hold on he wanna ask you something." He managed to get out through his heartfelt laughter. "He told me you were under arrest, that's the only reason I'd gotten smart with him. Then he said he was only going to give you a ticket." I tried to explain. "Technically a ticket is an arrest." He told me. His affirmation made me feel even worse. "Tay" He said with a surprisingly sweet demeanor. "Wassup?" I asked. My tone was soften and remorseful. "Listen they want a gun in order to release me." He stated. "Okay so what you need me to do?" I asked not caring about the consequences. "Go to the thing get the black jeans and drop it off at um." He instructed. "Thornton Park." I interjected. "Okay, they want a time." He asked. "Tell 'em thirty minutes." I responded. I went to the closet and pulled out a few Tim boxes. A gun was in one and drugs was in the others. 'imma fuck him up.' I thought. This boy got this shit in my house. I really couldn't concern myself with all that at that moment. I walked up the street to the plastic surgeon's office. I got back in the house and called

him back. "Yeah it's done. How you know they are going to let you go?"
I asked. "I have to trust them." He replied. I explained the exact
coordinates. I said my tearful goodbyes and impatiently waited for the
outcome. I heard the key in the door. My heart was filled with worry, my
eyes were filled with anticipation. He slowly pushed the door open. As
if was taunting me. He walked in his smile was radiant. My heart let out
a sigh of relief. I was still kinda afraid. I didn't know if he was mad at me.
He sat down and rolled up the weed. In our cipher we gained a new
respect for each other. We had each other back through it all. He knew
for damn sure I had him. And if for only that reason he had me. It seemed
like a day turned into three years overnight. With the same coming and
goings. Then I had gotten the dreaded knock. It was the kinda knock
you anticipate but you never really want to come. "Who?!" I yelled while
running to the door with my heart racing. "Gig." A girl replied. 'What is
she doing at my door.' I thought. I opened the door without hesitation.
"Yes." I asked calmly. "They just took Way to jail." She exclaimed. "What
happened?" I asked. My dismay was in my tone. "He got pulled over with
mad family size zip lock bags of crack." She explained. "About how
many?" I asked. "Like three or four of 'em." She finished. "Thank you for
coming to tell me." I said politely while closing the door. "No, problem
she managed to get out before the door closed. I could see the sympathy
in her eyes. I knew it was there because she could see the tears in mine.
By the time I got to the couch my phone was ringing. Dang it's Lamuziga.
I thought. I knew I had to answer the phone. "What's up with my son
yo?" She asked in an aggravated tone. "I don't know all the details but
someone just came and told me he got caught with three to four zip lock
bags of crack. Imma about to call the justice center see what his charges
are. Then Imma head outside and see what the local yokels say happened.
Imma call you back. It may take a minute though. It depends on whether
or not he in the computer. Sometimes it take a minute to update. Imma
call you right after I promised." I instructed. "Aight." She said while
hanging up. I took a deep breath and began placing calls. After following
the computer prompts they would transfer me to an extension that would
ring until a busy signal came on to disconnect the call. I repeated this so
many times I lost count. I looked at my cell phone to see how many times

I had gone through this process. 'fifteen, this is ridiculous!' I thought. Just then I heard a male voice. I gave his information and asked what his charges were. He started naming a list if things. Possession in this degree that degree, a violation of this and that also in forms of degrees. He was so short with me I was afraid to ask him to hold on to let me get a pen. I was running through house dumping whole drawers on the floor until I found a pen just in the knick of time I thought. I took a deep breath and asked him if he could repeat the charges. He wasn't happy but he did. I didn't get a call from Way. Dang. I thought. I called Lamuziga back. She answered on the first ring. I explained the list of charges. She then told me Way had contacted her and gave her a name of a lawyer he wanted to hire. She informed me that she would be able to attend the first meeting but every meeting after that she would advise him his aunt would be there. I was more than willing to step up. I knew she had to go to work. I went to court. Every hearing, every cancelled date, every adjournment, everytime they said it wasn't on the docket that day I was there. People would ask about him as they seen me coming and going. I would keep my answers brief. Few genuinely cared but most were just nosey. Girls trying to get his information so they could start a jailhouse romance. It was sickening. I'd just smile and tell them I'll tell him you asked about him. I would tell him but I knew he would be polite to them maybe even gave some of them some thank you dick, but he didn't care. I answered the house phone. "Hello." I stated nonchalantly. "You have a call from." A computerized voice stated. "Way." He said. "an inmate at New York state correctional facility. If you would like to accept the charges press one." The same computerized voice finished. I pressed one with excitement. "I don't have much time but I need you to do something for me. I need you to contact my lawyer. Ask him if I could get a Y.O. It's a youthful offender. It's only good until your twenty-one I'm cutting it close but I think it could be done. Be by the phone tomorrow night. I got to go someone let me cut in their time. You got it, youthful offender.l; Y.O." He instructed. "Yea I got it." I said. "You okay". I managed to get out. "I'm fine. I gotta go. Y.O. Tay." He hung up. My heart was overwhelmed with empathy. 'My poor friend.' I thought. I tried not to cry but I couldn't help myself. I wondered if he really was okay. I awaken bright and early to follow Way instructions. I called the lawyers office numerous times. I kept leaving messages for the lawyer to call me back. By midday I had decided to go down there just then the phone rang. It was the lawyer. I explained about the Y.O. the lawyer seemed apprehensive at first until I insisted upon at least a try. He agreed with no promises. I was gracious and kind every step of the way. I would drop off books and packages every Tuesday and Thursday. I tried to make sure he was in good spirits just by a card, letter something anything to show him how much he was loved. The whole process was taking forever. It's been about six months and Way was still in jail. The stress was beginning to show in my appearance. I wasn't going to get my nails and hair done because I didn't feel like it. I got up one day and decided to have a spa day. I was getting my nails, hair everything done. I'd remember a time before turning him into the best drug dealer he could be, it would be me having long talks trying to get him to change his ways. I began to flash back on all the conversations. The countless times I tried to talk him out of his way of life. Was all of this my fault? Perhaps I shouldn't have helped him to maximize this drug dealing thing. However I honestly tried to talk him outta his lifestyle. Just then I began reliving the conversations. "Everybody trying to be like Scarface but it's like you niggas didn't watch the end of the movie he dies." I protested. I flashed back to another conversation we had. "The streets don't love you. Every time you go to jail your not the only one who suffers. We suffer with you. It's only death or jail in those streets." I stated matter factly. I smiled when I thought of the look he shot me. 'he was mad as fuck.' I thought amused. I was watching television and decided my thoughts were consuming me. I'd figured I'd go to bed early. I stood up as I turned around he was standing there with that stellar smile I had become accustomed to. I wanted to run over and jump in his arms but I decided to play it cool. I just began to speak. "How? When? What happened?" I asked excitedly. "It worked." He stated. "I got the Y.O." He finished. I stood there and listen to the ends and outs of the case. It was back to business as usual. He was in and out handling business and I was sitting around getting high. One day Way came in and just blurted out a statement. "You should get a job or something. Sitting around all day is not cute." He stated in an annoyed tone. I looked up bewilder. I didn't know what had sparked this conversation. "Okay." I stated. The next day I began my job search. I didn't know where to start but I knew exactly what I didn't want to do. I was too embarrassed to work in retail. I mean if anybody came into the mall and saw me I would be the laughing stalk of the neighborhood. I had convinced Way to start looking for a job with me. Every day we would go out and look for employment. I found a volunteer position through the Americorps program. I was ecstatic. I couldn't wait to tell Way. I remember my first day of work him standing outside in the cold with me looking like a proud dad. I didn't know that was the beginning of the end of our friendship.

CHAPTER 14

Crossroads

Work was wonderful. I was learning a skill and helping people. Way was still dealing but that was something that I had to deal with at a later date. I was working at one of the local community health centers. I was super excited everyday to be doing something so amazing. I hadn't even notice that Way had stop coming in every night. I heard he had a girlfriend. Aw new love. I figured he wanted to be sitting up under her all time. I didn't mind, I had no reason to. My phone rang to disturbing news. Way was in jail again. By now I had the routine down although it still hurt. I started placing the calls to the justice center. Once I got all the information I called Lamuziga. She told me that she was on her way to the lawyers office. Again she explained that she had to work but we had to show him we supported him. In my mind not showing up to court was not an option. I went to every court date. The adjournments, rescheduled, him not being on the docket; I was there yet again. His mother informed me that he had decided to take boot camp. He qualified because the youthful offender was sealed so it was like he didn't have a record. The nine months of boot camp was just like his first bid. Letters, cards, books anything to let him know he was loved and missed. While he was away it was rumored that the girl he loved so much was cheating on him. His mother tried to plant the seed in my head, but I knew how manipulative she could be. I knew I was facing a difficult challenge. I couldn't decide if I should tell him or not. So I decided to do some investigating. I went to his mother house and picked up my goddaughter. I asked about his girlfriend and how things were going in the house. She explained how the girl would say she was here or there but the same person she was supposed to be with would call the house looking for the young lady. My decision was made. I couldn't believe in my heart that it was right not sharing the information I had learnt. I'd figured it would be best if I told him in person. I dropped her off and agonized over my decision. I knew what I had to do I just didn't want to do it.

It was graduation day. It rolled around pretty quickly. While Way was locked up I had applied for a job at the hospital. To my surprise the interviewer was an Americorps alumni. I got the job. I was so grateful for the opportunity. I would be doing patient registration in the emergency room. I had never thought any good would come to me in this life and now it had. I felt important. I felt like I mattered. I had friends that were doctors and lawyers. I felt like I had finally arrived. My life was fantastic. I didn't need God I had did it all on my own. Way had his coming home party and for once I was in attendance. His mother had started dating one of his friends again. But this time it seemed different. It seemed as if they really loved each other. I was watching Way expression to see if there was any animosity in his heart. He was good at hiding things so I couldn't tell either way. I tried to get him alone to have the ultimate conversation. It was harder than I had planned. I'd snuck up to his room and sat on the bed. He walked in smiling extra hard. "What the.. what you doing in here?" He asked still smiling. "I need to talk to you." I said returning his smile. "Bout what?" He asked. "Well." I managed to get out before I was interrupted. Lamuziga walked in telling jokes and laughing. Eventually we all ran down stairs. I figured it wasn't meant for me to tell him. I went home and knew the day would come for us to have the conversation. I anxiously awaited Ways arrival. So on the day I heard the key go into the door my body jumped. I exhaled as the door slowly crept open. I knew Way could tell I had something on my mind and he sat around all day trying to pull it out of me. I didn't want to be the bearer of bad news. I mean what if I was right and Lamuziga was manipulating this whole scenario. As Way got up to leave I just blurted out the information that was running through mind repeatedly. Way looked as if he would be physically ill. I let out a sigh at the sight of his dismay. He just walked out the door. Way went from him and his girlfriend to him and all of them after that day. I mean he did his dirt before but now it was apparent there was no love left in him. Not for the women he was dating anyway. We went back to the way things were but this time I wanted things to be different. I wanted Way to stop selling drugs and carrying weapons. I'd seen a life outside of the projects and it wasn't all that bad. Life could be exceptional, without all the glitter and glamour. I just wanted to live a simple life. Perhaps met a husband have a couple of kids. I knew he was attractive so meeting a wife wasn't going to be all that hard for him. I waited for Way. It seemed like that was all I did besides work. Way walked in and sucked his teeth at the sight of me. I knew Way wasn't going to like the conversation. I had been expressing my concerns in the letters I had been sending to the jail. I knew where he stood on the position of not selling drugs. He was totally against it. I needed to take him with me away from this life. I had just found a whole house that was rent to own. It was cute, quaint and the neighborhood was extremely quiet. "What?" Way asked not hiding his frustration. "I'm moving." I replied softly. "What? When?" Way asked in a curious and confused tone. "I should be out by next month. I don't plan on taking anything with me. I don't want anything to remind me of this place. The rats and roaches can have all of this shit." I exclaimed as if I didn't have any big news at all. As Way digested what I was saying I decided it was now or never. "I don't understand why you choose to sell drugs. I mean some people I get it. Their mother is on drugs or they are so dirt poor they barely have enough food to eat. You however just couldn't get two hundred dollar sneakers every month…" I started. My sentence was interrupted by Way sucking his teeth. I ignored the look that Way was giving me. The look was of a panther that was about to pounce on his prey. I decided to redirect the conversation slightly. "Don't you want more for yourself than the life you living in and out of jail?" I inquired. I knew the conversation was over as he began to head towards the door. "Look Taylor I'M A DRUG DEALER, that's what I do." His head was slightly down. I could hear the defeat in his voice. He knew I couldn't carry on with this lifestyle. However I was still optimistic about what was to come. I knew he was addicted to being "Way". The cute boy with money, nice clothes, jewelry, and cars. With all those things in play the women threw themselves at him. He enjoyed being him. I still had faith in our friendship. I wanted to get him out of the streets. I had seen a future where things weren't as flashy but he didn't have to worry about his freedom being jeopardized. We could make it by building and grinding slowly. We only had to be each other back bone like we've always been. Way left the house never to return again. I had the movers come and collect my clothes, purses, shoes, and closed the door to 1815 E. Fayette St. for the last time. I stood in front of the door misty eyed. I had so much fun here I thought. On the way out the building I threw the keys to the Jersey boys. I laughed and told them maybe it'll bring them luck. I figured Way was never coming back. I knew they were going to turn it into their spot, but I didn't care. It was the end of an era.

CHAPTER 15

The Beginning

My life was in a tailspin of horse shit. The job that I was so proud and grateful for I had lost. My rent was due. My car had died. I felt as though nothing else could go wrong until the phone rang. I was walking back from the laundry mat with a basket of clean clothes. In the new quiet neighborhood I liked that no one knew me and I could get away with walking down the street with a head scarf and slippers on. I made sure the scarf was Louis Vitton just in case someone drove by that I knew. I didn't want them to think. I had fell off or couldn't afford the finer things in life. I answered the phone in my now normal impatient tone. "Hello." "Did you hear what happened?" Way little brother asked. "No." I managed to get out over my heartbeat. "Way took the police on a high speed chase and when they finally stopped the car they pulled him out and started beating him bad. The ambulance was called and he wasn't breathing. Now every hospital we call they say they don't have no one there by that name" He explained. His voice sounded like a child who was trying to be strong. You could still hear the cracking in his voice every so often. "What? What the fuck you mean he wasn't breathing? Who was in the fucking car with him? How the fuck did this happen? Yo, I gotta go!" I screamed. I wanted to drop my clothes in the middle of the street. I took a deep breath and made my way to the house. I called all the hospitals except for the one I was formerly employed at. They all told me the exact same thing. They didn't have a patient with the name or description I gave them. I put my head down and decided to swallow my pride and call my former job. When they answer the phone they could hear the defeat in my voice. I heard the person ask "This Tay?" "Yes." I responded in a barely audible whisper. "He's at Crouse." I heard the voice whisper and then the dial tone. I couldn't make out the voice of the person who helped me but I was grateful. I called Crouse with some legal jorgan and empty threats and promises. Somehow it worked. I was able to get through to the nurse's station. "Hello ICU." The female voice said. I hung up immediately and called Lamuziga to my surprise she was already on her way up to the hospital. I rushed through the ICU doors. I looked down on my friend he looked so helpless. I began to weep quietly. The nurse came in to check his vitals. "You can talk to him you know." She stated. "I can." I asked. I couldn't muster up the courage to talk face to face with the nurse. I kept my head down towards the floor. I didn't want to be face to face with my weakness. There laying in the hospital bed was my weakness. I was lost I couldn't help him. "Way, Way can you hear me?" I said through my sniffles. The nurse made a strange face and began to speak. "Talk to him again." She suggested. "Way can you hear me?" I asked again. The nurse left the room. I began sobbing uncontrollably. "Way please!" I begged. He began moving his fingers. Just than the nurse walked back in the room. "We're going to take him off of life support." The nurse told me. "How if he is still unconscious?" I inquired. "Well we're going to see how he do? We can't explain why he stopped breathing?" She tried to explained. I couldn't understand why they would take such a risk. "No, what if something goes wrong. I'm not going to allow you to play rush and roulette with his life. What if your wrong?" I demanded to know. The nurse face displayed her aggravation with my adamant protest. She left the room and came back with two more nurse's. "Well visiting hours are over for the intensive care ward." One nurse had spoken in tone filled with authority. I knew they were bending the rules for the ICU and now they've decided to use their advantage. I wanted to issue a threat but I needed them to save him if need be. I apprehensively walked into the waiting area. I tried calling Lamuziga on the phone. I knew she wasn't answering on purpose. I kept hitting redial until the nurse came to escort me back into the room. They were smiling. I didn't like them taking such a risk. I just returned their smile. I didn't want them to put me out. My face must've spoke volumes because the nurse began to speak. "He is breathing on his own now. You can talk to him if you want to. I'm pretty sure he can hear you. He's awake." She stated. I was scared but happy at the same time. I began calling Way name. I could see his eyes fluttering under its lids. "Take your time." I instructed. His eyes were covered with dried up flaky white crust. That was making it difficult to open his eyes it seemed. I went over to the sink to rinse a washcloth with warm water. I gently placed the washcloth over his eyes. He flinched when the cloth first touched his face. I'd seen his body relaxing after he let out a silent exhale. I removed the washcloth from his face. As soon as the washcloth was removed he began fluttering his eyes again. "Wait a minute Way." I advised. He complied as he listened to my footsteps. Once I arrived to sink I rinsed the washcloth in hot water again. I came back and place the rag over his eyes again. This time he seemed to be anticipating the warmth of the washcloth. I gently massaged all of the left over film off his eyes. "Now try." I instructed as jovial as could. His eyes opened slowly. He began to blink rapidly. I'd guess to regain focus. I could see the drainage from his eyes. I kept patting it away before it could trickle down that far. "What happened?" He asked. "They said you stop breathing." I answered softly. "I WHAT?" He said in a panic stricken voice. "Your in ICU." I stated still maintaining my composure. Just then his girlfriend walked into the room. "Oh I'm so happy you're up? I would've been here sooner but I had to go to work." She explained. 'work! He is in here, in ICU, on life support and you went to work. Way this bitch don't love you!' I thought. I wanted to scream it to the top of my lungs. It wasn't my place though. We weren't around each other anymore. We were on different paths in life. We had come to our crossroads. The last time we spoke on the phone it wasn't pleasant. I passed the washcloth to his new girlfriend and headed out the hospital. He had asked me to do him one more favor. I did the favor. I knew he would spend more time in jail behind the chase he took the police on. That life was over for me.

I laid in the bed going through mental turmoil. I had been fired from the hospital. Every bill was overdue. I had all sorts of shut off notices. My mind felt as though it was slipping. I had decided to clean my house.

I just needed to do something anything. The house was so hot. It was a pretty enough house on the outside but the inside was small quaint and stifling. I poured bleach in a bucket and mixed it with ammonia. I'd heard that was something you weren't supposed to do. It just never really dawned on me at the time though. Just than I'd received a phone call. I had gotten the job at Rural Metro Ambulance Service. 'Yes.' I thought. I began cleaning the entire bathroom. I felt light headed so I opened up the window. I decided to lay down to take a nap. I figured the house would air out shortly. I fell asleep. I awaken gasping for air. I couldn't catch my breath. I reached for my cell phone. I dropped it once I realized I couldn't get a word out. It would've been pointless. I couldn't speak how could I give them my address? I looked up towards the heavens 'God please not like this!' I thought. My eyes returned to the darkness. I walked into work that morning with one thing on my mind. What had happened last night? It felt like a struggle walking thru the corridors where the ambulances were. I made my way to an EMT that I had become familiar with. I asked him to take my vitals just as professional courtesy. While I was telling him the story he seemed really carefreely listening to me. I explained how I felt like God had spared me. I thought perhaps he would think that I was crazy. I didn't care. I needed someone to know God had given me another chance. His face became puzzled. He had put the oxygenator on my finger to see my oxygen levels while I was talking. "Your oxygen is dangerously low. I think you should go to the hospital." He informed me. "Nah Imma work today." I replied. "But it's at eighty-three percent out of a hundred." He persisted. I knew he probably was right but I made my way to my desk. I knew where I needed to go. Whom I needed to talk to. Who I should apologize to and who I needed to thank; God. Yet again he had spared me. I had made a declaration that day that I would be all that God had sent me to be. I would love unconditionally and give relentlessly. I would show the world that God is love and his love lives in me. I would return to being the christian girl who trust God in everything. I had to reminisce on the things God had helped me through. I began to look back over my life. God had answered all of my prayers. Every last one of them. I'd constantly begged him to help while living with Kymela. I prayed from sun up til sun down. Then

I prayed and pleaded with God until I was removed. However once I was removed I acted as if I didn't get what I had been pleading for. I did this throughout almost every foster home. For whatever reason, but mostly to be closer to my sister's, or to see them. When I was in the group home, I prayed to get out of the group home. I was shuffled to a detention center and transferred to a residential treatment facility. Every step of the way he was there. He never allowed the cops to kick in my door, although there were drug dealers constantly running in and out my apartment. He never allowed me to experience any of the backlash from the stuff that I was doing. Stealing, lying, manipulating, he still chose to spare me. Time and time again. Despite all that I had said or done he still loved me. My Lord and savior Jesus Christ of Nazareth died knowing that I would make all of these mistakes. So that God would still have mercy on me. His love is truly everlasting. And if you believe in him he will help you along the way. Please take a lesson from me. Let him guide you. Lean not unto your own understanding and just when you think your in a storm know that your lifeguard walks on water. God got you and if he have to he will carry you just like he did Peter and me. You don't have to believe me, I'm just a nobody. I had to live this life to hopefully show you can make it. God has not forsaken you. If you would like to give Jesus a try and be saved repeat this scripture out loud believe it in your heart:

Romans 10:9-10 (KJV)

9 That if thou shalt confess with thy mouth the Lord Jesus, and shalt believe in thine heart that God hath raised him from the dead, thou shalt be saved.

10 For with the heart man believeth unto righteousness; and with the mouth confession is made unto salvation.

Now say out loud I believe Jesus died on the cross for my sins. You're Saved! Congratulations!

May God bless you as you enjoy your journey to Christ.

Printed in the United States
By Bookmasters